THE
MAN BEHIND
THE MIKE

THE
MAN BEHIND
THE MIKE

MIKE
TUCKER
The voice of
equestrianism

Jane Wallace

Quiller

Copyright © 2018 Jane Wallace

First published in the UK in 2018
by Quiller, an imprint of Quiller Publishing Ltd

British Library Cataloguing-in-Publication Data
A catalogue record for this book is available from
the British Library

ISBN 978 1 84689 268 4

Internal design by Arabella Ainslie

Printed in Malta

Whilst every effort has been made to obtain permission from
copyright holders for all material used in this book, the publishers will
be pleased to hear from anyone who has not been appropriately
acknowledged, and to make the correction in future reprints.

Quiller

An imprint of Quiller Publishing Ltd
Wykey House, Wykey, Shrewsbury SY4 1JA
Tel: 01939 261616
Email: info@quillerbooks.com
Website: www.quillerpublishing.com

Contents

Foreword

In November 2017 Mike and Angela came up to Scotland to stay with Jenny and me. The visit coincided with Mike's birthday and our anniversary. We had a wonderful few days, during which time Mike asked me to write this foreword. I was thrilled, surprised and honoured.

As we talked for hours, planning and discussing the future, little did we know that Mike would only have a few months left. This book has been brilliantly completed by Jane Wallace with incredible help from Angela and many memories from all his friends. Ironically, I doubt it would surprise Mike to know that I was the person Jane had to chase up to complete the text on time but I'm sure he would forgive me, as course designing at Tattersalls and Bramham International events were my excuse for tardiness. This year I really missed our annual drive around the cross-country course at Bramham, where Mike would quietly give me his appraisal – he never was shy of telling the truth!

I first met Mike in the early 1980s and we built a great friendship, culminating in working together for the BBC for ten years. We were described as 'grumpy old men', 'an old married couple', and even as 'Hinge and Bracket', but we had such a brilliant time covering some great events in different countries. Mike never missed a trick and, when we found ourselves covering the World Championships in Kentucky USA from a BBC cupboard in London, he suggested we go out for coffee. Although I should have known better, I was a little surprised that he asked the taxi driver to take us to Harrods. We had our coffee and he then spent over an hour talking with the head butcher about Wagyu beef. We then discussed, on our return journey, how he could increase his herd quickly enough to supply the store!

I'm so delighted that this book has been completed, as it tells of an incredible man, who lived a full and extraordinary life. He had time for everyone, never forgot a face or name, and always had a cheerful, if rather cheeky, smile. Always positive, with strong beliefs, he was never afraid to get stuck in. He chaired many committees and panels and was passionate about the future of everything he was involved in and how we could make improvements for future generations.

A dedicated family man, he was incredibly proud of his children, Emma and Andrew, and his four grandsons. We talked about our families for many hours during our trips and he always looked forward to returning home to find out what they were all up to and to be there to help and support them whenever needed.

Mike often talked of the similarities in our lives. We both competed, designed courses, commentated (though I was definitely not in his league), acted as field master for the Duke of Beaufort's and Duke of Buccleuch's hunts respectively, and had a huge love of racing, where we stewarded at many different courses. Over the years we became great mates — in fact, he was rather like a big brother, trying hard to keep me on the straight and narrow! There is no doubt that I miss him enormously but I feel very privileged to have played a small part in his life.

This book tells a great story and shows how much Mike was respected throughout the world.

I know you will enjoy it.

Ian Stark OBE

Acknowledgements

I would like to acknowledge with thanks the material kindly contributed by so many people who knew and worked with Mike, and their permission to use it in these pages, which was immensely helpful to the completion of this book. All such material is attributed where it is introduced on the page. The contributors include Jonathan Agnew, William Alexander, Clare Balding, Emma Barker, Sue Benson, Yogi Breisner, Nick Brooks-Ward, Simon Brooks-Ward, Mike Bullen, Virginia Caro, Simon Claisse, Lorna Clarke, Michael Cole, Tina Cook, Simon Cowley, James Dawson, Janie Dear, Guiseppe della Chiesa, Mike Etherington-Smith, Ian Farquhar, Kate Green, Lucinda Green, Tim Harding, Judy Harvey, HRH The Princess Royal, Elizabeth Inman, Cherry Jones, Alan King, Toby Lee, Chris Lewis, Charlie Longsdon, Harry Meade, Bruce and Jennifer Millar, Fi and Mike Mitchell, Phillip Mitchell, Gerry Morrison, Keith Ottesen, John and Betty Peacock, Mike Petre, Mark Phillips, Alice Plunkett, Lord Rathcreedan, Jim Reside, Giles Rowsell, Jane Sale, Richard Smith, Peter and Debbie Sidebottom, Katie Stephens, Gail Sturgis, Christopher Tar, Hugh Thomas, Liz Thorburn, Zara Tindall, Andrew Tucker, Angela Tucker, Georgie Tucker, Jane Tuckwell, John Tulloch, Sam Twiston-Davies, Lorenzo Soprani Volpini, Charlie Wallace, Malcolm Wallace, Tom Wallace, Johnnie and Wendy Watherston, Ray Williams, Jimmy Wofford, Jim and Beth Wright.

Jane Wallace

Preface

It was over thirty years ago when I asked Mike if he would walk the course with me at Badminton as a first-timer in 1986. I had decided that, with his many years' association with the famous horse trials as both rider and commentator, there could be no one more experienced to impart knowledge and advice. I felt rather cheeky asking someone I had never met before, but I thought he always sounded so charming when listening to his commentary! I was not disappointed and, thanks to his invaluable advice, I achieved a lifetime dream of winning a coveted silver horse trophy for a top-ten placing. Not only was Mike helpful and informative, he was also friendly and fun. He and his wife Angela have remained firm friends ever since.

The seeds of an idea for this book were sown at our dinner table during Burghley Horse Trials in 2015. At the time, Mike was contemplating his retirement as commentator from the BBC and he was regaling us with tales of a bygone era in the sport. It was after a series of particularly interesting reminiscences that our guests said in unison, 'You really should write a book …' and that was the beginning. The following year, after due consideration, Mike decided that he would indeed like to record his memoirs and asked me to help. I was honoured, flattered and indeed privileged that I was to be part of what proved to be an enlightening trip down memory lane.

The format that we decided upon for the book was that Mike would record his own memories into voice recognition software and, from the information provided, I would produce the overall narrative, liberally interspersed with his own verbatim recollections and anecdotes, which we would indicate by presenting them in displayed form. That was all proceeding swimmingly (we were 'kicking on', as Mike would have said) when I received the shocking news that Mike had died suddenly. In the aftermath, it quickly became apparent that there was a groundswell of support from Mike's family, friends, fellow competitors, former work colleagues – in fact from many people who had known him in various walks of life – to complete the biography as a tribute to a much-loved character. Accordingly, I am delighted to say that the latter part of this book has been completed thanks to the many contributions from which it has been possible to present the story of Mike's life from the time of his retirement from competitive eventing onwards. This has necessitated something of a change of style for the latter chapters (where recollections and reminiscences are introduced by their contributors' names in bold type), but I'm sure that readers will understand this in the circumstances. From Chapter Ten onwards, each chapter looks at specific facets of Mike's life and career.

Mike spent a lifetime in the horse world and has been witness to so many different aspects. I'm sure this book will be appreciated by all who are followers and supporters of equestrian sport in general, and the stories and reminiscences will entertain, amuse and fascinate, as well as giving an insight to the many changes that took place during Mike's long years of involvement.

CHAPTER ONE

Revisiting the Pinnacle

In every career there is a highlight, a moment that stands out from all others, an occasion that is just that little bit special. After some reflection, Mike decided indubitably that the one that stood out for him was the chance at the Rio Olympic Games of 2016 to commentate on Nick Skelton winning the individual showjumping gold medal. This choice did not diminish the achievements of the many other winners at top level but, for Mike, Nick's outstanding performance was unique. For over thirty years, Mike had commentated on Nick's showjumping career on numerous occasions. He had witnessed the highs and lows of Nick's various rounds on a multitude of different horses, from novices to Olympic contenders, at locations all round the world. There had been times of elation and moments of enduring total dejection, but nothing could have been bleaker than the aftermath of Nick's life-threatening fall in 2000. To return from such an injury and to win the most prestigious prize is a feat of monumental proportions. To be a part of one of the greatest achievements in the history of equestrian sport and to enjoy the privilege of announcing the result to the rest of the world has to rank as the pinnacle of Mike's career. It is a fitting way to commence this book prior to retracing the steps that guided him to that coveted spot.

Mike: 'It was when I was in the departure lounge at Heathrow early in the morning, waiting to catch my flight to the 2016 Rio Olympic Games that I was pondering over what might lie ahead for me in the coming weeks. It would be my tenth Olympic Games in all and my sixth with BBC television. It was then that I cast my mind back to my journey home from the London Olympics on a Saturday morning in 2012. I had countless memories that clearly made London the best of the nine Olympics I had worked at, in one way or another. I had come to realise that being part of an Olympic Games was something truly special. Not only the superb sporting moments that so often made history, but also the wonderful exchange of camaraderie and friendship with people from all over the world had made me a huge fan of the Olympic movement. London had it all; an amazing array of British sporting success and, despite all the critics, the Games were quite brilliantly produced and managed. The military personnel, deployed in place of the original contractor, had made such a great job of the security side of the Olympics. The new concept of volunteers guiding the huge crowd around the venues was an innovation that was successful beyond all dreams. It was on that morning on my way home after two exceptional weeks, that I felt truly proud to be British.

'At the start of every year after an Olympics there is an open discussion regarding the next Olympiad with the Head of BBC Sport. Do you want to go to the next Olympics? Do we want you? Well, that morning, coming home from London, I knew what my answer was going to be. I would confirm, if asked, that I would definitely be going to Rio in four years' time for what would inevitably be my final Olympics as commentator.'

That rosy picture in Mike's mind on his way home that morning was soon to change dramatically. Brazil's economy was to grow steadily worse; an unstable political situation meant plans would fall way behind and many cutbacks, accompanied by constant bad press, presented the Rio Olympic

Games as a gloomy prospect. Three of the team who had made the London Greenwich venue such a success – Tim Hadaway, Alec Lochore and Stephen Renoir – had been employed by the Brazilians to manage the equestrian side of the Olympics and they must have had their doubts on a number of occasions regarding their involvement. The scare of the Zika virus created another major problem, but gradually everything fell into place.

Hosting an Olympic Games in your home country certainly produces an enhanced competitive edge within all the equestrian teams and this was certainly evident in London. However, many situations had changed since then, with horses injured or sold and partnerships of horse and rider no longer intact. The selection of the right horse and rider combination is always such an important part of a successful team. Great Britain had shown consistent results in all of the three equestrian disciplines: eventing, dressage and showjumping. However, there had also been disappointments in the run-up to Rio and the chance of medals appeared less likely than at an earlier date. As always, there would be a seriously competitive challenge for the medals.

So, there was Mike, sitting at the airport, ready to take off and go.

Mike: 'As you can imagine, enthusiasm wasn't at its highest as we all set off for Rio from our various locations. It was not an auspicious beginning for me. I set off with my luggage but I arrived in Rio without it! I knew pretty quickly that my BBC colleagues were going to give me plenty of ribbing when I pitched up without my bags. Not the best way to start my tenth Olympic Games!

'One of the bonuses of being part of a BBC team at an Olympics is the number of famous people and voices that make up the sporting commentary world. It has been a true privilege to work with them. My first Olympics was in Atlanta with the great David Coleman, Harry Carpenter and Des Lynam and over the years there have been many more. The fact that a large group of us would be living together for the next two weeks, exchanging stories of the day's events, day in, day out, enjoying the camaraderie and excitement of all that went on, would make it very special.

'In Deodoro, one of the areas where there were a number of venues, the commentary teams from athletics, hockey, rugby sevens (first time in the Olympics), kayak racing, as well as the equestrian sports would gather. The dinners, the *caipirinhas* (the national cocktail) down on the beach just ten minutes from the hotel, were certainly a great way to relax after the long and hectic days. With the advent of the red button facility on BBC television, we were in the commentary box all day. Our average day meant an early start, a quick, snatched breakfast, and the rest of the day spent behind the microphone. Early bed beckoned after a demanding day!'

Rio is an enormous, sprawling city beneath the famous central mountain from where the massively imposing statue of Christ dominates the view. This mountain certainly hinders the crossing of the busy city, which is renowned not only for its expensive areas but also for the poor and dangerous ones, namely the infamous *favelas*, or slums. In fact, Mike and his colleagues could hear the sound of automatic gunfire from their hotel bedrooms on a regular basis, and considerable care was required in deciding where they went and their means of travel.

Mike: 'Ian Stark, himself an Olympic medallist, was already there when we arrived. I have always enjoyed working with him and relish his balanced views on the sport's progress. We only had two days before the eventing horse inspection, the first of the equestrian disciplines, was due to start. Our initial task was to find our way around, to discover the whereabouts of the commentary positions as well all the other facilities that are so important in producing a successful competition. The Brazilian management had surpassed themselves despite all the rumours of so much going wrong. The facilities were second to none, particularly for the horses, with great training areas, top-class veterinary care and excellent stabling. All in all the organisers had produced a superb venue, which was truly worthy of an Olympic Games. In Deodoro there was a military barracks and one of the key men leading the Brazilian team of organisers had been in the sport for a number of years and had put his experience to good use. The fact that he had the help of Brits Tim Hadaway, Alec Lochore and Stephen Renoir, as already mentioned, was very clear to see. Pierre Michelet from France was the course designer. With a wealth of experience and a definite style of his own, Pierre was notorious for producing a technical and often difficult track. The undulating terrain for the cross-country would prove important and influential and Pierre used it to full effect. The cross-country obstacles had been built by famous British course-builders the Willis brothers, from Malmesbury in Wiltshire. In previous years, Alan Willis and his brothers had built up a team that were not only renowned for the course at Badminton, but also for two other Olympic sites, Barcelona and Sydney, and the World Equestrian Games in Jerez. In Rio it was Alan's son, James, together with a selected international team who made an excellent job of producing a superb example of craftsmanship for the cross-country.

'My wife Angela was to be in Rio briefly, acting as trainer to one of the individual Japanese eventing riders. Angela's arrival highlighted one of the difficulties of an Olympic Games because she was in the equestrian base with one sort of accreditation and I was in the press and media with another, so chances to meet and talk were few and far between. It is always the same at an Olympic Games and puts enormous pressure on riders, managers, trainers and supporters alike. It emphasises why an Olympic Games is totally different from any other competition where restrictions are less rigorous.'

For a commentator, one of the important jobs is to walk the cross-country course to study the fences, walk the distances between elements in the combinations and to ascertain the course's overall difficulty. From the outset it was evident that Pierre Michelet had made strong use of the undulating terrain. His course presented difficult problems early on for those choosing to take the direct route and these questions continued as the course progressed. There were longer and easier alternatives, but the direct way created much the biggest track seen since the Sydney Olympics in 2000. All the riders and teams, having walked the course, considered that the Rio cross-country would play a huge part in the competition.

Mike: 'Angela was staggered by its size and complexity as was Tina Cook, who was not only the travelling reserve for the event team but also assisted Jonathan Agnew for Radio 5 Live commentary. Everyone felt the cross-country was going to be a serious test. One aspect of the selection for Rio, which I could never understand, was the perception that a good dressage and careful showjumping were going to be very important assets. It has always been the view in the past that while eventing was a three-phase competition, a good cross-country performance was crucial. The selection for Rio was a little different and the horses selected for the British team were not renowned for their experience across country. It is normal practice to hold a test event on the site the year prior to an Olympics to allow team management to assess the facilities and the terrain, and get an idea of what to expect in the future. However, only Brazilian horses had attended on this occasion, because, at the time, the disease "glanders" was a major problem. At that stage Deodoro was not a designated quarantine area because the army was still using it and, although foreign horses were allowed in, they were not allowed back out again. Also, it was hugely expensive – in fact no riders went from Europe and Yogi Breisner, in his role as team performance manager, was the sole British eventing representative.

'In the knowledge that Pierre Michelet is known for his testing courses, and bearing in mind the demanding, undulating terrain,

I had a feeling that the requirements for our team were very much underestimated. A bold, experienced and accurate cross-country partnership of horse and rider was going to be very important. There was a general concern that we might not have been well enough prepared.'

The story of the Olympic eventing of 2016 is now consigned to the history books and although the performance of Great Britain's team was a disappointment, the competition was adjudged to have been nail-biting from beginning to end, with many thrills and spills, but luckily few injuries to either horse or rider. The medal positions swung dramatically from phase to phase with all three disciplines playing their part but it was, as predicted, the cross-country that proved most influential – although an overall excellent performance was ultimately required. Only ten marks covered the top four teams at the conclusion of the competition. The French beat the Germans in style, but who could have predicted that result when the Germans had appeared invincible, having been unbeaten in championships since 2011. In the individual eventing, Michael Jung equalled Mark Todd's previous feat by winning his second consecutive gold medal riding the consistent Sam, adding no further penalties to his good dressage score. The young Frenchman, Astier Nicolas, confirmed his talents as a future star, winning silver, with the experienced rider Phillip Dutton salvaging a little American pride to take bronze.

> **Mike:** 'Scottie, Tina, Jonathan Agnew and I very much had our tails between our legs that night as we went down to the beach to drown our sorrows. The fact that it was the first time since 1996 that Britain had failed to win an eventing medal really did not go down well. Angela joined us to mull over the various disappointments of our British competitors.'

The next day was one of Mike and his team's two free days during the Games prior to the start of the team dressage. A meeting had been arranged with the British team management to discover how the dressage team had settled into their quarters and to unearth any news regarding the showjumping team. Richard Waygood, the chef d'équipe, attended the meeting and delivered an excellent briefing on the preparation of the dressage team. Although Britain had stayed high on the world stage, the Germans, proving they were worthy of the number one position they had achieved, had been successful in the major championships since the London Olympics, the Dutch always required respect and the Americans had delivered good performances since winning team bronze in the World Equestrian Games.

Mike: 'Just as the meeting in the media centre was finishing, there was a large "plop" about four metres away from us; something had dropped through the marquee roof and on to the floor. Our cameraman, Graeme Johnstone-Robertson, went to investigate. Quite calm, he came back to the group holding, would you believe, a bullet that had come through the roof. Unbelievably we all remained perfectly relaxed as we listened to the explanation of what had happened, but once it was reported to the media manager, all hell let loose!

'Immediately the officer commanding the Deodoro barracks was summoned to an impromptu press conference. He was put on the spot to report on the action. He made a statement that frankly told us little but "General" Jonathan Agnew (as we nicknamed him afterwards) took up the questioning on what was potentially a serious and frightening incident. It was as good as any episode from *Dad's Army*, but it rather highlighted the security problems that existed at all times while we were there. If you strayed outside limits there was danger afoot. One further bullet was found outside the stable boundary but that was the extent of any problem so far as we knew. However, I can't say that any of us were very confident of the military security system in place and we had little ambition to travel far in Rio!'

Britain's dressage team, despite changes, had shown that they were worthy of their élite status on the world stage in the four-year period before Rio. Interestingly, it was springtime 2016 when the main hope for a gold medal, Valegro, came back into serious work in his preparation for Rio. The partnership of Carl Hester and Charlotte Dujardin proved to be wise and experienced in their horse management and they had decided to give Valegro an easy period after the European Championships in Aachen 2015. This policy certainly paid off, with Valegro's top mark in the Rio Grand Prix helping secure a silver medal for the British team of Charlotte Dujardin, Carl Hester, Fiona Bigwood and Spencer Wilton.

Mike: 'Television audiences for dressage in the UK have grown considerably over the last ten years, mostly because of the British successes and, as a result, dressage enthusiasts are able to enjoy extended television coverage of championship competitions. In my years of covering dressage, I have been privileged to have the hugely knowledgeable Jennie Loriston-Clarke and more recently Judy Harvey as dressage experts to assist with the commentary. Unfortunately, Judy was unable to secure BBC accreditation for Rio (accreditation for an Olympic Games is notoriously difficult to obtain) so Ian Stark stepped in and although neither Ian nor I could regard ourselves as dressage specialists, we were thrilled to have the chance to cover the impressive silver medal team success. Luckily we had the benefit of former British National Dressage Champion Peter Storr's expert eye to guide us. Peter was in Rio as a reserve official for the dressage competition and he was a great help to us. Both Peter and Ian held the view that Valegro and Charlotte looked ready to defend their individual title won in London.'

The small crowd watching the dressage was a disappointment for the organisers, but many other sports around the Olympic city suffered from the same apparent lack of support. The Freestyle to Music competition, however, created plenty of interest and attracted increased crowd numbers although the stadium, in stark contrast to London Olympic crowds, was far from packed. The morning of the Freestyle generated excitement and nerves within the British squad.

Mike: 'We were all full of anticipation and nervously hopeful that Charlotte and Valegro could do it once again.'

Charlotte Dujardin's temperament under pressure has always been outstanding. Horse and rider had grown to know each other so well over the years and they formed the perfect partnership. The music was impressive and, although the floor plan was difficult, Valegro maintained a foot-perfect performance and the provisional marks that ran through the test looked most encouraging.

Mike: 'Peter Storr thought she'd done enough but of course it was the judges' scores that counted. When the marks finally appeared on the screen, there was a sudden large intake of breath around the stadium. Charlotte had made history yet again and, for the first time ever, a British dressage competitor had won back-to-back individual gold medals. It was an outstanding performance. We had arguably witnessed one of the best dressage horses ever seen, and an extremely talented rider. The celebrations had already started around the grandstands and the British followers were jumping up and down for joy. The BBC commentary box was electric too. Jonathan Agnew, Tina Cook, Ian Stark and I were in raptures over the outcome. "Aggers" had spent time with the Hester/Dujardin camp during the two-year build-up to his first Olympics as a commentator. The legend of *Test Match Special* had called an Olympic gold medal at the first attempt! His wife Emma, who is a dressage rider, would have been over the moon watching on the television at home. Celebrations went on long into the night, even in the BBC commentary base. By the time everyone had retired to bed, the parties had been richly enjoyed!'

However, a performance was yet to come that was to eclipse even Charlotte's outstanding achievement.

By the time Charlotte had notched up her win, the die had already been cast in the team showjumping competition, and it was not good news for Britain. The showjumping courses were big and technical and the British team of Nick Skelton, Ben Mayer and brothers John and Michael Whitaker failed to make the top eight places in the first round and so missed qualification for the next round. However, Nick, Michael and Ben had qualified with their individual scores to go through to the second round, from which the top thirty-five places would go forward for the individual competition, which started afresh on the final day of the equestrian Olympics.

Mike: 'It has to be remembered that Nick and Big Star had not jumped a course of that size since Aachen in 2013, when Nick achieved a rare feat of adding a fourth Aachen Grand Prix to his four at Calgary. Nick was respected by the very best from all round the world. His determination was legendary. He had experienced several low moments in the build-up from 2013 to 2016 but he never lost faith in Big Star and had mentally planned every step of the way to that gold in Rio, and was still on target. Nick had been to eight Olympics. He'd won a World Cup and ridden successfully all round the world on such horses as St Jones, Apollo, Dollar Girl, Tinker's Boy and Arco, to name but a few. To see Nick in "full cry" in a jump-off was something very special, often crouched low over the horse's withers with an amazing eye for a stride and with total control despite the speed. His ability to keep the horse balanced on a tight turn was all part of his skill as a horseman and he'd been a regular winner wherever he went. During my commentary career I had witnessed some of his great wins and spectacular rounds. I had commentated on his multiple wins of the Hickstead Derby and King George VI competitions. I was behind the microphone at the London Olympics where he played such a major part in winning the first gold medal for the British showjumping team since 1952. One moment that particularly sticks in my mind was when he rode Arco in the Athens Olympics as an individual and he made it through to the final round with a possible chance of a medal. Although Arco had two fences down and ended up down the line, it was only thanks to Nick's exceptional ability that Arco was close to winning a medal – but that made Nick even more determined for the future.

'That, remember, was the Olympics four years after a very black time for Nick. In September 2000 he had the most horrific fall at Park Gate in Cheshire. On that day he landed on his head as he fell into a triple bar and broke his neck. He never lost consciousness and was in tremendous pain but, more importantly, could not move. Riders and helpers ran over and were horrified. Nick was flown off the showground in a helicopter to Chester Hospital. The world of showjumping held its breath. The accident was reported in all the main news bulletins, both on radio and television. The prognosis was serious. He had indeed broken his neck but the surgeon proclaimed that, if fitted with a special metal halo, he should make a full recovery in time. That was promising news but it was a long and painful recovery.'

The showjumping world, led by the Hales family, Nick's loyal owners, rallied round and supported Nick in those dark and difficult days. Despite some serious setbacks during the recovery period, which included warnings that he should never ride again, Nick was still determined to make a complete recovery. More consultations with specialists, including a trip to Nuremburg, led to a better prognosis and, within days of that particular visit, he was back riding Arco, the horse the Hales had kept especially for him.

Mike: 'Indeed it was one year, eight months later, that Nick took Arco to a show. The fierce determination was still there. It was not long before he was back on the county circuit and furthermore, winning. An occasional fall caused panic stations, but the progress was good. First trips abroad came in the spring of 2002 and Nick realised his aim of competing at the Horse of the Year Show, held for the first time at Birmingham, where he was thrilled to finish in third place in the Grand Prix. It wasn't much later that Laura Kraut, America's showjumping superstar, found Big Star for Nick in Germany. Soon the talents of the young Big Star and Nick were making headlines and there was a hint of a dream that came to fruition in London when he was part of the gold medal winning team.

'For Nick and Big Star, the dream in Rio was still alive. The first round was big – exactly what Nick had hoped for – and Big Star was back to his best and jumped one of thirteen clear rounds. Nick's faith and confidence in winning gold never faltered and he jumped clear again in the second round, this time making it look easier than ever. His foot-perfect round this time was one of five of the best in the world going through to the jump-off for one of the three medals. The horsepower on show in Rio was out of this world. I have never in my life seen such a set of horses in one competition. We were all getting more and more nervous as the hour approached but "Skelly" and Big Star looked remarkably cool and calm. They had been drawn first to go, which was just what Nick had hoped for.

'Nerves were at fever pitch, not only in the stands but also in the commentary box and Andy Austin, my co-commentator for the showjumping, and I felt that Big Star was jumping better with each round. Pictures of Gary and Beverley Widderstone, Big Star's owners, showed them apparently very relaxed, but I bet in their heart of hearts they were very, very tense!

'I'd had a bet that morning that Nick would win, whereas

others thought Eric Lamaze would repeat his London win. Lee McKenzie, who had done a wonderful job interviewing for all our television programmes from Rio, also had her money on Nick. So everything was set. The course had everything in size and technicality but with such a high-quality field, Nick was going to have to risk all to have a chance of winning. It was how he liked it and how he would have wished it, but it would put his faith to the test. The atmosphere was electric. The crowd was totally silent the moment the bell went. Nick set off purposefully, not going flat-out but keeping Big Star in a lovely rhythm. Big Star looked alert and manoeuvrable and appeared to be jumping for fun. This amazing horse always seemed to be at his brilliant best when it mattered most. His round was clear and quick – not unbeatable but fast enough to force the challengers to take a risk or two. The next two riders both made mistakes and it became apparent that Nick would certainly win a medal. He'd already stated that he didn't want the "rusty" one!'

The Swedish competitor Peder Fredricson, riding All In, who was yet to have a fence down in the whole of the Rio tournament, was the penultimate to jump. Peder, who had ridden in the three-day event in the Barcelona Olympics when trained by dual Olympic gold medallist Mark Todd, was highly respected for his horsemanship and skill and had been most impressive. He now rode a beautiful clear round but everyone heaved a sigh of relief when he was one second slower than Nick. So Big Star was guaranteed silver. What a moment it was, waiting for the final competitor, the Canadian Eric Lamaze. Turning too tight into an upright was an error and he accrued four faults.

Mike: 'Nick Skelton had won gold! The crowd went mad. In the commentary box, we all went mad. "Skelly", Big Star and Great Britain had won one of the most exciting individual gold medals we had ever seen in equestrian sport. The emotion all around us was staggering. Several of us, including me, were in tears, with my old voice showing signs of croaking as I announced the result. Nick, understandably was also shedding a tear of joy. There are pictures of him walking round the collecting ring in disbelief as he came to terms with what he'd achieved. Having ridden at international level myself, albeit not at an Olympics, I can understand what it takes to compete at high level and how the good times are inevitably mingled with those that are disappointing and frustrating. There is no doubt that to win an Olympic gold under circumstances such as this is a fairytale come true. We had witnessed a horse and rider, as good as any, who had overcome adversity and, against all odds, won the one title they both so deserved. I have never commentated on such a thrilling competition, nor one that gave me so much satisfaction. The *caipirinhas* flowed freely that night in the celebrations. It was certainly a night to remember and treasure, although we all felt a bit the worse for wear the following morning! For me it was the culmination of an Olympic Games that did not carry the highest expectations when it started but produced two of the greatest-ever equestrian Olympians and I was there to witness them. What an honour and privilege to be doing a job you love at the highest possible level.

'The BBC had taken me round the world on some outstanding trips, but this had to be the occasion when the curtain came down for me on the Olympics. It simply could not get better than that.'

CHAPTER TWO

To Be a Farmer's Boy

S o this is where the whole story begins:

Mike: 'Farming had been deeply ingrained in both my parents'
families for several generations. My father's father, George Tucker,
farmed at Langridge Down south of Bath. Very sadly he lost his
wife through illness early on in his farming career, so he wanted
to make a new start and have some bigger challenges. He decided
to move some fifty miles north to take on the tenancy of Church
Farm, Long Newnton, Tetbury, where he nearly doubled the size
of his former farming enterprise.'

George Tucker came to Church Farm in 1900 as a tenant and then
later as an owner. He found a lovely new wife, Margaret Knight, who
in 1907 gave birth to their only son, Bertie. He had three sisters, two
of whom married well-known local farmers: Gwendoline married Dick
Bevan and Gladys married George Ponting. Olive, the youngest sister,
married Ewart Bosworth, from near Stratford-upon–Avon, who worked
in the agricultural engineering trade.

Mike: 'Church Farm was alive with the sound of children but there was an awful lot of work to be done and everyone had to muck in. Farming was tough in those days, running a herd of some sixty cows. Even in winter, provided the weather was reasonably favourable, the cows would be put out in the fields every day which, of course, meant they had to be brought in twice a day for hand-milking. All the family would go out and help get the cows in. Any cows with calves would have the calf tied alongside them, so that the calves would get the first chance of having milk. The cows would all be tied up by chains in the long, Cotswold stone sheds, where they were milked by hand into buckets. The milk was then carried nearly a hundred yards with the buckets hung on yolks balanced on strong shoulders up to the dairy! Father's sisters were delighted to help the two or three milkers do all of that.'

It was long, hard work milking twice a day. Some of the milk was turned into cheese in one of the rooms at the back of the house and the rounds of cheese were then taken upstairs into a special cheese room to mature. The left-over milk was put into heavy ten-gallon churns which, in those days, were taken by pony and trap to the local dairy to be sold.

On the other side of the lovely old farmhouse were the cart-horse stables for the six horses that carried out all the heavy farm work. The carting, ploughing, and cultivating work was all done by these six powerful but loyal Shires and they had their own staff to look after them. In the 1970s, the stalls in those Cotswold stables were changed back to the individual stables that are still used at Church Farm for the competition horses today.

Mike: 'Father was never frightened of hard work and was always active. He went to school at Cirencester Grammar but yearned to come home to do jobs on the farm. He developed an interest in hockey as well as becoming very keen on hunting.

'My mother, Betty, was an only child and her parents also came from farming stock. My grandfather Ted Jones (J.E. Jones) came from a long line of successful and respected farmers, who originated in the Vale down by the River Severn and was actually born at Court Farm, Horton in 1889. Grampie Jones, as he was always known to me, married Edith King who was from another big farming family down in the same vale in 1912 and they set up their home at Court Farm.'

The newly married Grampie Jones's first farming venture was on a Badminton Estate farm, which is where Mike's mother was born in 1913. She was an only child, but with countless relatives. Indeed, it was one of those relatives, Uncle George, who caused the next move for the family, up to the top of Horton Hill to a farm right on the edge of the famous Badminton Park. It was the death of Uncle George in 1918 that meant the Jones family was set to move to the seven hundred acre farm called 'Little Badminton'. At that time this farm was regarded as one of the best on the estate and Uncle George had farmed it extremely well, so this was to prove a high-profile test of the young Jones's farming skills.

After the First World War, it was a regular occurrence to see six or more teams of three horses on this farm, ploughing, carting and working the land. In Uncle George's time the farm was always held up as an example of a well-kept farm with good crops and timely cultivations. The fences and gates were well maintained and in good working order. To encourage soil fertility, mixed farming was the way forward in those times and so Ted Jones kept beef shorthorn cattle with which he won top prizes, not only at local shows but also at the big Smithfield Show in London. He also ran a flock of Hampshire Down sheep and a small herd of Gloucester Old Spot sows – the latter played a useful role in clearing up any unsold corn and also supplied litters of piglets. He firmly believed in good rotation for the production of prize-winning crops and keeping up the soil quality.

It was soon obvious that Grampie Jones was up for the challenge of running a successful farm. Only a year after he took up the tenancy, he won the prize for the Best Farmed Farm in the category of over two hundred acres in the Gloucestershire County competition.

As if that wasn't a big enough achievement in its own right, he went on to win it again in 1922, and three more victories up to 1926 meant four on the trot. Hardly surprisingly, the judges decided enough was enough. They asked the organisers of the Gloucestershire competition to tell Mr Jones that he was not to enter again, but presented him with the splendid silver trophy to keep, as it was deemed that he had won it outright. That cup stands proudly on the sideboard at Church Farm to this very day.

Not satisfied with that tremendous record, he decided to take on the well-known Castle Barn Farm, named after a castle-like tower in the middle of the farm buildings. This was designed by an earlier Duke of Beaufort as a feature of the Badminton Estate and remains part of the famous farm buildings to this day. That meant that Grampie Jones was now farming well over a thousand acres, which in those days was an enormous acreage. He supplied all the hay for the Badminton stables and it was a common sight to see ten ricks of hay, each one beautifully thatched and neatly lined up for the year ahead.

Grampie Jones retired from the tenancy of Little Badminton Farm in 1932, with Mike's mother having had a dream childhood in the midst of the Badminton Estate with horses, dogs (and hounds!) galore, which revolved around a life of hunting and farming.

Mike: 'Grampie Jones was not only an out-and-out farmer and a true countryman who loved his hunting but he was also a fine sportsman. He owned a winning racehorse as well as a champion greyhound and when he retired from hunting, he became a renowned shot in a number of shoots in and around the county. He was a total perfectionist and I was privileged to see this for myself as a small boy in his later years and I believe he set an example that I unwittingly strived to follow as I grew up.'

Mike's mother's parents were legendary within the local community and the fact that, following retirement from Little Badminton, they were moving only a couple of miles as the crow flies to Woodway House, just outside Didmarton, and would still be farming the acres of Castle Barn, meant that not much would change and the local community was delighted with that. The lovely Woodway House was built in the mid-eighteenth century and had a very well-tended walled garden. There were twelve acres around the house for the two Channel Island house cows and a whole host of poultry, all of which provided excellent fare for the prolific kitchens.

> **Mike:** 'Between Ted and Edith there were few jobs that hadn't been taken on around Badminton. Mum was nineteen and had not long left Badminton Girls' School near Westbury-on-Trym, Bristol. She had made many friends there but, interestingly, when it came to talking about school, it was reminiscent of St. Trinian's because there was little mention of any academic achievements but she had clearly enjoyed her tennis and hockey! Hockey was one of Mum's passions and it was to play a significant role in her life in years to come.'

Her own mother had been a very good goalkeeper for Luckington Ladies' hockey team and so daughter took up the club tradition and proved to be a talented and popular member of the club. The team were reputed to be a fearsome bunch and in one particular spell had a two-year unbeaten run. The club was only a stone's throw away from their new home and not long after they moved in a mixed Luckington hockey team was started up – and who was there to play as well? A certain Bertie Tucker who, within a decade, was to become Mike's father. He and two of his tear-away mates from Long Newnton very much enjoyed their hockey and were members of Tetbury Men's Club. Having heard about the new mixed team at Luckington, they decided to take their chance. In the late 1920s and early 1930s, although Bertie's life was hectic, with much to do, he was never short of energy and still found time to enjoy some hunting and hockey with his two inseparable mates, Harry Brown and Henry Witchell. They really did live life to the full. In fact, it could be said that life in the 1930s must have been great fun for them. The crowd of like-minded young people thought nothing of hunting on a Saturday morning, playing a hockey match in the afternoon and then setting off for Bath Pump Rooms to dance the night away, despite the fact that Bertie had to be up at dawn to milk the cows!

Mike: 'Dad was not keen on dancing but this beautiful young lady had dazzled him to such an extent that it was very obvious to one and all that a wedding might well be on the horizon. The wedding day was chosen for the ninth of October 1940, the very same day that mother and father Jones had married all those years before. Despite the gloom and effects of the Second World War all around, it was a fabulous occasion and it seems as if half of Gloucestershire's farming community were there to share the celebrations. They were married for fifty-four years and I recall memorable wedding anniversaries, highlighting to all present what a wonderful loving couple they were and what a host of loyal friends they had around them. They were so special and set us, their family, the most perfect example of what a marriage should be.'

Times were still very tough but Grandfather George Tucker wanted more of a challenge and, with his son's marriage pending, he wished to further increase his farming enterprise. So he took on the tenancy of Slads Farm in the beautiful park just outside Tetbury, part of the Estcourt Estate.

Mike: 'It meant Mum and Dad would be setting up home on three hundred acres right next door to Church Farm, which must have been so exciting for Grandfather. It was essentially a stock farm that had been in the same Estcourt family for twenty-eight generations, in other words nearly seven hundred years, and Dad would be farming it in addition to helping his father. Dad was truly in seventh heaven! It was an idyllic setting with some lovely parkland to turn out the dairy herd, so ideal for what Dad had learned to manage with his own father before he got married. He was certainly up for the challenge.'

Mike's father never shirked hard work and he joined forces with his own father to tackle the exciting and demanding project. The team of horses from both farms was stabled mostly at Church Farm for ease of management. Mike's parents gave up hunting to concentrate on the farm and Grampie Jones, who was always very forward-thinking, was instrumental in helping modernise and make progress on the farm. During that time, working horses were gradually phased out, to be replaced by tractors and machines.

Mike: 'All Dad's sisters were by now married with their own families and indeed two of them, Gwennie Bevan and Gladys Ponting, were farming other tenanted farms on the Estcourt Estate, less than a mile away from Slads Farm, so everyone was still very close. At the end of the Second World War, Grandpa Tucker was over seventy years old and had decided it was time to retire. The staff now comprised ten people and sometimes more were needed to run the two farms, with the remaining teams of horses still stabled at Church Farm.'

Farming as an industry played its part in the importance of community work and back-up during those dark days of the war, with Mike's two grandfathers and father all serving as churchwardens in their various parishes for a total of eighty-four years! They had been on the Parish Councils as well as serving in the Home Guard and did a tremendous amount to serve their country in the industry they loved. They were never called up for National Service because farming was seen as vital to feeding the nation. However, other special wartime efforts were requested and Granny Jones, for instance, took in four evacuees from London to help the situation of the thousands who were in the centre of the bombing in London. There were many nights when the bombing of Bristol could be heard clearly at Woodway. In fact, a German warplane came down very close to Woodway itself, reminding everyone of the horrors of the war. Local farmers were asked to take on German prisoners of war from the small local prisoner of war camp at Easton Grey to work on the land to make up for those young men and women who had been called up for National Service.

One man who came to work for Mike's father was Curly Herzog. He stayed for two years during the war and then for another two post-war years before going back to Germany to find his wife Ingeborg. He was a very good workman and an excellent craftsman and, having found his wife, came back to England for a further seven years. They lived in the house at Slads, with Ingeborg helping in the house and Curly helping on the farm. They were a tower of strength to Slads and the local community and became very much part of the family. They stayed on locally and raised a family, integrating well into the community. This was a real eye-opener for Mike as a young child and made him wonder how England could have been fighting a war against a country that included people as lovely as Curly and Ingeborg.

Mike: 'Four years after Mum and Dad were married, I came along. I was an only child but born into a solid family environment and indeed with so many of Mum's girlfriends marrying locally, there were plenty of trips to children's parties in the area. There was also the ritual of the weekly trips for tea at Woodway, normally on a Sunday, which were just heaven. Granny Edith was a great housekeeper and wonderful cook so any meal from the Woodway kitchen was always a very special treat, relished by the many visitors entertained there. My Mum had been well trained by her own mother and there were always favourites that invariably revolved around baking.'

There would be home-made butter and cream from the house cows, plenty of fresh eggs and all sorts of wonderful fruit and vegetables from the garden. The list would go on, with the opportunities for delicious meals being endless. Perhaps best of all were the legendary fruitcakes that were made on a weekly basis, with mother passing on the recipe to daughter and so on. This ritual lasted for two more generations and still goes on today! Manners at table were high on the agenda, with strict discipline.

Mike: 'One stricture in particular created much mirth. Started by Granny Edith (although Betty also stuck to it rigidly), it was that we did not cut the butter at both ends because it brought bad luck. She was really strict about this, as became apparent one lunchtime, when my Grandfather had invited a big boss of one of the large cattle feed companies to meet my Dad. The aim was to obtain a better feed price now that they were milking double the number of cows. I was lucky to be allowed to sit at table on that occasion and I remember being under particularly strict instructions to behave. However, when the "big boss" went to cut the butter at the wrong end, Mum let out a shrill cry and really berated the poor man. Initially, he had no idea what he had done wrong but he soon realised, whereupon Father Jones gave his daughter a major lecture on how to behave. Sad to say, the rest of us were splitting our sides in trying to hold back the giggles until we could hold them no more and everyone burst out into raucous laughter. It was always a family joke from that day forward and on any occasion when Mum had guests, wherever they came from in the world, they were told the story about one of the captains of industry cutting the butter the wrong end and the pandemonium that followed.'

Church Farm had its share of great family parties, particularly at Christmas, when all four Tuckers with their young families came together and a great time was had by all.

Mike: 'Granny Margaret was not a big person and I remember how on these big family occasions, she had to get the coal-fired Rayburn properly stoked up for the feast ahead. She would fill the Rayburn with coke from a large scuttle and despite her lack of stature, there was no doubt where the coke was going. The end result was a red-hot cooker that would deliver a huge family feast. We would all move from the dining room to the drawing room for games of cards after the meal. It was a real learning curve for me as a young Tucker because there was fierce competition between the families, but at the same time lots of leg-pulling, fun and laughter, which was what the Tucker family was all about.

'As a small boy, there was little doubt where my heart lay at that time. I was always out and about on the farm watching the cows tied up in the barn, inspecting the calves and watching the milking and the milk being brought up to the dairy. I loved the magnificent power of the heavy horses, not as many as there once were because the use of tractors was beginning to make an impact. Horses were used, often set up in tandem with one in front of another, for pulling the big loads of straw and hay into the stone barns, which were unsuited for tractors in those days. Tractors, however, were already appearing on the binders to cut the corn and tie it into sheaves, then a team of men would work on stacking the sheaves into stooks (tight groups of sheaves) to dry out. I was riveted by the huge threshing machines, driven by mighty steam engines, which separated the actual grain from the straw, whereupon the straw was put into ricks for the winter. The grain itself, whatever the crop, was put into huge two-hundredweight bags, which were trucked off (in two-wheeled trucks pushed by the workmen) to be stored in a dry area before leaving the farm. There were so many exciting things to see but my complete joy was in the dining room at Slads Farm, where I had a big table with my own model farm laid out and I spent hours and hours playing (and talking to myself!) and enacting the various farming tasks.

Next door in the drawing room, there was a rocking horse, a present from Lady Helena Gibbs, the Duchess of Beaufort's sister, who lived in the lovely property on the other side of the river from Slads. She felt that it was a way of getting me interested in riding since, at that point, I had shown no real signs of enthusiasm. From time to time, I did sneak in there and have a play on it but the model farm took pride of place and was always the centre of attention when guests came!'

In 1949, when Mike was five years old, there was an important introduction of a competition that was to have a big impact on him. At that stage of his life, there were still no ponies and actually no interest either. In 1948, London had hosted the Olympics and there had been a disappointing result for Britain in the eventing competition, particularly on the cross-country phase, held at Tweseldown. In those days, three-day eventing was practised more on the Continent than in Britain, and was known as 'the Military', since it had its origins as a military sport and invariably involved military participants.

In response to the poor showing by Britain, the 10th Duke of Beaufort, known as Master, offered his estate as a venue for an event similar to the Olympic one, the aim being to help improve the performance of the British horses and riders. The Duke, who was a great all-round sportsman and a most impressive, upright man, summoned Colonel Gordon Cox Cox and Colonel Trevor Horn to help organise and direct a three-day event in Badminton Park. The Duke was the most famous huntsman of his time and had a great reputation for crossing the country fearlessly behind his beloved pack of hounds. He believed that, with such a great tradition of hunting in Great Britain and crossing the many and varied hunting terrains, the British should have a strong advantage in this particular phase. Of the three phases, namely dressage, showjumping and speed and endurance (which, in those days, included the cross-country phase), he was most keen to see the cross-country improve.

All the phases would fit into the park superbly. The dressage would be on the lawn, right in front of Badminton House; the speed and endurance course would weave its way around the magnificent park and through famous woods such as Allengrove and The Verge, and the lake could be used to full effect. The final day's showjumping would be in a roped arena up by Badminton Lake. Grandfather Jones was soon to be heavily involved. The planned cross-country course, more than four miles long, went around the park through the woods and then came to an old quarry right at the back of Grandfather's buildings at Castle Barn. This was cleared out and it became one of the fearsome sequences of fences on the cross-country course that was to be a feature phase of this multi-discipline competition. The Quarry was the first big feature fence on that very first course and Grampie Jones was asked to provide wagons with straw bales for The Duke's special guests to sit upon so they could watch and enjoy the spectacle and excitement that was expected there. There certainly was to be plenty of action!

The Duke of Beaufort was 'Master of the Horse', a royal appointment to oversee the royal family's extensive stable of horses. One aspect of that role was to ride alongside any coach or horse that the monarch was riding in or on. As a result, the Duke and Duchess had a very strong connection with all members of the royal family over many years. Since the royal family had a passionate interest in horses they were invited to join the Badminton house party to watch this exciting new competition.

Mike: 'I had never before seen the royal family in real life and so with a wagon for Grandfather Jones's family nearby, we had a wonderful view of the royal party watching the thrills and spills, of which there were many, at this spectacular new fence. Although I found the rules complicated, I was mightily impressed and really enjoyed the action of some of the riders falling off, remounting and carrying on again!'

It was an achievement just to get round the course that day, which not all succeeded in doing, but the best went fast and clear. Since the event took place in mid-April it was certainly 'wrap up warm time' but the crowds clearly enjoyed this inaugural event and it was obvious that those in the royal party had also enjoyed themselves. At the end of the second day, there was work to be done for Grampie Jones and the farm staff who, that evening and the following morning, had to move the wagons and straw bales from the cross-country course to around the roped ring for the final showjumping phase.

> **Mike:** 'Mum had made an exciting-looking picnic so I was persuaded to go and join Grandfather's party on his wagon to watch, but the showjumping was nowhere near as exciting as the cross-country the day before.'

The general consensus was that this was a competition that might be repeated on occasions in the future, and it certainly caused plenty of chatter in the horse world. Little did anyone know at that stage what a world-famous event it would become!

Grampie and Granny Jones had made a big impression on Mike's childhood years, but in 1954 there was more excitement around the corner. In the New Year's Honours of 1954, it was announced that Her Majesty Queen Elizabeth II was to bestow on Mike's grandfather the Member of the Order of the British Empire (the MBE) for his work with the 'War Ag' Committee and his contribution to farming during the Second World War. He and other prominent members of the agricultural world had formed a committee that advised farmers and their families regionally on how best to achieve improved yields to help feed the nation during that time. It had been a very successful campaign and Ted Jones, as he was known to the farming community, along with Professor 'Bobby' Boutflour, were two of the men honoured locally for their hard work during that campaign. (Professor Boutflour, at that time Principal of the Royal Agricultural College, was one of the great farming legends owing to his ground-breaking work to increase yields in Britain's dairy herds, which was to change and advance dairy farming.)

Mike: 'It was hailed in the local and agricultural press as a great honour that was richly deserved so, as you might imagine, the whole family glowed with pride at what my Grandfather had achieved. The presentation was to be made at Buckingham Palace by Her Majesty the Queen in the summer and arrangements were made for Grandfather, Grandmother, Mum and Dad to splash out and stay the night before in the Cumberland Hotel by Marble Arch and then go to the ceremony the next day. Only two family members, other than Grandfather, were allowed to attend the ceremony so Dad missed out and had to twiddle his thumbs while the two girls watched every moment of it. Quite rightly, there was a second night in which to celebrate this great occasion in town and the three who attended had to give Dad a blow-by-blow commentary of what happened and who said what. I was away at boarding school in those days and so it was Mum who wrote one of her lovely, long, detailed letters telling me all about it. Although when I got home on my next exeat weekend, I heard all about it again and there was little talk of anything else for several weeks!

'The Jones tradition was never to do things by halves, so up went the marquee at Woodway, which was made to look spick and span. All Grandfather's farming friends, plus relations from far and wide, together with the Duke and Duchess of Beaufort and Professor Boutflour were invited. Everyone came and it was a wonderful celebration party. Despite it being mid-week I was given permission to come out of school for the night to share a very special occasion. It is one that has always stuck in my memory to this very day and it was definitely one of those not to be forgotten memories.

'My Grandfather's influence was immense, very much through my parents but also through his outstanding example. He was a gentleman, countryman and sportsman who could walk with kings and queens yet not lose that common touch, and my

Grandmother was always there too, providing such outstanding support. How lucky was I to have such role models.'

CHAPTER THREE

Schooldays and Pony Club

Mike: 'When Grandfather Tucker retired from Church Farm in the mid-1940s, Dad inherited a most loyal and dedicated workforce. He wouldn't expect them to do anything he wouldn't do himself and as a result they trusted him and worked every hour asked of them.'

Mike's grandfather found retirement difficult and although he and his wife would venture forth in the car to visit relations, he would always find himself keeping an eye on happenings on the farm. His health was poor and he died in 1953, leaving his wife in a rambling farmhouse, which she loved, so the large size was of no concern to her. The family rallied round and she was determined to stay where she was and enjoy life to the full in Long Newnton. It was always Mike's grandfather's wish that Mike's father should be given the option of buying the farm from the rest of the family. There was, as is so often the case in family matters, plenty of wrangling and it took several months to negotiate a successful sale.

This started a new era and Mike's father and Grampie Jones were already making plans for the future. They intended to modernise the milking and were looking at some of the new inventions such as a modern milking parlour. This layout allowed all the cows to pass through the one building, with eight cows being milked at any one time by only two men working the equipment. That project entailed extensive planning and it would take several years to become a reality.

Mike's mother played her part in helping his father overcome all the work involved in running accounts for the two farms.

> **Mike:** 'But Mum always had time for her large circle of friends and there were a few who were very special and nearly always on the phone.'

Her greatest friend in those days was Rosemary Alexander, called 'Rojoe' for short, whose husband was killed in the war in Holland in 1944. Their first son William was just two years old when his father died and their second son, Roger, was born the following July. From then on Bertie and Betty, Mike's parents, became almost surrogate parents to the two boys, being incredibly generous and thoughtful toward them and making them feel part of the family. The Alexanders lived locally at Westonbirt, so the fact that they had no car was not a problem because they were mostly able to cycle everywhere, except to school.

> **Mike:** 'Mum drove the three of us to school in our trusty Rover 90. We all went to Courtfield School, Hampton Street, Tetbury, which was run by quite a fearsome lady called Chrissie Rymer. We all dreaded forgetting our seven times table because the punishment was standing in the corner for what seemed like forever and the only escape was when Mum came to pick us up at the end of the day.'

Often, after the boys had been collected from school, they were brought back to play in and around the farm buildings – not something that would satisfy the modern health and safety risk assessments! This rough and tumble would be followed by a vast tea with lashings of bread and home-made jam and slabs of delicious fruit cake. The farming life dictated that lunch was always the main meal of the day and because of the very early starts each morning for milking, supper was minimal, and so teas were important and hugely popular, particularly for the youngsters.

Mike: 'That Rover 90, which was so much part of the two boys' and my childhood, took us everywhere including on holiday to Weston-super-Mare where we always stayed in the same guest house. I remember one particular occasion when we were playing on the crazy golf course at Weston and Mum had given Roger a golf club to putt the ball all of ten yards. Well, he took a practice swing as if he was going to whack it miles and managed to crack my head open with the club on the backswing. Roger could do no wrong, so I was asked by Mum why on earth I was standing so close behind him! I still have the scar to this day! I did get my own back, however, when I challenged Roger (who couldn't ride) to a "have a go" on the donkeys on the sands at Weston-super-Mare. Instructions from Mum were simple, "No more than a walk boys", but it wasn't long before we were gaily cantering along, at which point Roger's saddle started to slip and off he came, wallop, onto the hard sand! He was bruised but no real damage was done other than to his pride. Eventually we got back to Mum and she had her "fierce face" on for all of five seconds before bursting into laughter. Dad meanwhile had missed all of this action. His love, when there was nothing better to do was to sit, sound asleep in a deckchair, trilby over his eyes, in theory relaxing and listening to the band after all the long hours on the farm.'

The time came when there was more and more talk about ponies and whether it was time for one to be bought for Mike. It was on one visit to try a pony that the Rover 90 played another part in the life of the

Alexanders. The boys would often go along just for the ride in the car when Mike was taken to view potential purchases.

Mike: 'On one particular trip Roger and William had come along with us. Mum was driving sedately through the middle of Chippenham over the bridge when I piped up "Mum why is there a wheel coming past us?". Yes, it was our wheel bumping along beside us! That turned out to be a very long day's journey en route to seeing a pony called Peggy at Calne, but we all still managed to enjoy ourselves.'

The trip to view Peggy had been set up by another of Mike's mother's great friends, Kay Stokes (née Daniels), who came from a particularly respected family in both racing and hunting in the Berkeley country. Kay had married John Stokes, who farmed at Biddestone near Chippenham and they had a young, pony-mad daughter called Gillian. The family's passion was showing ponies and they went to shows all over the country. On occasions Mike and his mother would go with them, sometimes staying in the trailer overnight in readiness for an early start the next day. The Stokes's ponies were extremely successful with Gillian and they qualified for the famous International Horse Show at the White City, London, in 1953 where Mike and his mother went in support.

Mike: 'The show at White City was really good fun and I thoroughly enjoyed the occasion. As a result, I was getting a lot more interested in the fact that Gillian Stokes went each year to the famous Beaufort Pony Club camp just outside Tetbury. Becoming a member of that same Pony Club and booking into camp soon became the next goal for one young Tucker!'

The Pony Club was first started in 1929 and set out to teach children and young people between the ages of eight and twenty-one how to ride and look after horses and ponies to best advantage. It was based around each of the hunting countries up and down the land and had proved extremely successful. To this day, one of the annual highlights for any keen member is the week of Pony Club camp. In Mike's era the Beaufort camp was held at Highgrove in Gloucestershire, now famous as the home of the HRH The Prince of Wales. It was an ideal venue, having plenty of space to accommodate everything required to run a successful camp. It was non-residential so the ponies and children were boxed or trailered in daily for tuition and all the other activities of the day. The venue provided all the facilities required to look after children of varying ages. There were over a hundred ponies and children there every day for seven days, grouped according to their age and ability. The venue also had miles of post and rail fences where all the ponies could be tied up over lunchtime. There were jumping lanes, cross-country fences and plenty of covered stock yards, ideal for wet days, lectures and the tedious tack cleaning.

Mike: 'So our trip to see the pony Peggy was successful because it was decided that she would be an ideal confidence-building pony for me and it was that pony who took me to my first Pony Club camp at Highgrove in 1954.

'A lady called Greta Phillips, who had recently been teaching a family called the Bullens in Dorset, was our instructor that first year in the bottom ride and there was a lovely gentleman by the name of Reg Brice who made us all feel very welcome. His grandchildren were there – namely Julian and Howard Hipwood![1] Their background was the polo world[1] and they were very competent riders indeed and were soon moved up to the ride above me. It left me as the only boy in my ride and I wasn't happy about that. The girls, mostly with pigtails, talked about nothing other than their ponies, tack cleaning or grooming, which all seemed very unnecessary to me. I found it difficult just to ride my pony, particularly since this was quite uncomfortable anyway,

---

1   They later became world-class players.

especially when we were encouraged to do sitting trot! However, what was fun were the picnic lunches on the ramps of the trailers parked all around the grass surrounding the glorious Highgrove House. At the end of lunch there was always an ice cream van in the park, and this quickly attracted a long queue before we went for our afternoon lecture followed by tack cleaning – ugh! I was nine years old and despite my limited talents, I amazingly passed my "D" test at the very first attempt, which certainly pleased Mum and all her friends, who had loved every minute of it, and so there was no doubt I would be coming back next year whatever I thought!'

It was in 1954 that Mike went away to Wycliffe College at Stonehouse in the Stroud Valley, a boarding establishment that had preparatory, junior, and senior schools. His friends the Alexander boys started there with him initially, but after preparatory school, they went on to Wellington College while Mike remained at Wycliffe College on the proviso that he passed the necessary exams. The Alexander boys never shared Mike's interest in riding, but they all remained friends and have kept in close touch over the years. Being sent away to school was going to be a real wrench for Mike, and whether he could cope with riding only in boarding school holidays and on exeat weekends would depend upon his enthusiasm and ability to work.

Nevertheless, Mike started hunting that autumn on Peggy, although he considered his father a disgrace the day he borrowed a skewbald pony called Sherry to escort Mike at the first meet in Estcourt Park. Sherry was far worse behaved than Peggy and in the end reared, nearly going over backwards, before Mike's father decided it was best that they went home before anything serious happened. Peggy had been ideal in that she gave Mike enormous confidence, but she was not a very good jumper and was rather sluggish, so it was decided that a new pony should be found in readiness for Pony Club camp in 1955. The next pony was soon bought, a 13.2hh part-Fell pony called Puck, who was strong but a good jumper and had been quite successful locally. Grampie Jones was thrilled with this acquisition because he could really see Mike hunting properly for the very first time, and the first meet was planned for Hawkesbury Monument in the autumn of 1954, a day that Mike remembers all too well.

Mike: 'Mum had got all the right gear and she had made sure the tack was absolutely gleaming and jodhpur boots shining because she knew that her father was going to be there proudly watching his grandson. Things didn't work out too well because the pony was very strong and very enthusiastic. Add to that the hills all around Hawkesbury Monument and I quickly knew I wasn't in control of the situation. This was my first serious meet even though it was autumn hunting and, despite my best endeavours to stay behind the field master (a fact that had been drilled into me by both Mum and Grandfather) I was not being very successful and suddenly Puck took off and galloped straight through hounds and away. I heard "Master", who was hunting hounds, bellowing at the top of his voice and when I eventually got Puck under control and came back behind the field master, I had a serious dressing down from "Master" himself and was told that if I ever did anything like that again I'd be sent home and not come out ever again! I came home with my tail very much between my legs and Grandfather was absolutely mortified so there was a big review of the situation regarding what should happen next. The former owners said that we shouldn't be worried and that, as I grew stronger, I would be able to hold Puck and he really would be a wonderful pony for my confidence in the future. And that, thank goodness, was exactly what happened.'

For Mike, riding was becoming more fun despite the disaster of that first day's hunting. He made loads of friends, enjoyed some delicious picnic lunches and, although Puck was unable to do dressage too well, he was quick and agile in gymkhana. He could certainly jump, which meant the chance to compete at plenty of hunter trials, and Mike was learning to enjoy the competitive aspect of riding.

Mike: 'So with Land Rover and trailer "roadie Mum" (and sometimes Dad) started to take us to hunter trials and local shows, especially those including gymkhana and jumping, in the Easter and summer holidays. As long as I didn't have to jump off and then get back on again (I was useless at doing that) Puck was proving very successful, particularly in hunter trials. I will always remember my first Berkeley show doing the gymkhana with two slightly older children called Terry and Tony Biddlecombe who, with their father Walter, were absolutely red-hot at the gymkhana. Puck and I had enjoyed a good run of success until we went to the Berkeley show, but there the Biddlecombes showed us how much we had to learn about the world of gymkhana and riding. They were showing their racing skills in abundance already!'[2]

On the educational front, Mike completed his first year of preparatory school in the Grove House as a boarder. It was an idyllic start to being away from home for the first time as the school had some wonderful facilities to take his mind off home, horses and the farm. It had good sports grounds, which were a novelty for him. He particularly enjoyed cricket and – amazingly for him and his family – made it into the team. Here, Mike's mother once again acted as 'roadie' and took the team in the farm's long-wheel-based Land Rover to away matches at schools such as Dean Close, Dauntsey's and Stouts Hill. Courtfield School had given Mike a good start and so, during that first year in the preparatory school, he was able to take the new education system in his stride. A year later Mike went on to Ryeford Hall, one of two houses in the junior school, which introduced

2   Tony rode 100 winners over fences, was champion amateur rider in 1961/62, and was stable jockey to Hawick-based Ken Oliver in the Borders. Terry was three times National Hunt champion jockey in 1965, 1966 and 1969 and after he retired, married Henrietta Knight, trainer of Best Mate, three-times Cheltenham Gold Cup winner for his owner Jim Lewis.

him to more sport, including football, rugby and swimming. By this stage schoolwork at the junior school was becoming more difficult and it was obvious that he was unlikely to be a scholar, but he relished sport and all the other activities at Ryeford Hall, in particular, roller skating. This was held on an area central to all of the buildings, providing enormous fun but an awful number of sore legs!

As Mike's schooling progressed, the Beaufort Pony Club was continuing to flourish. The Pony Club movement had, over the years, attracted many military personnel, often trained at the famous Weedon Military Equitation Academy in Northamptonshire, as instructors, and the Beaufort Pony Club was one of the major beneficiaries of such well-trained individuals. Just a few of the names who taught there included members of the Lowsley-Williams family, Colonel Babe Moseley, Colonel Alec Scott (who was a member of the Olympic squad in 1948), and Colonel Morgan Jones. The Beaufort members were further spoilt by benefiting from the knowledge of two equestrian heroes, Colonel Frank Weldon and Major Laurence Rook, who were both team gold medallists at the 1956 Olympics in Stockholm. Much was happening in the Duke of Beaufort's country as, not only was it one of the most famous hunts in the land, but the Badminton Horse Trials was gaining in stature and popularity year by year.

On a wider front, the fact that the British team had made it to the top of the world in Stockholm demonstrated that Weedon was playing its part in educating riders for the sport of eventing. Also instrumental in this success was another famous riding academy in Somerset named Porlock. It had been started by Captain Tony Collings, who helped to train the British team that included Weldon, Rook and a young farmer showing great talent named Bertie Hill. The work undertaken at Porlock during 1951 and 1952 in preparing for the Helsinki Olympic Games had laid a strong foundation of training, which contributed to Britain's modern, successful horsemanship. It was a tragedy that Tony Collings died prematurely before the academy at Porlock was really established, because he had achieved so much in such a short time.

As a result of all this progress, many well-known families started to move to the Badminton area. In 1959 the Bullen family moved from the well-known Catherston Stud in Dorset to the Manor House in Didmarton. Colonel Frank Weldon, Commanding Officer of the King's Troop Royal Horse Artillery, one of the very few people to have escaped from a prisoner of war camp in Germany, also moved to Didmarton with his wife Diana and their two sons, George and David, who became members of the Beaufort Pony Club. A young Mark Phillips, whose family lived in Somerford, joined the Pony Club with another great friend from the same village, Toby Sturgis, who was also to have a successful career in eventing,[3] and Bridget Long who, as Bridget Parker, was to win team gold at the Munich Olympics and later became chairman of the Senior Selection' Committee.

Mike: 'We were so spoilt to have such a wonderful array of talent to help instruct us, but at the same time it was all very competitive. About the time I was getting towards the senior rides Colonel Frank Weldon, Chief Instructor of the top ride, and Major Laurence Rook, who had moved from Kent to Beverston Castle just outside Tetbury with his wonderful wife Jane, both became a key part of the Pony Club's discipline and etiquette. They quickly became extremely influential over the Pony Club team training squad. Colonel Weldon made learning such fun and he would often bring one of his young horses to demonstrate correct presentation to an obstacle over the cross-country fences around the park. We all hung on his every word and were mindful of the fact that this was the man who rode one of the best event horses

---

3 He did, indeed, but things didn't always go smoothly. Gail, who became Toby's wife, recalled that: 'It was either 1968 or '69 when Mike and Toby set off to a competition together up in the wilds of Herefordshire, full of hope and expectations. Boys being boys, they chatted about this and that before they jumped into the lorry to set off – and off they went. It wasn't until about half an hour later that Granny Tucker asked me which horses had they taken, as there were plaited ones in the stables tied up. Yup … they had gone without their horses. No mobiles then. Two very sheepish boys returned later in the day – they never did that again!'

in the world, Kilbarry, and was winning major steeplechases with his super horse Snowshill Jim.'

Highgrove had been the location for the Pony Club Championships of Great Britain so there were all types of cross-country fences around the park that were used for those capable of jumping them during Pony Club camp.

Mike: 'Colonel Frank had us all going down the jumping lane with no stirrups and singing songs as we went and he had some amazing phrases that made us laugh, but actually had an impact when we had them interpreted by him and really drove home what was required. Those phrases might have been fairly rough and ready but my word, we did remember them. One was "Keep kicking" and another, very much related, which I remember to this day, was "One in the kisser and two in the guts!" As you can imagine, we loved hearing him call them out!'

By this time Mike was fourteen; he was really enjoying his riding and gaining a certain degree of success which, in turn, triggered more ambition. His parents were hugely supportive and his mother was a great organiser and recruited local help with the horses to keep them in work while Mike was away at school so, when he did get home, he was able to continue enjoying his riding. Willie Donaldson and his working partner, Theo Butchart, who together had one of the top local showing and breaking yards in Malmesbury, became very important stable advisers and helpers. Their enthusiasm and knowledge would be essential if Mike's growing equestrian ambitions were to be achieved.

At school, Mike managed to squeak a pass in the exams to move up to Haywardsfield House, one of four houses that made up the senior school, the biggest part of Wycliffe College. Four very happy years were to be spent in there, where a new science block meant the additional teaching facilities offered a great opportunity to move forward. He also made the best use of the excellent sports facilities at Wycliffe College, which allowed him to enjoy team game success in cricket and rugby. He travelled to some of the local schools in the Colts team and the Seconds for both rugby and cricket.

However, despite enjoying many aspects of his schooling, it became clear before long that the opportunity to move on to higher education was not a route to be taken by this particular pupil. After two years in the senior school the decision was made that Mike should leave school at sixteen. Then, after a family discussion, which included Grampie Jones, it was decided he should aim for the Royal Agricultural College at Cirencester as the next planned educational move. This did not come as a surprise, bearing in mind Mike's grandfather's relationship with the former Principal, Professor Bobby Boutflour. Fortuitously, in addition to the science and sports facilities at Wycliffe College:

Mike: 'There was another facility, which was just up my street. They had a small farm that was overseen by the woodwork teacher Mr Parrott, a farmer himself. That gave me my first opportunity to understand about the feeding of poultry, pigs and a few cattle, and gave me a basic understanding of some of the principles behind the care and welfare of stock. I made many new friends whom I was to meet again over a number of years in different parts of the world and they were very happy days. I was able to get sufficiently good exam results (the exams weren't that difficult) to get me an entry into the Agricultural College. This allowed me the next year, having left school, to be farming at home to complete the practical experience which was needed before college. I remember being given a serious lecture from both Mum and Dad that this was going to be a year's working at home and although I would still be allowed to ride it would have to be on the basis that I had to put sufficient work into the farm.'

In 1958, with Mike's pony Puck becoming outgrown, and having proved more effective at cross-country than at the other phases of eventing, Mike's parents had bought him a 15.2hh mare called Turkish Delight from Reg Brice, who ran a popular riding school on the edge of Minchinhampton. Turkish Delight had been ridden in the Beaufort Pony Club team by Reg's head girl, Rosemary Calvert, who succeeded in getting through to the Pony Club Championships on her. Whereas Puck had certainly fulfilled his role in getting Mike enthused and competitive, this new mare could perform all three phases of eventing proficiently. Puck was retired and stayed with the Tucker family until the day he died.

> **Mike:** 'I found dressage difficult and painful, my showjumping was agricultural to say the least, but it was cross-country that I found really exciting and challenging so that is why I needed a schoolmaster (or, in this case, mistress) to help.'

However, Colonel Frank's jumping tuition was beginning to produce some improvement in the young Tucker and, even in the mysterious world of dressage, Major Rook's wise words were helping to improve his marks and so it was, in 1959, that he made his first Pony Club team.

The same year saw the Bullen family's first appearance at Pony Club camp at Highgrove, in the persons of sisters Jennie and Jane with their lovely ponies (younger sister Sarah attended a year or two later). In the big family there were also three boys, one of whom, also a Mike, was training with Colonel V.D.S. and Mrs Williams and hoping to make the British eventing team.

Jennie and Jane Bullen were quickly selected for the Beaufort Pony Club team, along with Rob Erswell, and Mike's selection with Turkish Delight to join these three for the inter-branch competition at Trewsbury near Cirencester was a huge boost to his confidence. However, although it was a great honour for him to be chosen, it proved to be a nerve-racking experience. Not surprisingly, because of their lack of experience at this level at the time, the team failed to qualify for the finals but finished in third place, giving them real encouragement for the future. Pony Club eventing was growing in popularity and very competitive but at the same time it provided a platform for making many new friends and created great camaraderie.

Mike: 'There is absolutely no doubt that the phrase "Friends you made in your Pony Club days are true friends for life" is absolutely correct.

'Colonel Frank was a true inspiration to us all. I'm not sure that we really understood how privileged and spoilt we were, not only to have him but also Major and Mrs Rook all taking an interest in us. They made a wonderful combination with all three of them looking after the team, giving us the best instruction not only in riding skills but also life as well. By now we had the bit firmly between our teeth and Turkish Delight was developing into a star as she took me to my first Pony Club Championships in 1961 at the fabulous venue at Burley-on-the-Hill in the County of Rutland. The standard was very high but on our first appearance at the finals we didn't disgrace ourselves even though we didn't win a prize. In fact, it was a culmination of a dream to get to the finals at all and served as yet more encouragement for me to go further and higher.'

Messrs Rook, Weldon and Hill were known as the 'Laughing Cavaliers' and to have these members of the British team as mentors for the Beaufort Pony Club team was something to treasure for all involved. Regular conversations with Colonel Frank, in particular, encouraged the Tucker clan to progress to the British Horse Society eventing circuit:

Mike: 'Mum was going to have to get out the roadmap and become a roadie again to drive me around the country to the events.'

The campaign started in the spring of 1962 with Crookham Horse

Trials, held at Tweseldown, being Mike's first-ever BHS event. Riding Turkish Delight, he finished in second place in the novice section, an exciting result and all the more so because of the presence of Colonel Frank to witness it. This was the moment when ambition began to grow in the direction of what was known as the 'Local Gymkhana', namely the Badminton three-day event. It was growing in stature year by year and, as a result, with the encouragement of his parents and grandparents, Mike's one aim was to ride there one day. However, although Turkish Delight had given Mike huge confidence and experience around a number of novice event courses, she had now reached her limits and, with the talents of Jennie and Jane Bullen and Mark Phillips all beginning to come to the fore, she was no longer good enough to make the Beaufort Pony Club team.

So, in the autumn of 1962, Mike and his parents started scanning the 'For Sale' columns of *Horse & Hound* for his next horse and discovered one that might fit the bill owned by the Acheson family in Norfolk. They were part of the very successful West Norfolk Pony Club and their son George had been a member of the British Universities team in Europe, riding a Swedish Warmblood called The Viking. George had to give up riding to concentrate on studying medicine and the horse had to be sold. This was the most expensive horse the Tuckers had ever looked at, so they took the experienced Willie Donaldson with them for advice and drove all the way to Norfolk to try him. The horse was considerably bigger than anything Mike had ridden up until then, and was quite flashy, with a reasonable but not over-scopey jump. Jock Ferrie, Riding Master of the Household Cavalry, was team trainer of the West Norfolk Pony Club and also George's trainer. Despite his sixteen stone he was a seriously good dressage rider and displayed The Viking to his best. They had put on a good show, but Mike managed to enjoy his ride and coped reasonably well.

Mike: 'To cut a long story short we bought the horse and this started a long friendship with Jock, who shortly after leaving the Household Cavalry became dressage trainer for the Irish three-day event team. Once again my parents were wonderful and had come up trumps because this was not a cheap acquisition in those days, but he turned out to be the best schoolmaster possible for the keen, now ambitious young Tucker.'

By the autumn of 1962 Mike was taking the work at the Royal Agricultural College seriously but, by going into lectures from home on a daily basis, he was able to keep riding and got to know his new horse. Academia did not come easily to him, but the ability to ride before he left for lectures or after he had finished in the afternoon, gave him the encouragement he needed to cope with all the work about the farming industry. He was embracing this new life with the definite aim after two years of achieving the National Diploma of Agriculture (NDA).

Mike: 'We took our time to find the buttons to make Ben *[The Viking's nickname]* tick and I spent time getting to know him in the hunting field as well as having some dressage lessons with Molly Sivewright at Talland School of Equitation, close to Cirencester. The partnership began to develop in the correct way and so it was a case of making plans for the year ahead. The aim was to compete at some BHS events in the spring of 1963 and then perhaps have one last crack at getting to the Pony Club Championships again.'

Mike turned seventeen just two months into his first term at Cirencester and girls had barely featured in his life up until then. His new mates at college soon made him realise that he was missing out and, with the college a male-only establishment, it was decided that something needed to be done about the situation! Rumour had it that there was a bevy of lovely girls at the Cirencester Operatic Society, which was held in the Beeches Centre in the centre of town.

Mike: 'So a gang of us went and it was certainly true that there were some lovely girls there, but the only problem was that they were casting for the Gilbert and Sullivan production of

The Gondoliers. I had done a bit of drama and was even in the choir at Wycliffe and had benefited from elocution lessons at Courtfield. I thought it would be the chorus for me, which would be fun, but that was not to be because they were really struggling to find some of the principals in the cast. I had never been able to read music or know what notes I was trying to sing but I was always encouraged to have a go. It proved how short of talent they were when they encouraged me to try for the part of the Duke of Plaza Toro, a pompous character who was the lead role of *The Gondoliers* production. Amazingly I got the part and had to put in hours of homework. Actually I loved it and was reported to be making a reasonable job of it. The final result can't have been too bad because I was given leading parts in four productions in all, two Gilbert and Sullivan, the second being *The Pirates of Penzance*, and the other two were Rodgers and Hammerstein productions of *Oklahoma* and *South Pacific*. We rehearsed throughout the winter in the evenings and the productions ran for a week in May each year. Performances were held in the Bingham Hall and attracted nightly audiences of about three hundred. It was hugely rewarding and great fun, all the more so since a number of mates joined in the excitement of being involved in the Cirencester production. These included Jane Bullen, some of the staff from Didmarton, Mike Petre, a great Pony Club mate, along with other locals. Eventually I could no longer spare the time but it had given me so much confidence in performing in public and undoubtedly played a part in shaping my future career as a commentator. Although I didn't realise it at the time, the great Dorian Williams, perhaps the greatest-ever voice of equestrian sport, was a Shakespearean actor and his theatrical background played a huge part in his outstanding career.'

In 1963 the plan was to concentrate on competing at some intermediate events with Ben and to try to qualify for the Pony Club Championships at

Stoneleigh, the home of Lord Leigh, in what was most certainly going to be Mike's last year in the Pony Club. Colonel Frank was still team trainer and, with his help, Mike and Ben won an intermediate class at Downlands Horse Trial at Liphook in Hampshire that spring and also achieved several good places elsewhere, so by the autumn the partnership was looking quite promising. The area trial was at Wells in Somerset and two great friends of Mike's, namely George Weldon and Mark Phillips, were fellow members of the team. Sadly the team did not qualify, but Mike and Ben won the Associate section and so qualified as an individual for the finals. It was a great thrill to qualify but the whole team all had dreams of higher accolades.

Mike: 'It was very hot competition and although the day didn't work out the way we had hoped, we finished fifth in the midst of some very well-known names. What we didn't realise until after the Championships was that, earlier in the spring, Ben and I had actually qualified for Badminton, would you believe? In those days – it's a bit different now – all you had to do to get a Badminton qualification was to win a prize of fifteen pounds or more and go clear around two intermediate cross-country courses. I had done both in 1963, so I then asked Colonel Frank whether we would be silly to contemplate going to Badminton in 1964. I suspected he would just laugh at the suggestion. To my delight, his answer was to go to Chatsworth Park at the end of the autumn season that year and then, depending on performance, make the decision of whether to go or not.'

Before Mike's final Pony Club camp he decided to try for his 'A' test. It has always been regarded as a very stiff exam to pass and candidates have always had to take it at an outside venue, and not at camp. The number of passes has never been high, even in those days, so it was a big surprise to his parents and a proud moment for everyone when Mike came home with his 'A' test certificate, rounding off what had been a wonderful time of his life in the Pony Club.

Mike: 'The 1964 season was far from over as we made the long journey from Gloucestershire to Derbyshire to what must be one of the most beautiful venues for an event anywhere in the world. It was without doubt the biggest and grandest competition that I'd ever seen. We had made many friends on the circuit and several of them were also competing at Chatsworth for the first time, including Mary Macdonnell, Edwin Atkinson and a number of riders from the King's Troop, who were also successful competitors in the sport. As a guest at the splendid cocktail party in Chatsworth House my eyes popped out of my head – it was truly amazing. Luckily we all managed to keep our heads and not get carried away, so we were keen and ready for action the next day. The Chatsworth hills have always been demanding for the cross-country, so I could see why Colonel Frank had suggested this was a good trial for Badminton. All went well in the dressage in front of one of the biggest crowds I'd seen and I finished with a reasonable mark. I was more than happy with the showjumping round, with just one rail down, but about halfway around the cross-country, Ben rubbed the top of a big drop rail and out the side door I went. It was a long way down and it really hurt when I landed, but we had always been encouraged to jump back on quickly if possible and finish the course. That we did, but I was so bitterly disappointed because I thought that was the end of the Badminton 1964 dream and it meant a long, quiet journey home.

'I rang Colonel Frank to ask him his thoughts and was very much taken by surprise when he suggested that it would be worth preparing for Badminton. He suggested we see how I fared at the pre-Badminton competitions before taking the final decision whether to run. This was music to my ears and I decided to give Ben a rest until Christmas, then make plans for the spring competitions leading up to Badminton, incorporating yet more dressage and jumping lessons in preparation for the possible goal ahead.'

In the first two years studying at the RAC, competing on one horse and studying for the NDA had all gone well and Mike was feeling confident about the future. The dual challenge had been successfully accomplished by Scotland's John Tulloch when he completed his land agency exams and managed to ride at Badminton. Mike was well aware that, if 1964 was to be successful, he had to work incredibly hard. Not only was Badminton a real test, but passing his college exams was of vital importance to guarantee the continued support of his family. The only other person that year to be attempting the same feat was Bill Leigh, Lord Leigh's son from Stoneleigh, on his horse Marshall Tudor.

Badminton was growing in popularity year on year and the number of entries had increased to such an extent that the organisers decided to divide the competition into two sections run over the same course. The most experienced and highest prize-winners were put in the top section, which was called 'Great Badminton', and the less experienced and lower qualified partnerships were in the second section for the 'Little Badminton' title. In 1959 Sheila Wilcox (later Waddington) won her third Badminton on Airs and Graces and Shelagh Kesler on Double Diamond was the winner of the first 'Little Badminton' competition. In 1963 Badminton suffered its first cancellation for bad weather. The event was, at that time, held in April and in fact only changed to the current May date in 1988 following the need to cancel on several occasions. (The division of the competition was abandoned in 1965, since when the dressage phase has been held over two days to more readily accommodate the number of entries.)

At the time when Mike was contemplating his first Badminton, three-day eventing was a true all-round test of horse and rider via the dressage, speed and endurance and then, provided the horse was still fit and able, the final showjumping phase. Without doubt the most influential phase was the speed and endurance, which was made up of five phases. The first phase (A) was 4,500 metres of roads and tracks, mostly taken at a trot as a warm-up before the 3,000 metres (phase B) of steeplechase, with eight or nine steeplechase fences taken at the fastest speed of all the phases at 690 metres a minute. The next roads and tracks (phase C) was nearly 10,000 metres and was used as the recovery phase after the speed and exertion of the steeplechase. This phase was the time when riders had to judge how well their horse was recovering before trotting on to arrive without time penalties for the cross-country (phase D). There was then a compulsory ten-minute halt including a brief veterinary inspection to ensure that the horse was fit to continue onto the cross-country test. This was a huge welfare factor for any horse taking part and there were a good number that were not allowed to proceed to the cross-country phase.

The cross-country consisted of more than thirty numbered fences but, because several were combination obstacles, more jumping efforts were required than the fence numbering itself suggested. The course covered a distance of over four miles with an optimum speed of around 570 metres per minute. It was a demanding test of guts and determination of horse and rider and both required supreme fitness.

Phase E was still in existence in 1964. This was 1,500 metres long and had to be completed at a slow canter, with the object of winding down the horse prior to the finish. This final phase was abandoned in 1965 to allow for a more exciting gallop to the finishing line for a fit horse and, at the same time, was deemed unnecessary for a weary one.

Mike: 'The sight of the thrilling finish to the Badminton speed and endurance test was by all accounts magical, and a daunting but exciting challenge lay ahead for The Viking and me if everything fell into place in the next few months. I couldn't wait.'

CHAPTER FOUR

Eventing
Begins in Earnest

The year of 1964 dawned with potentially exciting challenges or possible disappointments. During the winter months, plans were laid in preparation for the eventuality of Mike and Ben attempting their first Badminton, but nothing was yet finalised. It was also the second and final year of the National Diploma of Agriculture course at Cirencester, with mid-summer exams in Leeds. Hours of hard work and revision would be required if Mike were to achieve both goals.

Mike: 'It was a real pleasure to be doing the agricultural course at Cirencester in those days, enjoying the wisdom of the very best lecturers. Geoffrey Craghill was a great countryman and lectured on animal husbandry, my favourite subject. Vic Hughes was farm manager, taught farm management and few would be more qualified to teach this important topic. Di Barling, extremely well respected in the academic world, made grassland management so interesting. These were just a few of the subjects and, at a time when there were many changes afoot in the industry, there was no doubt that a huge amount of time for revision would be required for all the papers.'

Although Mike and Ben had qualified for Badminton it was questionable whether the relatively inexperienced partnership of a nineteen-year-old Mike and Ben should be taking on this massive test, the most challenging part of which comprised over seventeen miles of speed and endurance.

Ben was brought back into work just before Christmas with the idea of giving him some short days hunting to help with his fitness, a crucial requirement for the future action. Colonel Frank Weldon, Mike's mentor, was riding Young Pretender in the 'Great Badminton' competition, one of the big final trials for team selection for the Olympic Games in Tokyo that October, so he would be fully committed to his own preparation and perhaps less available to help Mike prepare for 'Little Badminton'. To give Mike a full opportunity to achieve his aims, Ben was sent to livery at the Talland School of Equitation, just two miles from the Agricultural College. This short distance allowed Mike to attend important lectures and have more time for revision as well as being able to work with Ben. The added bonus was that Ben would be looked after professionally in a yard with very good training facilities. Mike's dressage was also able to benefit from Molly Sivewright's teaching skills.

Mike: 'All the plans were laid for Badminton but to ensure that we were well enough prepared, we had to go well at two important spring events. A good performance would give me a real chance of realising my dream to ride at Badminton. Crookham Trials, held at Tweseldown near Aldershot, was always one of the first competitions of the eventing calendar and that year it was a two-day event. We did dressage and showjumping on day one and an extended cross-country with some short roads and tracks before and after the steeplechase on the second day. It was an important exercise for me to be riding steeplechase fences for the first time and overall a really good practice for Badminton. Many of the famous names were competing at Crookham and so we had no chance of finishing in the prize money, but confident clear rounds in both the showjumping and the cross-country, plus a reasonable dressage, meant we went home with a huge amount of confidence and a feeling that the goal was still a possibility.'

Two weeks later was Downlands Horse Trials in Hampshire. This competition held happy memories for Mike after his win the previous year. This time the class was open to the top horses and riders, with a more difficult dressage test and a bigger showjumping course but not the highest level of cross-country. The decision to run here was part of the plan, believing it was better to go to Badminton full of confidence, rather than risk losing it over a more difficult track.

Mike: 'All went well and so it was thumbs-up for my first attempt at the famous Badminton, but instead of being over the moon, I found it a very tense and nervy two-week build-up to mid-April and the actual competition. Pauline Smith looked after Ben while he was at Talland and she was to come as groom for me at the event itself. This was a dream come true for her, being in charge of a horse at Badminton. For me it was a real treat and a novelty because I had always been my own groom up until then. Pauline was absolutely magnificent, making sure Ben looked at his very best and had everything that he needed.

'In many respects the whole Badminton week was like a haze. It was hard to believe that it happened at all as the time passed so quickly. There were too many competitors for all their horses to be stabled in the magnificent main yard so a few of us were stabled nearby in a small yard behind the Badminton estate office. It was wonderfully quiet and ideal in allowing Ben to relax. The moment it actually sunk in that we really had made it, was when I led Ben through the lovely arch into the big Badminton stable yard for the first horse inspection. There were far more people there watching than I ever expected.'

For every competitor horse inspections have always been (and always will be) one of the most nerve-racking parts of a three-day event. The purpose of the initial inspection is for the ground jury (the judges) and the appointed veterinary officer to ensure that each horse is sound and fit prior to the first of the three disciplines, the dressage. It is easy to forget just how much work goes into preparing a horse for any three-day event (a point especially relevant in the days of the long format of roads and tracks and steeplechase), so there is relief all round when a horse passes.

Many of Mike's new friends made since he started eventing were, like him, having their first experience of that big occasion: Mary Macdonnell, Tom Durston-Smith, Alison Oliver and Eric Thompson were all in the 'Little Badminton' section. So was Sheila Waddington, who, under her maiden name of Wilcox, had won the main event twice in 1957 and 1958, and again under her married name in 1959, but this year now riding her new, young and promising prospect, but relatively inexperienced Glenamoy.

Mike: 'I will always remember the very first night after we had taken Ben to the Badminton stables. It was a Tuesday evening and I decided to go to the Hare and Hounds Hotel at Westonbirt, which was known as the headquarters of the Badminton Horse Trials. I walked into the bar and there was a loud shout from the other end. I wasn't quite sure who it was but on investigation it was none other than the man who found Ben for me, Major Jock Ferrie, with his Irish riders Tommy Brennan and John Harty, all thoroughly enjoying their glasses of Guinness. Jock exclaimed very loudly, "Here Tucker, what are you doing here at Badminton? I sold George Acheson's Ben to you to go Pony Club eventing not to come to Badminton. I can't believe you've got him this far!" It was a wonderful welcome and we had a great night together and, what's more, I still felt fine the next morning! This really was the start for me of the great camaraderie that I have enjoyed in the sport wherever I have been all over the world.

'The dressage was quite scary and I got really nervous. The main arena was in the middle of the park with proper grandstands all round and no longer Grampie Jones's farm wagons. I ended that phase about halfway down the order but it was the next day that all the talk was about. The speed and endurance phase took a new route through the park and didn't go to the old quarry at Castle Barn, but a new Quarry obstacle had been built at the other end of the park. There were plenty of other famous fence names in the course – the Coffin, the Luckington Lane crossings, the Irish Bank and the Open Water – the fence I particularly didn't like. The cross-country course didn't frighten me too much but the combined length of the two roads and tracks phases, the steeplechase (Ben was no racehorse) coming before the cross-country followed by the final fifteen-hundred-metre run-in, made me wonder whether Ben would be down to a walk by then.

'What I do remember of that day – and I would have to admit it was all a blur – was the steeplechase. We had a maximum score[1] but he did pull up blowing quite hard so I let him walk for about ten minutes while he got his breath back. Then, by trotting and cantering on some good ground to keep up to time at each kilometre marker, we found ourselves on target for the time on phase C of the roads and tracks. One of the great monuments in the park is called Worcester Lodge, which was about two miles from the end of phase C. You saw very few people on roads and tracks and it was quite a lonely ride really, but you could get the feel of how your horse was coping and the Lodge was a good landmark to ascertain how fit he felt. Actually, Ben was fine, but

1   Compared to the current scoring based solely on penalties, scoring was different in the early years of Badminton.

I felt sick because the closer you drew to the finish the more you could smell the hot dogs and burgers being cooked in the main arena area and it was not a nice feeling!

'Luckily there was so much happening in the ten-minute break after phase C and before the cross-country that any thought of sickness had disappeared. Ben had to be inspected by an experienced panel which, in those days, was made up of two vets and an experienced horseman. That year it was Bill Bush, a top point-to-point jockey who gave me a confidence boost by being very complimentary about how Ben was looking. So, with horse freshened up and jockey briefed, it was time to girth up, get legged-up and, with a short warm-up, we came under starter's orders.'

The start was down by the front entrance to the park by the Badminton stables and a large crowd had gathered to cheer the competitors on their way. The memories of riding Badminton for the first time are vivid for most riders and Mike can remember the course in detail. He recalls the three straightforward fences going away from Badminton House before encountering the famously difficult Coffin combination, which always caused problems early in the course.

Mike: 'Already I was aware of the big crowds and I realised I had to have Ben's full attention. He was an honest, genuine horse and all I had to do was ensure the correct speed for each fence. He jumped a sequence of rails downhill to a ditch, followed uphill to another set of rails really well and I had Colonel Weldon's words "Keep kicking" ringing in my ears. We negotiated the Luckington Lane crossings then galloped back to the Open Water which, despite my misgivings, Ben jumped like a stag. I began to think I should go a little quicker but I still wasn't halfway round and had yet to jump the biggest fence, the Irish Bank, so decided to keep the same pace for a little longer. He scrambled up the bank over the ditch, onto the top and quickly popped down the other side as if he had been doing it all his life.

'Then it was out through Allengrove Wood towards the new Quarry, which was just a sheer maximum drop of one-eighty metres to the bottom! It looked huge from the top of Ben but I gave him a big kick and down he popped, clean as a whistle. We were well over halfway by now, not quick on the clock but still clear and as long as I kept my head, I felt we could get home and possibly even stay clear. Fence by fence we closed in on the fantastic sight of the last fence, the Whitbread Bar. I so nearly wrestled him to the ground, trying too hard to meet it right, but Ben did what he thought was right and we slithered over! But that wasn't quite the end because we still had some fifteen-hundred metres of the run-in. We turned away from the finish box and Ben suddenly decided he'd had enough and broke from canter into trot and I had visions of us picking up time faults in this last phase. It was quite a struggle to get home but in the end we made Phase E inside the time; I wasn't sure who was more tired, me or Ben. What a wonderful experience it was and my dream had been realised! All the family and support team, including Grampie Jones, were over the moon. Ben was washed down, rugged up and put into his cosy stable looking pretty weary but seemingly fine. At the end of the day, a tea in the stables' canteen revealed some very excited competitors including this one, as well as some disappointed ones, all full of stories.'

Sheila Waddington was leading Mike's section, in which he had managed to pull up into eighth place after the cross-country. James Templer on M'Lord Connolly was leading the big section. Mike had supper that evening with Grampie Jones at Woodway. Now widowed and in his seventies, Grampie Jones was in great spirits because this achievement was something he had wanted as much as his grandson, and he demanded to hear how Ben had jumped every fence on the course. Mike had one important job before bedtime and that was to check his horse and hope that all would be well for the final horse inspection and showjumping phase the following day.

Mike: 'I didn't sleep much that night, so with the adrenalin still running, getting to Badminton for seven o'clock to ride that morning was no problem. Pauline had taken Ben for a pick of grass at six, ready for me to go for a short hack to help him loosen up. He was tired and stiff, which I'd never experienced before, but when he went out into the park and heard the Beaufort hounds in their kennels he suddenly livened up. I began to realise that there might be just enough energy left for the jumping. So, it was then breakfast for both of us (although I can't say I was feeling hungry) while Pauline prepared him gleaming and polished for the final inspection. If the first horse inspection was nerve-racking, the second was a thousand times worse. We had practised for these inspections while at Talland and my word did it pay off. It's all too easy for a horse to fail by not trotting up well in front of the inspection panel. Several horses did fail but Ben wasn't one of them so we moved on to that final phase.'

Before the showjumping begins, there is always a parade of all the remaining competitors. It is inevitably a stirring experience and the rider has to try to conserve the horse's energy and attempt to remain relaxed – never easy with bands playing and crowds clapping and cheering! This was Mike's first experience of showjumping after a demanding speed and endurance test and he discovered a totally different Ben:

Mike: 'After the exertions of the day before, the horse is unlikely to feel his normal self and the only comparison I can make is to say it was like driving a car with a flat tyre because Ben didn't turn and respond to the aids like he normally did.'

The Sivewright team was there to help Mike in the collecting ring during the important warm-up. All the scores were very close and the course was not proving easy. Ben tried hard and, despite rattling a few poles, only had one down and the partnership moved up two places to eventually finish sixth. This was a truly creditable performance for a first attempt. Sheila Waddington won the section and James Templer won the 'Great Badminton' title, with Colonel Frank in fourth place on Young Pretender.

> **Mike:** 'What a thrill it was when Colonel Frank came up and congratulated us. There was one even bigger thrill to come when Her Majesty the Queen, escorted by the Duke of Beaufort, presented the rosettes. He was delighted that I, a Beaufort Pony Club member, was in the final line-up. What a dreamy week it had been and everything had lived up to my expectations.'

There was little time for much in the way of celebration because it was less than six weeks to Mike's final exams, held at Leeds University. Two of Mike's great pals on the course were Paul Thain and Ken Davies and they had arranged to travel to Leeds together and stay in Pontefract with a school friend.

> **Mike:** 'I'd never been good in exams at school and although I loved the class work at Cirencester there was no guarantee I could get it down on paper and my two mates rather feared the same. By the time we'd come out of the first paper, morale had dropped even further but there was time for a quick pint before we were back to last-minute revision. We thought the papers were a little easier but none of us was banking on a pass. By the time we'd spent three full days doing exams we were ready to celebrate on two levels. One: that we had lasted the full two years without being kicked out and two: there would be no more exams! And did we celebrate before we left Yorkshire! We were not in the

best of condition to make the journey home the next day but we survived. It was agonising waiting for the results but when they eventually came, I was mightily relieved to learn that I had passed my National Diploma of Agriculture. This was a really important result for me. I had so wanted to reward my parents for all the sacrifices they had made to enable me to study at the RAC and continue riding at the same time.

'Meanwhile, life at home had not stood still and the dairy cows' new milking parlour and covered yards at Church Farm were already showing practical advantages and financial returns for Dad. He had also asked Estcourt Estate to give permission for the same improvements to be made at Slads Farm.'

On the riding front there was disappointing news, since Ben had picked up an injury at Badminton and consequently would be sidelined for the autumn events. Plans to enter Burghley three-day event would have to be put on hold. Mike and his parents went on a trip to Ascot Sales to look for a suitable replacement, but these sales were not renowned as a place to find an event horse in those days. There was, however, a two-year-old up for auction, by the good Cornish stallion, Little Cloud, out of a Cleveland Bay mare. This youngster was related to a very good horse called Viscount, on whom Lars Sederholm had enjoyed much success.

Mike: 'When we got there we were disappointed to find the horse was enormous for a two-year-old and had two bony growths on his hind legs just below his hocks called curbs, potentially a sign of weakness. We thought that was that but, out of interest, watched him go through the auction ring with his breeder. The bidding stuck at 250 guineas and I couldn't believe it when Dad stuck his hand up. Sold! Dad had bought the horse, but what on earth were we going to do with him? We eventually got him home and once again Willie Donaldson was called upon to give his opinion. He was prompt in saying that there was only one thing to do and that was to call Jeffrey Brain, the well-respected vet, to seek his advice. I suspect Jeffrey was pretty shocked at what he saw but he said there was only one thing to do and that was a treatment called firing *[no longer legal in the UK]*. He said the horse should then be left out in the field for a year and we would see what results we had after that.'

The horse was called Farmer Giles and, despite his unpromising start, he was to become one of the stars of Mike's riding career. As a result of the successful operation, Jeffrey became the Tuckers' horse vet and a very dear friend for many years.

Autumn 1964 was a busy time on the farm for Mike, with many exciting new projects and the farmyard seeing some major changes, with the power of the industry coming from mechanical sources rather than horses. With such changes came changes in the workforce, particularly on the milking side, where a milking machine was installed and a new herdsman named Mervyn Arthurs took control of the Church Farm herd.

Mike: 'Socially, I was still enjoying being part of the Cirencester Operatic Society but had also joined the local Young Farmer's Club (YFC) in Malmesbury. Many members of the local farming community were involved in this active youth movement, which in many ways was taking over from the Pony Club in my life. I was still young enough for the Pony Club, but no longer an active member. The YFC had lots of inter-club competitions, and I became particularly involved in the debating and public speaking side. I remember a gentleman by the name of Michael Copland setting me off by asking me to speak for two minutes about toilets – and that is how it all began! My first public engagement was when I was asked by the Beaufort Pony Club organisers if I would commentate at their hunter trials, which is exactly where ideas for my career were started.'

On the horse front, while Ben was recovering from his injury, Mike was given an ex-racehorse, Northern Saga, by a friend of his father's called Henry Witchell, a member of the famous Balding family from the racing world, and this horse became Mike's next project, being the only horse he was riding that autumn. Despite being less active in the Pony Club, he still kept in touch with his Pony Club friends, in particular Charlie Bullen who, unlike the rest of his family, was not over-keen on riding. Charlie loved machines and helped his family at the Manor House stables in Didmarton by keeping the machines, many of which were his own, in working order. He and Mike would spend time together on the two neighbouring farms. Meanwhile, Charlie's brother Michael had been picked for the British team for the Tokyo Olympics on Sea Breeze, along with James Templer, Ben Jones and Richard Meade, with Colonel Frank Weldon as team manager.

That October, everyone was eager for news of the Olympic equestrian events in Japan. Although expectations of the British eventing team were high, things did not go well. Both Mike Bullen on Sea Breeze and James Templer on M'Lord Connolly were eliminated and, as a consequence, so was the team. Ben Jones and Richard Meade, despite their good performances, were not in the medals. It was while discussing the disappointments of that competition that Charlie informed Mike that all the Australian Olympic team horses were coming to spend their quarantine period at Didmarton when they returned from the Olympics in late October. Mike Bullen was a director of Pedens, one of the main shipping agents of horses worldwide and instrumental in the horses being shipped to the UK. At that time, and for at least two more Olympics, strict Australian laws meant that, before the horses could be shipped back to Australia from abroad, they had to spend a compulsory eleven months of quarantine based in the UK (which was deemed to have strict disease controls in place) before they were allowed home.

The Australian team already had connections with the UK, having previously campaigned here, from a base at Brian Crago's yard near Aldershot, in preparation for the Rome Olympics in 1960. One member of that team was the legendary 'iron man' Bill Roycroft who, despite having had a nasty fall on the cross-country, remounted and finished the course. He was later taken to hospital, but discharged himself the next day so he could ride in the showjumping phase to help secure team gold! Another of that team, Laurie Morgan, remained in the UK after Rome not only to win Badminton in 1961 with Salad Days but also to win both the Cheltenham and Aintree Foxhunters' races on a hunter-chaser called College Master. What a horseman!

The Australians' arrival at Didmarton caused much excitement and although they had failed to win an eventing medal in Tokyo, they had been much talked about because three of the four horses in their team were only six years old. Also included in the squad was John Fahey who, with his diminutive horse Bonvale, had competed in the Olympic showjumping and jumped-off for the bronze medal against Britain's Peter Robeson and Firecrest, with the latter partnership proving successful.

Although all the Australian squad of horses had to come to the United Kingdom for the full quarantine period, not all the riders came. Of those who did, Bill Roycroft was 'team leader', having been one of the earlier visitors to Britain in 1960, in fact winning the Badminton title that year with the brilliant little horse Our Solo. He knew Badminton and its surroundings and, having made many acquaintances, was able to introduce his team to the area. Charlie Bullen introduced Mike to the gang, which included Bill's three very talented sons, Barry, Wayne and Clarke. Barry, the eldest, had been in the Olympic showjumping team with a lovely horse called Genoe. The reserve horse for that team was Peter Winton's Brahmin, and Peter came over to the UK to compete on him during the quarantine period.

Mike: 'Bill was fifty years old, six feet tall, with not an ounce of fat on him. His lovely wife, Mavis, a real pocket dynamo, was chief organiser of family Roycroft and the squad here in Britain, and was to arrive some six weeks after the others. By the time the horses had completed their rest post-Olympics, the Aussies had got to know the area, had met many of the locals and were coping well with an English winter and even with the warm ale! The showjumpers planned to jump on the British summer circuit as well as competing in one or two of the Nations Cups in Europe, which would not be breaking quarantine rules. The Roycrofts had owned and produced at least four of the event horses in the squad and it was Bill's intention not only to try to compete at and win Badminton again but he also wanted to race the Thoroughbred event horses, just as Laurie Morgan had done before him. Bill's horses were quality and well-bred from Sir Alec Creswick's stud in New South Wales. He had ambitious plans; not only did he want to run in the Aintree and Cheltenham Foxhunters' but he also wanted to run Stoney Crossing in the Cheltenham Gold Cup against Arkle and Mill House, a little grey stallion called Avatar in the Champion Hurdle and Eldorado in the Grand National. Many people could not understand how this Australian was going to multitask with his horses between racing and eventing but he soon showed them how and I was able to enjoy a close insight into his talents.'

Bill had planned to ride in several races in the build-up to Cheltenham but first some essential paperwork failed to arrive in time and then a meeting at Doncaster was cancelled because of snow. So he set off to the Cheltenham Festival in March with no race under his belt and furthermore his ride on Avatar in the Champion Hurdle was to be the first time he had ever ridden competitively in company! Amazingly, he coped in a big field and although he did not feature in the finish, he learned from the experience and was not disgraced. In the four-runner Gold Cup against Arkle and Mill House, being unused to the starting procedure, Stoney Crossing was left by some twenty lengths and finished a well-beaten third, thirty lengths behind the great Arkle. However, Bill was convinced he would have beaten Mill House and finished second had he not lost those early lengths.

It was one of Bill's ambitions to ride Stoney Crossing in the Aintree

Foxhunters'. Unfortunately, he was jumped across at the famous Chair fence and was brought down but Bill, in typical fashion, caught his horse, jumped back on and finished a gallant fifth. The sporting press was full of this man's wonderful spirit and Bill himself suggested to the Aintree stewards that they should be encouraging jockeys to jump straight by penalising them if they did not!

After talking to his fellow showjumping team members, Bill withdrew Eldorado from the Grand National and opted to ride him instead in two Nations Cup showjumping teams for Australia in London and Dublin – an extraordinary feat.

The qualifications for running and riding horses in races in those days were considerably less stringent than they are nowadays, but Bill's achievements were still remarkable and demonstrated the natural talent of a superb horseman.

Mike: 'For me to be around the "boys" when all that was going on was immense but it did not end there.'

Just over a month later Bill entered those two Cheltenham horses and Eldorado at Badminton and he was to be the first man to ride three horses in the competition. With Bill catching the imagination of the horse world and the great Colonel Frank Weldon designing the cross-country course for the very first time, the publicity surrounding Badminton certainly gave the sponsors, Whitbread, excellent coverage. Colonel Frank had ridden all over Europe and made it known that he was planning to incorporate some of the special cross-country fences, seen on his travels, into the 1965 Badminton course.

Mike: 'Despite all the distractions from down the road at Didmarton, I had The Viking (Ben) back in work and fit with the intention of making a second appearance at Badminton in the spring of 1965. Even though I only had the ex-racehorse Northern Saga to keep my hand in while Ben was off the road, everything seemed to slip back into place. New events appeared in the spring calendar and we tried to be a little more ambitious in the warm-up competitions leading to Badminton. Ben showed that he was not only sound but was as honest and genuine as ever.

'Having done few competitions since the previous spring, I was in the "Little Badminton" section again, up against Bill on Avatar. With three horses for him to ride, one had to be in the less prestigious section. Colonel Frank had certainly put his mark on the cross-country course, which was stronger and more testing than the previous year but, having done it once, I felt confident that it was all possible again. I did ask Bill if I could walk around the cross-country course with him to have the benefit of his wide experience. Looking back, it was probably a mistake but it was fascinating to see his planned routes through some of those interesting new complexes.'

Ben's dressage test was an improvement on the previous year and Mike finished in the top third, but there was no doubt the cross-country would prove to be influential. The course designer initiated changing the direction of the course each year, so instead of starting off in front of Badminton House, the course started out past the Hunt Kennels to the new feature of Huntsman's Close.

Mike: 'There was a small rail in front of a big gulley, which you couldn't jump as one. Bill's advice was to "Collect Ben together, just pop over the rail, down through the gulley and away." When it came to it, I approached the rail without enough energy, leaving Ben not sure what I was asking of him and so we had a refusal. We turned around and I attacked it with much more energy and although it wasn't a stylish jump, at least we were on our way again. It was only the second cross-country penalty I had ever had on Ben and I was determined then to jump clear round the rest of the exciting new course. That refusal was my fault and I experienced huge disappointment. In the sport of eventing, or any sport in fact, you have to learn to take the rough with the smooth and move on. Sport can be a great leveller, whoever you are. That was the end of any hopes of being in the prize-giving but Ben did finish the competition sound and healthy so I could make plans to compete at Burghley that autumn.'

Bill and Avatar finished in second place behind Captain Martin Whiteley riding The Poacher in the 'Little Badminton' section. In the 'Great' section history was being made because Bill, 'The Legend' managed to take Stoney Crossing to the top of the leader board after cross-country, followed by Major Eddie Boylan from Ireland on Durlais Eile, with Bill's third ride, Eldorado, in sixth place. The royal family, together with the biggest crowd ever seen at Badminton, were treated to a spectacular competition. Stoney Crossing's exertions in the Gold Cup the previous month took their toll in the final showjumping phase. He had several fences down, which dropped him to sixth place, but Bill jumped a great clear around on Eldorado to climb up to second place behind the popular Eddie Boylan.

Badminton had first been transmitted on BBC television in 1956, thereby giving the sport a higher profile, and the classic competition of 1965 attracted one of the biggest sporting audiences of the whole year. Furthermore, that quarantine period for the Australian 1964 Olympic horses was giving the British 'horsey' public a huge treat wherever they went. The Australians made use of the summer's county show jumping circuit and John Fahey on Bonvale, Barry Roycroft on Genoe, Peter Winton on Brahmin and the legend himself, Bill on Eldorado, provided tough competition for the likes of Harvey Smith, David Broome, Alan Oliver *et al*. Mike joined them whenever he could and relished the time spent with them all.

Mike: 'I remember in particular a tremendous Royal Show Grand Prix when Peter Robeson on Firecrest jumped off again against

John and Bonvale for the title. This time it was John and the "little black spider" who won and we had a big celebration.

'Those months when I had got to know the Aussies were very special and we talked for hours about Australia; what was it like, what was there and would I go? The answer was – although I told no one, not even my parents – that I was beginning to think it was something I should consider, especially since I had never been outside Britain.

'All was about to change though, and one of the reasons for our celebration at the Royal Show was because I had a foreign trip on the horizon and the Aussies, too, would soon be on their long boat journey home.'

Mike had received an unexpected invitation from the Pony Club to go on an international exchange for three weeks, at which there would be teams from Australia, New Zealand, Canada, Great Britain and the host nation USA. Mike was to be one of seven British Pony Club representatives, along with Judith Garrad, Rachel Watherston, Minette Harding, Kate Gould, Vanessa Friar and chef d'équipe Mary Martin-Hurst, who later became Mary Anderson, and chaired the Pony Club. It would be a wonderful experience, with five days sightseeing in New York including the World Fair, followed by an international eventing competition on borrowed horses at the Potomac Centre in Maryland and the opportunity to hunt with several different packs in the final week.

Mike: 'I so wanted to go but part of the last week clashed with Burghley Horse Trials, my autumn target, so I tentatively asked whether I might come back three days early. I had a horrible feeling that Eileen Thomas, the then Pony Club Secretary, would say it has to be one or the other. Imagine my joy when a letter from the Pony Club dropped through the door and said yes you can do both, but if both of these were to work there had to be some good plans in place. So I rang Mary Wettern, a fellow competitor working at the successful stables of Sarah Whitmore, to ask if she could prepare Ben in the three-week build-up to Burghley.

'Ten days later, the six of us met at Heathrow to fly to New York where we would meet the other teams. We were billeted with Pony Club families in and around downtown New York, where we spent two days at the amazing World Fair and in general sightseeing. The trip to the United Nations building was one of the highlights and, as country people, our eyes were opened at the thousands of people and the massive skyscrapers.

'From there we headed south to the Potomac Equestrian Centre, a very well-appointed facility in Maryland, where enough horses were loaned for all of the teams. We were all divided into teams made of members from different countries, which gave us a chance to mix and hear all about the Pony Club in other parts of the world. Riding borrowed horses was fun, but soon showed up the more experienced riders. The British girls were very amused that my ride was a little palomino, but he was honest and genuine, which would be a help to me. We had lots of laughs and although it was somewhat competitive, it was all in very good spirit and made the exchange visit a real success with all the countries mixed up and communicating with one another. All our girls were experienced riders and put up a good show for their teams. Roger Haller, who came from Far Hills, New Jersey, and I soon became friends. He was already making his name in eventing with very much the same sort of enthusiasm as me. I also made friends with an Australian, Sam Campbell, who I was to see often in the coming years.[2] From Potomac it was a short trip to Washington to see the capital city, with a very memorable moment in the White House, when quite unexpectedly we bumped into the President himself, Lyndon Johnson. Some great parties and barbecues were laid on for us and the week went by far too quickly. We then headed off

2   Sam rode for Australia in the 1972 Olympic showjumping in Munich, on April Love.

for the final stage of our trip to see some of the lovely hunting countries that exist in the States. I only had two days hunting, with Mrs Bedford's wonderful pack of hounds at Chesterlands in Pennsylvania, which were followed by a typical hunt breakfast with the Elkridge-Harford. The other teams were to have two more days before the final farewell. It was particularly special to meet the organisers of this international exchange, which was such a good idea. It went on around the world for a number of years and will never be forgotten by those of us who took part.

'Despite Mary Martin-Hurst's best efforts to keep us all in order it was a tiring trip and, combined with the jet-lag, I was not totally switched on to compete at Burghley the week of my return. Mary Wettern had done a great job on Ben and he arrived there in good shape. The terrain of Burghley, with its ridge and furrow, was more testing than at Badminton. It was an important factor to take into account and, coupled with the fact that it was my first ride there, it was going to be a challenge and a good experience.'

At Burghley, Ben was his usual honest self and produced one of the best tests the pair had done at that level, but on cross-country day Mike was unable to do him justice. The horse made no mistake cross-country, jumping all the famous Burghley fences designed by Bill Thomson but, at the second of the Capability Crossings, he stumbled crossing the road and, in his attempts not to fall off, Mike tore a groin muscle and was nothing more than a passenger all the way home.

Mike: 'It was pretty painful and slowed me down enormously, which made me feel guilty in letting everyone down, particularly Mary, who had done such a good job. I had an injection next morning to help with the pain. Ben passed the final horse inspection so I did the showjumping but had two fences down. At least Ben had kept up his good completion record.

'It had been a manic twelve months for me. I had completed

my exams, ridden at Badminton and Burghley and been to America. At home, the farm had a younger labour force and its future looked well established. I had given much thought to my future as a result of the discussions I'd had with my Australian friends while they were over here. I was an only child and felt that it would be good to get out and see some more of the world. Australia particularly took my fancy. I decided that I had to pluck up courage and tell Mum and Dad that I planned to spend perhaps up to a year in Australia, but did not want them to think that I was leaving home for good after all they had done for me.

'It was a very difficult afternoon tea that day when I chose to explain my thoughts and plans. As usual, my parents were totally understanding and, having made friends with Bill and Mavis Roycroft, were planning a trip to Australia to see them. This was great news to me because as a married couple, Mum and Dad had never been out of the UK. We talked it through and discussed the immediate goals for the farm. We decided that I should aim to get on a ship sometime in late summer 1966. I would then make my way down to Australia to stay with the Roycrofts and some of the other great friends that I'd met in the last year. For me, it had been a year when I had learned a lot, made contacts and forged friendships around the world and, at the same time, I'd had a lot of fun.'

CHAPTER FIVE

Antipodean Invasion

A combination of nearly three weeks in the United States on the memorable Pony Club International, followed by Burghley three-day event with Ben meant that Mike had been absent from work on the farm for four weeks. A wet autumn meant that harvest was still in full swing halfway through September, no longer with a binder but now with the latest additions to the farm's equipment of a small combine harvester and a couple of corn carts. These carts transported corn from the combine back to the corn store. A newly installed drying machine brought the moisture content of the corn down from its harvested content to fourteen per cent moisture. This enabled storage for the winter months in special storage corn bins without the risk of mould developing.

> **Mike:** 'It was all very exciting. By now the chaps on the farm had already got a firm understanding of how it all worked but it was very new to me and they so enjoyed telling this newly "trained" agricultural student how it all worked!
>
> 'Father was delighted with the way the new milking unit and cattle housing was being run by the new manager, Mervyn Arthurs. I was given the job of being relief milker, which meant

that at least one and sometimes two days a week I would be in the milking parlour with the second person milking. I had to help get the cows in, take off the milking units and let the cows out. It was all a very new routine for everyone, including the cows, but it certainly saved labour and meant the milking and caring of the herd was much easier and more cost-effective.'

As a result of Mike's memorable afternoon tea with his parents, when he announced his plan to go to Australia later in 1966, the family had a discussion on how he would fit into the farm in the future, and the labour requirements in his absence. As a consequence, it was decided that the farm would employ a young person recently qualified in agricultural training. Over the coming years there were several, including Charlie Bullen and Mike's ex-college friend Paul Thain among others, who did a great job as assistants on the farm.

This extra labour allowed Mike the time to follow his passion for the sport of eventing. Throughout his Pony Club days, Colonel Weldon had always encouraged him to spend time whenever possible with Bertie Hill at Great Rapscott in North Devon. Bertie was famous as one of the best three-day event riders in the world and was also an outstanding point-to-point jockey in the West Country. Frank Weldon always said that Mike needed to improve and strengthen his cross-country position and considered Bertie, with all his racing experience, the best person to help.

The ex-racehorse Northern Saga was showing improvement as an event horse but he lacked the talent to take Mike to the higher echelons of the sport. Attention was turned to how Farmer Giles, the two-year-old acquisition from Ascot, was progressing. By now he was rising four years old and, although his 'curby' hocks looked unattractive, they had strengthened and Willie Donaldson, who had broken him as a three-year-old, was more impressed with him than he ever envisaged. Giles was big and gangly and therefore would need time to mature, but he had a lovely temperament, was a good ride and these qualities indicated it would be worth spending time and effort on him.

Plans were quickly made for Mike to take Northern Saga for a week's training with Bertie Hill in that October of 1965. Mike would stay with Bertie, his wife Mary and their two children Tony and Sarah in their lovely home, which nestled in the steep country just a few miles from South Molton. It was a typical North Devon farm, with sheep and beef cattle and had several buildings which, in time, would be converted into accommodation for the increasing numbers wanting to train at Great Rapscott. At the time of Mike's visit all the students[1] lived in the house, but Mary was a great organiser and her easygoing manner made it all great fun. There was also a stock building that had been converted into a rather small but effective riding school and a large area of flat land in the valley, some two or three hundred feet below the farm buildings, which was used for schooling on the flat and jumping, both showjumps and cross-country fences. The surrounding land was extremely hilly, perfect for getting horses fit, and provided a picturesque backdrop for the house and stable yard.

The main aim of the week at Great Rapscott was for Bertie to get to know Mike's riding ability and for Mike to understand Bertie's method of teaching and working horses.

Mike: 'It was so interesting because it soon became apparent that the most valuable lesson was to watch him ride my horse. He had the wonderful ability to make any horse work to his very best and he could explain clearly how he was able to achieve such considerable improvement in the horse's movement and balance. It was important to grasp that information. We all got on really well and although we soon agreed that Saga wasn't the star we were hoping for, he proved an excellent conveyance to get to know the genius of the man.'

---

1   One fellow student at Great Rapscott was Mark Phillips, who recalled: 'After leaving school I went to train with Bertie Hill and had no idea that a cow had to have a calf before it produced milk. Mike used to pull my leg unmercifully and never let me forget it – one of many stories that kept me in my place with Mike!'

Michael Trickey was Bertie's assistant at that time. He had recently attended the Royal Agricultural College, but returned to Bertie's yard to help with the point-to-pointers and was proving an excellent addition for breaking-in the young horses. Already the list of Bertie's potential eventing students was growing and included Mark Phillips and two local boys, Tom Durston-Smith and Stuart Stevens, who looked exciting prospects.

Mike: 'That week was more than sufficient to make up my mind to be back again next spring before the 1966 season started.'

Mike spent many evenings that winter writing to the Roycrofts, to John Fahey and to Peter Winton trying to establish a plan for the trip 'Down Under' in the autumn of 1966.

Mike: 'It was all coming together but what wasn't quite so easy was the planning of the trip down there. Eventually I found a passage on a ship from the Greek company the Chandris Line, which left from Southampton at the end of September. The route was through the Bay of Biscay into the Mediterranean calling at Piraeus, then Beirut, into the Suez Canal down past Cairo then on to Aden, followed by Colombo, the capital of Ceylon (now Sri Lanka) in those days, before the long sea journey to Perth, finally docking at Melbourne early in November. It was six weeks in all and I wasn't sure that I could be cooped up on a passenger ship for that length of time. However, there was still plenty to think about before I finalised it all.'

That winter, Ben's legs were beginning to show a lot of wear and tear after his two three-day events in 1965. He had been a tremendous schoolmaster for Mike and everyone felt he should be found a home where he could hopefully give another young rider confidence and enjoy a quieter life. As a young horse, Farmer Giles would only be lightly worked in the first half of the year and aimed, if deemed appropriate, at a few small competitions in the autumn. Northern Saga, who had already completed several novice events, would hopefully progress to intermediate level and be aimed for the new Punchestown three-day event in August that year. As an ex-racehorse, Saga's temperament was not ideal for eventing but he gave Mike experience and competition practice. Mike went back to Great Rapscott with Saga and also Farmer Giles to allow Bertie to cast his eye over the young horse.

Mike: 'Bertie was finding some lovely young horses and we decided that maybe this was the route we were going to have to take if we were to find another future Badminton horse. The result of another very productive and fun week with Bertie and Mary was that Saga was put on a list for Punchestown, but with considerable reservations as to whether he would be well enough qualified to go. On the other hand, Bertie's view of Farmer Giles was much more complimentary than we could have dreamt of, and was without doubt the positive message to come out of that spring visit.'

Bertie was appointed as trainer to the British team for the first-ever World Eventing Championships at Burghley that coming September. The chef d'équipe, Colonel Bill Lithgow, was another former Commanding Officer of the King's Troop, Royal Horse Artillery, who had ridden at Badminton and had already acted as chef d'équipe to the British team in the 1965 European Championships in Moscow.

Mike: 'Bertie knew how enthusiastic I was and, in conversation whilst staying with him in Devon asked whether, if he could organise it, I would be interested in being part of the back-up team at Burghley, filling haynets, carrying water buckets, etc. for the British squad. There would be twelve riders, with four in the team and eight riding as individuals. As you might imagine, I jumped at the idea because there would be several riders competing whom

I knew and, as long as I watched and listened, I could learn a tremendous amount from the best event riders in the world.

'About a month later I had the phone call from Bertie that I was waiting for, which was positive news. I was so excited and decided, with all that was planned for the months ahead, that I should sell Northern Saga and would go to Punchestown on my feet to help friends competing there. We advertised Saga, who had good racing breeding and he was soon on his way to a new home as a hunter chaser, where he proved very successful in winning three races on the trot.'

On the home front, Mike's father was very happy with the progress of the two farms. The Estcourt Estate had given their permission for a new milking parlour and some covered yard space for winter housing of the herd at Slads Farm to be completed by early 1967. With Saga sold and only the promising Farmer Giles to ride there was plenty of time for Mike to be involved on the farm and to be the regular relief milker with the Church Farm herd.

Of course, 1966 was the year in which the World Cup was held in England and it was a memorable one for football fans.

Mike: 'It all came down to that exciting match between England and West Germany. I listened to the final while helping to milk the cows with Mervyn Arthurs that Saturday afternoon and it was one of those moments when you can say "I remember where I was at that particular moment"! I'll never forget the immortal words of commentator Kenneth Wolstenholme as Geoff Hurst so nearly put the goal in the net but then recovered to kick the winning World Cup goal past the goalkeeper: "The crowd think it's all over", followed by, as Hurst actually put the ball into the net, "It is now". The cows didn't appreciate our cheering and enthusiasm but there really hasn't been a moment in football to celebrate like that since.'

Soon Mike's plans were finalised and the ticket bought for his trip to Australia. He was to leave Southampton on the twenty seventh of October, arriving in Melbourne on the third of November to be met by Peter Winton, one of the members of the Australian event team who had previously been quarantined in the UK. However, two more quick adventures were to be experienced before his departure, in the form of trips to Punchestown and Burghley. Punchestown was hosting its inaugural eventing competition, and this was to be the first of Mike's many memorable visits to the famous racecourse. It turned out to be a proper adventure because rough seas prevented the horses travelling over by boat, so the Irish organisers flew planes over to England to transport the horses back in time for the competition. This avoided the loss of twelve entries, which would have made too great an impact at that late stage for Punchestown's first competition.

Mike: 'It was the first time I'd ever flown with horses and it proved to be an interesting and rather frightening experience, because Pru Cawston's little mare Charm tried very hard to kick her way out of her stall! Luckily no one, not even the vet who was trying to treat her, was injured but it was certainly a scary moment. Helping some of the competitors at the event was a good introduction to my future duties at the World Championships at Burghley a fortnight later. I also had a chance to assess the questions that the course set out for both horse and rider and to meet and enjoy the company of the wonderful characters within the Irish sport.

'I had agreed to meet Bertie the week before things became busy at Burghley so I could understand from him and Colonel Bill what I was to be expected to do. It turned out I was "errand boy" for the team, which included our team vet Peter Scott-Dunn and his wife Anne, who was the team's equine physiotherapist and something of a pioneer in the equine use of Faradism, a pulsing electronic stimulation of damaged muscles. With the best competitors from all over the world, including the Russians, who were quite strong in the sport at that time, I was really at the heart of all that was going on. At the same time as doing my job, I was able to watch the different types of horses and the various ways they were prepared and worked. I was able to witness the pressures that existed behind the scenes (and there were plenty) as well as seeing how the officials were running the event. I had never seen the sport from that angle before and it was truly fascinating.'

The cross-country course, built by Burghley's course designer Bill Thompson, was the biggest ever seen. Bill was also the course commentator, so he was kept busy. The course proved as difficult as it looked, with only two teams completing (three riders were needed to get a team score) and Britain was not one of them. The Irish had the reputation of being brilliant cross-country riders, although this was not matched by their dressage skills, despite Jock Ferrie's best efforts. Nonetheless, winning the competition here was undoubtedly their greatest team victory with Eddie Boylan, Penny Moreton, Virginia Freeman-Jackson and Tommy Brennan defeating the Argentinians, the only other team to finish:

Mike: 'I remember watching the most beautiful horse called Chalan ridden by Carlos Moratario from Argentina putting up the most brilliant display to win individual gold, beating Richard Meade on Barberry.

'As it turned out, it was one of the most influential weeks of my sporting life. I so enjoyed the experience of meeting people from around the world, but it was the result of a conversation with Colonel Lithgow, when I went to thank him for letting me be involved with the team, that I initiated a life-changing experience. I said my "thank-yous" and then asked him whether there were any riders who might need a groom for a championship team competition, because I would be interested if the opportunity arose. He kindly said how useful I had been and that, should such a position arise, he would put my name forward. I did admit that

Left: Nick Skelton on the podium at Rio – 2016 Olympic showjumping gold. [Courtesy of Peter Putnam]

Below: The BBC TV and Radio commentary team at Rio. *Back row left to right* are the Radio 5 Live team of Tim Allen (engineer), Tim Peach (equestrian producer) and commentators Tina Cook and Jonathan Agnew. *Front row left to right* is the BBC team of Graeme Johnstone-Robertson (cameraman), Lee McKenzie (presenter), Andy Austin (showjumping pundit), Liz Thorburn (producer) and Mike Tucker.

Above: Harvest time in the 1920s.

Right: Grampie J.E. Jones – a real countryman.

Below: 'Master', 10th Duke of Beaufort.

Above: Grandpa's wagon acting as grandstand for the royal party at Badminton.

Below: Grandfather's MBE celebration – Mike is in short trousers!

Top: Mike competing at the 1956 Chavenage Hunter Trial on Puck. [Courtesy of Peter Harding]

Below: The 1959 Beaufort Pony Club team *(left to right)* Jennie Bullen, Mike, Jane Bullen, Rob Erswell. [Courtesy of Peter Harding]

Above: 'The Three Laughing Cavaliers' *(left to right)* Major Laurence Rook, Bertie Hill, Colonel Frank Weldon.

Below: Mike at the BHS Horse Trial at Tweseldown, 1962. [Reed Photography]

Above: Cirencester Operatic Society; *The Gondoliers* – Mike third from left.

Below: Mike on The Viking jumping the Open Water, Badminton Horse Trials 1964.

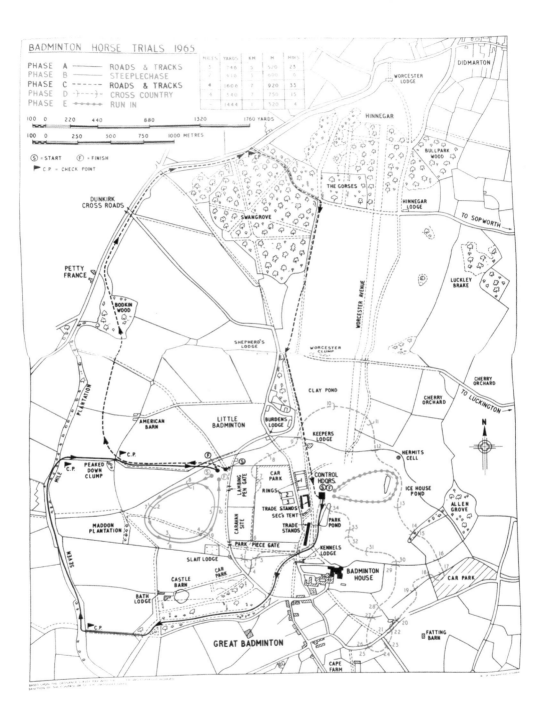

Map of the cross-country course from the Badminton programme, 1965.

Above: The 1962 Australian showjumping team *(left to right)* Peter Winton, Barry Roycroft, John Fahey, Bill Roycroft.

Left: Bill Roycroft – the world-class horseman in his everyday gear.

Below: Brisbane Show.

I still couldn't plait! I never imagined that I would ever hear from him again.'

It was now less than a month before Mike was to board ship to head south to Australia. His father had the farm well organised, but the best way forward to develop Farmer Giles's career had yet to be decided. Willie Donaldson and Molly Sivewright were both consulted and they unanimously agreed that, as a backward four- rising five-year-old, he should not have a hard year and a little hunting with Willie and some dressage work with Molly would be ideal in helping him strengthen up.

Mike: 'Packing done and finances organised, my parents and I set out early on the twenty seventh of October for Southampton Docks as we didn't really know where we were going. We followed instructions, parked the car, found the terminal and had a little while to say our farewells, which weren't going to be easy. There was a small coffee stall near the gate and so we headed there for the final goodbyes. The ship looked enormous to me but, as liners went apparently, it wasn't that big. As we were discussing its size, I saw someone I thought I recognised. He looked as if he was about get on board too. By coincidence it was an old boy from my year at Wycliffe College, a farmer's son from Herefordshire called Clive Snell, who I hadn't seen since leaving school and who was also heading to Oz. Mum was absolutely thrilled because I'd organised no contacts between Southampton and Melbourne and we were all a bit concerned about the journey. Clive was in exactly the same situation, so that chance meeting meant the goodbyes weren't quite so difficult now I had someone with whom to share the long journey.'

Being country boys, neither of them knew how they would cope with being stuck in the confines of a ship for six weeks, and being on the ocean was a new experience. They quickly discovered the need for sea legs when crossing a very choppy Bay of Biscay, which cleared the restaurants for a couple of days and, although they both felt distinctly queasy, they retained their appetites!

Mike: 'The first half of the trip was the most interesting and at times our eyes were out on stalks. We visited Piraeus, and the Acropolis, we walked round Beirut where we saw extreme wealth alongside abject poverty. We took trips round the Pyramids and Cairo. Then it was back on the boat to the Red Sea for a brief stop at Aden then to Colombo until we finally and thankfully arrived in Australia.

'That section of the journey did keep us from getting bored and it was interesting, but then for the next three weeks we saw nothing but sea and we were fed up with the same deck games time and time again; swimming in the pool had become tedious and we'd read all the books. The relief at finally arriving at Melbourne was huge and was made even better when I could see Peter Winton waiting on the quay to pick me up. Peter had been on the boat that brought the Olympic horses back from quarantine in England after the Tokyo Games, so he understood what it was like, although they used to ride the horses on deck for exercise on their journey back to relieve the boredom. I spent three days with Peter at his family home in Melbourne getting my land legs back, seeing his horses and stables as well as some of the sights of this attractive city. Then it was off with Peter a hundred miles due south from Melbourne to Boonabaroo, the home of the Roycroft family. They lived in a typical Australian country home: a bungalow on a small dairy farm with almost as many horses as dairy cows all housed in outside yards or corrals, with no riding school of any sort in view.'

Since Bill and Mavis Roycroft were frequent visitors to Mike's family home when they were in England, the welcome given to Mike really was like being home from home.

Mike: 'There was no definite timescale to my trip to the southern hemisphere, but there was an outline plan to ride a horse of the Roycrofts called Kingdom in some events and, if I got on with the horse I could take him to the three-day event at the Royal Sydney Show held in April over Easter 1967. My only other definite engagement was to go on tour around the shows for two or three weeks with John Fahey in the New England part of New South Wales near the Queensland state border.'

It was already high summer 'Down Under' and haymaking was under way on another of the Roycroft's properties, which was about ten miles away.

Mike: 'The day after I arrived another Olympic rider, Brian Cobcroft, and his brother John were bringing down a trainload of two hundred cattle to Camperdown, and they had to be walked back from the station to their summer grazing at the Roycrofts. It was about a ten-mile walk in all and would take most of the day in hot sunshine and I was expected to be part of the team! We did it, but not having ridden for a while, sitting on a stock saddle, under hot sunshine with just an Aussie hat for protection, I was saddle-sore, sun-burnt and exhausted to boot. I already knew better than to argue with Bill; you came off worse! His tough upbringing, coupled with his time spent signed on for the Second World War effort, meant he did not suffer fools gladly. If you did argue it was not unknown for him to unbuckle his belt and give you one, which I did witness on occasions, and the boys could verify that. Despite all that, I was hugely privileged to be there with the chance to benefit from an all- time "legend" of the horse world. Bill was largely self-taught and was so generous in sharing his wide knowledge and helping others. Mavis was a "Mum" to me and a real worker, and she organised the day for her men down to the last minute.'

Mike and the Roycrofts rode in the morning after the cows had been milked. They took advantage of the relatively cool temperature before the intense heat of the day built up. They schooled the horses in one of the fairly small but flat paddocks or, if the horses required cantering, they would work them alongside the road outside the house. This track climbed steadily uphill for a mile or more, so was ideal for improving fitness. Avatar, the horse who ran in the British Champion Hurdle, Dupeche a lovely young horse, Cop This Lot an advanced horse, and Kingdom, the horse earmarked for Mike, were all being trained for the coming event season. After riding, all hands turned to haymaking for the rest of the day, although one member of the family would undertake putting the cows through the parlour for their evening milking.

Mike: 'There was not a lot of rocking needed to go to sleep at night despite the heat! To be fair it was the busiest time of the year on the farm, but there wasn't a competition until two came in February to be used as a build-up to Sydney in early April. If we wanted to travel anywhere with the horses it was invariably in open-top trucks with six to eight horses all tied up next to each other with no partitions. It was quite an eye-opener for me but it worked!'

Australia had an equestrian centre at Bowral, where an ex-instructor of the Spanish Riding School, Franz Mairinger, was based. Franz was the master figure, not only for improving dressage but also competitive riding in general. Bill wasn't Franz's biggest fan and undertook most of his own training, but who could argue with the Austrian's successful record?

Mike: 'Christmas was a bit different in the heat but Mavis still cooked the traditional Christmas roast. To celebrate New Year, Peter Winton picked me up and we went off to Sydney. It was the first time I realised the huge distances involved in getting anywhere in Australia. It took us two and a half days to drive there, but it was worth it. I certainly got a great feeling for the country and its people and of course had my first glimpse of Sydney Harbour Bridge. We had a lot of fun and certainly saw in the New Year in style before the long journey back home.'

Mike forged a good rapport with Kingdom, and Bill was happy with the partnership. They completed their first event with clear rounds in the showjumping and cross-country and had a respectable dressage. During the next three months the horses targeted at Sydney were in good form and Mike was progressing with Kingdom. Bill took Mike on sightseeing trips when there was time, including a visit to Gawler in South Australia, the site of one of Australia's biggest three-day events. They regularly went to Camperdown market together, one of the important social gatherings for the farming community. This was a big stock area and one of the major grass-growing regions of the country. Bill would meet up with his farming colleagues to discuss trade over a pint or two. It was fascinating for Mike to listen to them talking about farming, which differed so much from home.

Sadly the opportunity for Mike of a possible ride at the Sydney three-day event did not materialise.

Mike: 'There were about eight horses trucked up to Sydney, Kingdom being one, with the plan to compete in a one-day event on one of the many Sydney racetracks as a warm-up. One of the cross-country fences was a series of three angled metal rails covered with white planks with no ground line. My eye was never that good for a stride and Kingdom hit one of the rails all ends up and although we did not part company he was not sound enough to compete again while I was there. I got a major telling-off and from then on I was a spectator at one of the greatest stock shows in the world. Consistent as ever, Bill won the three-day event for the umpteenth time! We stayed up for the two weeks of the show, which in those days was close to Randwick racetrack, and we slept in bunk beds above where the horses were stabled.'

When the horse and farming world congregated at the Sydney Show to demonstrate their skill and high-class stock, it made for a wonderful spectacle. Several classes were judged simultaneously in the huge arena so there was always something happening to entertain the spectators.

Mike: 'Showjumping was always one of the highlights and the New Zealanders, who were huge rivals of the Aussies, had sent their top riders Graham and Bruce Hanson and Stuart Mitchell to do battle. There was a high standard of jumping and the Aussies Johnny Fahey and Kevin Bacon together with their top lady riders Fiona Hyem and Toots Murcheson gave the Kiwis plenty of competition. All in all it was a very social scene and I made some great contacts from New Zealand and decided that I was going to visit there on my way home, probably in late May 1966.'

Mike said his sad farewells to the Roycroft family at the end of Sydney's Easter Show. He had enjoyed the most wonderful time with Bill and his family. He had learned much about life and witnessed the harsh world of the Australian farmer and horse coper. The plan now was for Mike to accompany John Fahey for two weeks on the New England circuit in northern New South Wales, prior to a visit to New Zealand and then home to England. First, he travelled with John in his lorry to John's home in Taree, New South Wales.

John's great attempt at a medal on Bonvale in Tokyo had been a boost for Australian showjumping. Like the Roycrofts, John would carry eight horses on a truck and travel from show to show, competing not only in showjumping but also campdrafting. This competition involves working cattle with horses around a set course for valuable prize money. John was one of the best in Australia in his time and it was a spectacular sport to watch.

Mike: 'It was a fabulous two weeks going to Guyra and Glenn Innes shows and, much to everyone's amusement, I even won a dressage class on one of John's campdrafting mares. I had a chance to catch up with Sam Campbell, who had been on the same Pony Club exchange as me in America and who was just bringing out the wonderful grey mare April Love, which he went on to ride in the Munich Olympics. Being involved at those shows, there was no better way to see and hear about the very different farming methods and meet the Australians on their home ground. Those two weeks were one of the highlights of my whole trip.

'The decision to start wending my way home was based on my yearning to start working my own horses. So I booked a flight to Wellington, New Zealand and organised a lift to Rotorua to catch up with Stuart Mitchell, one of the top showjumpers in New Zealand, who found and broke his own horses as well as being a very good stock farmer. Stuart gave me a guided tour around some of the tourist highlights near his home, including the amazing town of Rotorua, which has hot sulphur-smelling baths as a result of the volcanic activity in the area. A tour around Cambridge, one of the top bloodstock areas of New Zealand, was another interesting day. It whetted my appetite for wanting to come back to this spectacular country one day.

'I was enjoying every moment of my gap year, but then received some news from home that shook me to the core. Grampie Jones had passed away very suddenly. My parents were adamant that I should stay in New Zealand and not come home but it was a difficult time for me. He had been such a major part of my childhood years.

'After some thought I decided to go to Blenheim in the north of South Island for the New Zealand Pony Club Championships before catching the plane back home in late June. Stuart organised a lift down to Wellington to allow me to cross to Blenheim by ferry. I caught up with two of the New Zealand Pony Club team who were with me in America on the exchange and still buzzing about that memorable trip. They introduced me to some of their

Pony Club organisers. I was really impressed with the standard at those Championships and I thought the cross-country was more testing than our finals at home. What struck me most was the high standard of riding and I clearly remember thinking that, if these Kiwis ever took up international eventing, look out world! Their riding was so natural and skilful, particularly in the cross-country.

'What a wonderful way to finish a trip! The whole adventure had surpassed all my expectations and I had forged long-standing friendships, which would play parts in my future riding and commentary careers.'

But now it was time for Mike to catch up at home. His mother's letters had given him progress reports about Farmer Giles, and also about the farm: the new milking parlour was up and running and the newly erected cattle sheds were ready for the silage cuts (cattle fodder in place of hay), but he was keen to see it all for himself. His mother had also written about the successes of his fellow Pony Club members Jane Bullen and Mark Phillips in British Horse Society events, which made Mike all the more determined to aim for Badminton again.

Mike: 'It was the middle of June when I was given a wonderful welcome home. Although we had constantly written our news from opposite ends of the world, everyone was keen to hear again of the fun and excitement, so I had to recount it all over again.'

Mike soon settled into a routine at home that allowed for a couple of hours riding in between the work on the farm. It was pleasing for him to see the great morale of the farm staff, who were enjoying the new machines and gadgets, but the best moment came when Willie Donaldson delivered five-year-old Farmer Giles back to Slads — the horse appeared to have grown even more than his 17hh, having furnished and matured in Mike's absence.

Mike: 'I was keen to catch up with my Young Farmer friends who, I was surprised to hear, wanted me to be Chairman of the Malmesbury Club that October. It was an honour to be asked and, with a good secretary and committee behind me, I decided to take it on.

'When news spread that I was back in the country, I received a couple of requests to commentate on the cross-country for a Pony Club event and a local unaffiliated event, both of which I really enjoyed and they went quite well without too many *faux pas*!

'Not long after I was back, Mary Hill asked me if I would take a ride at their Pony Club camp in early August. It presented an ideal opportunity to take Giles with me for Bertie to assess. The camp was great fun and I enjoyed teaching as well as spending time with the Hill children, Tony and Sarah, and the resident riders Stuart Stevens and Mike Trickey, who were helping to promote Rapscott as a training facility. Mark Phillips had recently stayed and impressed us all with a horse called Rock On, as did Jane Bullen and Our Nobby, despite Nobby being little more than a pony. The other great character to arrive at Rapscott was Hendrick Wiegersma, from Holland, who was quickly making his presence felt.

'What excited me most was that Bertie was now extremely enthusiastic about Farmer Giles who, as a five-year-old had matured, jumped well and (despite his ugly hocks) was looking quite a prospect.'

CHAPTER SIX

The Mexico Olympics

Autumn was turning to winter. The cows were housed indoors and hunting was under way. Mike's Young Farmer commitments meant few evenings in at home.

Mike: 'Luckily I was in the evening Colonel Bill Lithgow rang. He was in a very chatty mood, wanting to know about my Australian experiences. I was longing to know why he had rung and eventually he explained that Richard Meade, who would most likely be in the eventing team going to the Mexico Olympics, was looking for a groom. Because of the high altitude, it would mean a minimum of two months' commitment for both horses and riders to acclimatise, starting in September, and would I be interested? He hardly had the chance to complete the question before I said a very definite "Yes!" He seemed pleased and I was delighted!'

Mike's mother and father were thrilled and were more than happy to release him from his farming duties. His Young Farmer duties would be finished by the beginning of September and a programme for Giles's eventing campaign as a six-year-old was organised to finish in time. 1968 promised to be an extremely exciting year – although any plans involving horses tend to be somewhat precarious!

Mike: 'My first call was to thank Bertie Hill for instigating this for me and to book in Farmer Giles for a week in March 1968 prior to our first BHS event at Penzance. Many of the Rapscott pupils were competing because it was the home of Bertie's head girl, Pippa Tomlin, girlfriend and future wife of Hendrik Wiegersma. The long journey was worthwhile because it proved to be an excellent first novice event for Giles as well as being tremendous fun. Giles had certainly benefited from hunting and performed well to finish second, justifying hopes and enthusiasm for his future. We were all over the moon, which made the long journey home a happy one. Giles proved he had ability and, before a well-deserved rest, spent the next five months competing consistently and successfully. Dad was very happy with his acquisition, as Giles had cost only two hundred and fifty guineas, and I was dreaming of another ride at Badminton.'

Mike's year as chairman of the Young Farmers had been hugely rewarding, with the club winning competitions in south-west region debating, the County Rally and National Entertainments; the last-named was as a result of team effort and spending time with the Cirencester Operatic Society.

The full Burghley three-day event was the final designated trial for the Olympics. There were already several changes to the short list, which had been drawn up after Badminton that spring. Barberry, Richard Meade's intended ride, and Ben Jones's Foxdor were lame and had been withdrawn from the list. Richard switched to Lady Russell's Turnstone for Burghley but only competed in the dressage phase. Ben rode Cornishman V and, albeit with a refusal, finished in a creditable eighth place, having had little time to form a proper partnership. Sheila Waddington was the winner on Fair and Square, Jane Bullen and Our Nobby confirmed their fine form by taking third place, with Gill Watson on Shaitan finishing in sixth position, also with a refusal. The biggest drama attended Martin Whiteley on The Poacher, when he unwisely wore leather gloves for the cross-country. He had an extremely difficult ride, hampered by lack of grip on the reins, which culminated in an unexpected refusal. This combination was thought to be a definite choice for the Olympics, having won individual silver and team gold in the European Championships of 1967.

Colonel 'Babe' Moseley, as chairman, with his fellow members of the Selection Committee had some difficult decisions to make after the Burghley results. All the team possibilities were waiting anxiously in the stable yard. The first names announced were Jane with Our Nobby and Derek Allhusen with Lochinvar.

Mike: 'Then came the first surprise, which was the selection of Richard Meade to ride Mary Gordon-Watson's Cornishman V. I thought at that stage my trip to the Olympics was definitely off. The next surprise was when Colonel Babe told Martin Whiteley that the selectors wanted to put Ben Jones on The Poacher because Martin's performance on the horse at Burghley was not of Olympic standard. Martin was absolutely devastated but behaved like a thorough gentleman and agreed that it would be in Britain's best interests. Those of us who were nearby were embarrassed and sad to witness a piece of history that would not happen today in the modern sport. Another surprising decision was the choice of Mark Phillips as reserve rider[1] since, at that time, he had never ridden in a team championship and he had never sat on any of the horses before they left England! The reserve horses were Turnstone and Shaitan.'

That evening, the team horses and entourage travelled down to

---

[1]   Mike was talking here of the eventing competition. As a matter of interest, Mark was also reserve rider for the showjumping team!

Mr and Mrs Reg Hindley's Ribblesdale Stud near Ascot for final training prior to departure for Mexico. It was a very quiet evening while everyone absorbed the consequences of the Olympic selection.

> **Mike:** 'I felt that my trip to the Olympics would be over, but it had been arranged that I would travel down to Ascot with Richard's horses and it seemed the decision over his Olympic groom was yet to be made.'

All the horses who arrived for the final training at Ribblesdale were passed fit and sound after the rigours of Burghley, which was a relief after all the earlier soundness problems.

> **Mike:** 'Once we had unpacked, I was summoned to a meeting with Colonel Bill and he made it clear to me that Richard wanted me to be his groom for Mexico. I felt so sorry for "Mouse", the Gordon-Watsons' and Cornishman's usual groom, but she took the news very well and helped me to get to know "Corney" in that Ribblesdale period, which was hugely helpful. I had been given serious responsibility and I needed to know exactly what to do.'

The stables at Ribblesdale were superb, and all the facilities required for final team training were just a short hack away at Smith's Lawn in Windsor Great Park. Any fast work could be done on Ascot racecourse but, as most horses had competed at Burghley, there was little need for much training at this time. Riders brought in other horses so they could maximise the time working with team trainer Bertie Hill. There were two important objectives during this period. First, the horses needed to get accustomed to drinking purified water because there was a possibility that the water in Mexico, which was of poor quality, could be harmful to them. Second, because the squad would be together for a total of six weeks before the Games, the chef d'équipe made it clear to everyone that it was crucial to build up a team who would work cohesively in all respects.

Mike: 'The great thing was that the riders and grooms had all competed against each other in previous years, so there was an understanding within the whole team. Jane's sister Jennie was grooming for her, Bez Thomas not only groomed for Derek but also rode his young horses and was well known to all of us. Michael Herbert, who was grooming The Poacher, had produced Martin's young horses for a number of years and was a successful competitor. The same was true of Gill Watson who, having been sixth at Burghley on Shaitan, was now to be Mark's groom for both that horse and Turnstone. I suspect there has never been a team with so many grooms who had also ridden at international level!'

From all angles the team was beginning to gel and the horses were taking well to the purified water, which had been a possible concern. It wasn't long before all the Olympic kit was being handed out and the big trunks were being packed for the long flight to Mexico. The horses, including the showjumping team, were to fly from Heathrow, which was only a short journey from the stables. A convoy of horseboxes drove onto the tarmac close to the plane in readiness for loading. The operation was soon under way, with each horse unloaded from the box, led into a stall on a pallet and locked in. The pallet was then lifted up to the height of the plane and pushed on rollers into its fuselage.

Mike: 'I was amazed how these fit horses were so placid and reacted so well to all that was going on. There was a crowd of some two hundred watching this procedure unfold and Corney was one of the last to go on board. Lochinvar was the horse before us and was becoming a little agitated. Bez was doing her best to calm him down as she led him up the ramp but suddenly he stopped dead and pulled back violently. To everyone's horror his bridle came off and there he was, loose on the tarmac at Heathrow, not a million miles from the active runways. Some very quick-thinking people linked arms and quietly and effectively surrounded him, allowing a much-relieved Bez to catch and secure her precious charge. Disaster, thank goodness, was averted but it was a very anxious moment!'

The long journey to Mexico City was completed by a chaotic arrival when, accompanied by a lot of shouting and Latin-American excitement, and to everyone's fury, all the kit was chucked in a great heap by the baggage handlers. Fortunately, the horses arrived in excellent condition at the main stables, where they were to spend the first ten days before going to the eventing base at Avandaro. In fact, it was the grooms who were fractious and fatigued, but there were a few easy days to allow everyone to settle down and establish a new routine. The grooms were billeted in the Olympic Village, which was close to where all the Olympic horses would be stabled.

Mike: 'How exciting was it for me, at my first breakfast, to be standing in the queue beside a British girl whom I instantly recognised at Lillian Board, the four hundred metre runner! She was really friendly and asked me what I was doing and what chances we had. I was so impressed!

'It didn't take long to discover the effects of being at high altitude because we easily got out of breath, although we were told that we would acclimatise given time. We didn't have much chance to look around, but in any case there were student riots going on in the city and a large number of heavily armed soldiers. Security in general didn't seem that tight, so we decided we wouldn't take any chances!'

Once all the equestrian teams had arrived, horses and kit were loaded onto trucks and transported the one hundred miles north to the site of the eventing competition on a golf course in an area called Avandaro, where the organisers felt the altitude could have less effect. The stables were adequate and the grooms, along with Colonel Lithgow and Peter and Annie Scott-Dunn (the team veterinary surgeon and physiotherapist), were housed nearby in little chalets. The riders and Bertie Hill remained in the Olympic Village. The area of flat ground around the golf course appeared small to fit in both training facilities and competition requirements. The region beyond was very hilly and stony, apart from a flat area several hundred feet higher up, which was the site of phase A, the first roads and tracks, and phase B, the steeplechase. Phase C, the second roads and tracks, was down a track to the start of the cross-country where the terrain was full of ditches and water gullies. These were to prove very influential with the prevailing tropical climate. The weather was generally warm but with heavy downpours every afternoon. The horses were therefore worked in the mornings and were back in their stables before the rain came. The routine worked well and both Peter Scott-Dunn and Bertie Hill were satisfied with how the horses had travelled and the way they had settled back into full work.

Mike: 'Every morning an ex-RAF Squadron Leader called Billy Clyde would gallop down into the stable area on his donkey. He knew the area and locals like the back of his hand. He was a real character and was incredibly useful to Colonel Bill when extra hacking and galloping areas were needed, because many designated routes were stony and the canters provided weren't really up to the Ascot standard. Billy would locate the best areas and then lead our string of horses on his donkey. On several occasions one or more of the horses came back with a scrape or bang requiring treatment from Peter or Annie, but fortunately nothing serious. Mark rode the reserve horse Shaitan most days in case of mishap to a team horse, but luckily a reserve was not required because Shaitan had to be rested after developing a sore back. Our days started at daybreak when we would hurry down to the stables before Bill and Peter arrived to see us jog each horse in hand to monitor his condition and soundness. All our hay and hard food had been shipped out so the horses had no change of diet and they were content to drink the purified water.'

There were forty-nine competitors from thirteen countries and there was strong opposition from the USSR, America, Australia, France and the World Champions, Ireland.

Mike: 'Whenever there was time, we had many friends to catch up with and find out the latest news. In the build-up time there was only one party that was attended by all officials, riders and grooms, held at Billy Clyde's lovely home up in the mountains, which commanded stunning views. We had all been lectured to keep off the alcohol but, on that particular occasion, it was impossible! We were each handed a tall glass of what appeared to be gin and tonic, perfect for a sunny evening, but were then handed the tonic bottle. The original glass was all gin! It was a great evening as you might imagine but, as we were leaving, we heard a huge crash. Mark had walked through a plate-glass window. Frankly, it could have been any one of us, but it was Mark who had to go to hospital to be stitched up. Not unsurprisingly, that brought the curfew down in a big way and some strict words from our chef d'équipe (and he could be strict!) put the fear of God in us all, which was perhaps no bad thing at that stage! Mark was soon back on duty supporting the team.'

Britain's Laurence Rook had a difficult task as the international technical delegate and one of his roles was to be solely responsible for the standard and safety of the cross-county course. The weather pattern could present a potential problem with the heavy afternoon rain. In addition, the going was far from ideal on parts of the course, which included many obstacles involving water.

Derek Allhusen and Lochinvar, as the most experienced partnership[2], was chosen to be our pathfinder, followed by Jane on Our Nobby, with Richard, who was really enjoying Cornishman, going third and then Ben with The Poacher going last.

> **Mike:** 'As grooms we were all so involved with our horses that we weren't able to watch much of the competition. We had one request from our chef d'équipe, however, which was to ensure that Ben ended up the night before his dressage in a relaxed state ready for his test. He admitted afterwards that the grooms had done a first-class job! The weather was becoming less predictable and on occasions quite ferocious and when Ben and The Poacher went in for their dressage, the heavens opened with thunder and lightning such as we had never seen before. Under the circumstances Ben did a fantastic job in what was more like a ploughed field than a dressage arena.'

After dressage Britain was halfway down the team classification but well in touch, particularly as it was felt that the cross-country course was going to be very influential.

Because of the worsening tropical weather, Laurence Rook, as technical delegate, decreed that the cross–country should start early in the hopes that everything would be finished before the rain started.

> **Mike:** 'The day had to be organised with military precision and Colonel Bill held an important briefing so we all knew exactly what we were doing and when. The horses had to be taken up the mountain for the start of phase A without us, the grooms, and we would wait in the starting box to prepare them for phase D, the cross-country.
>
> 'The day dawned bright and fine as usual, but there was a

---

2   Derek was fifty-four, and a grandfather, at the time

distinct feeling of tension in the camp. Colonel Bill had not received distinction in his military career without showing his leadership skills and that morning he was at his best. Peter and Annie were efficiently prepared as usual for what the day might bring and Bertie was giving last-minute briefings as news came back of how the course was riding. As grooms, we had to concentrate on our own horse and rider and make sure that everything was fully prepared. Richard was known to be at his best under pressure but we needed no silly mistakes.'

Communication was not as sophisticated in 1968 as it is nowadays, but news arrived that Derek and Lochinvar had completed the roads and tracks and steeplechase but had picked up an early refusal on the cross-country. They then settled down to jump fast and clear over the rest of the course and looked none the worse on return to the stables.

Mike: 'We had learned the sad news that Loughlin had suffered a heart attack and fallen with Penny Moreton for the Irish, but we didn't tell Jane any of that before she set off on Nobby. Jennie was distinctly nervous for her, but Nobby, not much bigger than a pony, looked ready for anything and set off boldly, perhaps too boldly and fell early on the course. Jane was back in the saddle in a flash (those days, that's what you did!) and completed the rest of the course in a good time without further problems. As the third rider from each team came onto the course, with heavy black skies overhead, the rain started coming down in torrents. The rain was relentless and news came back that the gullies and ditches were filling up very quickly. I, quite frankly, was getting very nervous for dear Corney. However, Richard was a hunting man and a superb cross-country rider. With his steely nerves, he was the man to tackle the course when things were getting tough. The pair worked miracles between them and jumped an amazing clear round in the worst of the storm. Corney was big and strong and really showed the guts and stamina that made him a true champion. That round put Britain very much in the hunt for a team medal.'

Around the course, fences began almost to disappear under the rising floods. The latest news from the Irish was that Tommy Brennan on March Hawk had fallen jumping into water at fence four and was swept downstream shouting 'I can't swim'! Fortunately, he was fished out safe and sound! Other teams were having their problems but British fortunes depended on Ben and The Poacher.

Mike: 'I was straining to hear any news as I was making Corney comfortable after his amazing round. Jennie shouted that Ben was nearing the last fence, which was situated near the stables. It should have been an Open Water but it had totally disappeared under the floods. I couldn't believe what I was seeing. Somebody had planted branches along the take-off bank so you could see where the metre drop was. Now, however, it was not a jump but a drop into the water followed by a scramble out as the last fence to finish the course. We didn't know whether he was clear or not but we were all shouting instructions to Ben to slow down. He had lost his riding hat (no chinstraps in those days) but he managed to just lower "Poach" into the water, sat very tight and scrambled out to finish. I had never seen anything like it in my life before and thankfully for the sport, never since.'

Despite all their exertions that day, the British horses were in good fettle the following day and any stiffness was soon walked off in time for the second veterinary inspection.

Mike: 'Annie and Peter Scott-Dunn had worked their magic so we were able to have some hours of sleep before getting up very early to have the horses out for the all-important trot-up.'

The showjumping phase was in a big arena, with the going looking more like hunting conditions than the final phase of an Olympic Games. Britain was one of the teams in contention for a medal and Derek and Richard were in the top ten individually.

Mike: 'Once again, with all our efforts concentrated on our steeds, we didn't witness much of the dramatic action that was to unfold. The horses were in wonderful condition for that final day and all were to improve their position by their jumping round. Everyone's hard work that had gone into the whole preparation was paying off. It was a long course and by the time Ben came in on The Poacher, Britain was in contention for team gold. He was under intense pressure yet managed to jump a clear round.

'The drama wasn't yet over because Jimmy Wofford on Kilkenny for the USA had a fall in the showjumping, giving Britain the gold. The USA won silver and France bronze. Celebrations didn't start immediately because the last to jump was the individual leader Pavel Deev from the USSR. It was an excruciating moment when he took the wrong course and was eliminated, which gave individual gold to Frenchman Jean-Jacques Guyon on the lovely Pitou. Derek and Lochinvar climbed up to win silver and Michael Page from the USA won bronze with Foster. I was so proud because Corney finished fourth. One memory that will never leave me was holding Cornishman during the medal ceremony when the National Anthem was being played. I can remember those goose pimples now and the thoughts ran through my mind that I would love to have some of this for myself one day. It was an amazing effort from everyone. It was without doubt one of the best team performances and I was so privileged to be part of it.

'Once the horses had been put to bed, the whole group was invited to the villa where HRH Prince Philip was staying. We had the most wonderful barbecue around a beautiful swimming pool and enjoyed a special time, where all of the squad who worked so closely together were included and were able to celebrate the achievement. There was hardly anyone who didn't get thrown in, even HRH himself, although Scotty-Dunn managed to keep us all at bay!'

The final week was spent back in Mexico City where the horses were allowed to wind down. Mike had the treat of riding Corney on easy exercise every day.

Mike: 'We were able to watch the Olympic showjumping, which provided further thrills with David Broome and Mister Softee winning individual silver and Marion Coates bronze on the diminutive Stroller. The fences were enormous and I even remember Harvey Smith saying just how big they were.

'For me there was one more unforgettable reception for all the equestrian teams and followers at the British Embassy in Mexico. Purely by chance, this was to provide a huge opportunity for me. There were a number of star names there, including Dorian Williams and Raymond Brooks-Ward, and they came to talk with all the eventing grooms, congratulating us on the work we had done to help secure the outstanding team gold medal. They were genuinely thrilled with the result. During the conversation with Raymond, I asked how it was possible to get involved in the commentary profession. He suggested that I join him in the commentary box at the Bath and West Show the following May to see what went on. I said I would love to and would follow it up, not thinking for a moment that anything would come of it.

'I was sad to say goodbye to Corney, but delighted to hand him back to the Gordon-Watsons in good shape and now an equestrian star. We were able to enjoy several weeks of celebration on our return and I had quite a task settling back to farming after all that.'

CHAPTER SEVEN

Return from Mexico

Mike: 'I came back from Mexico on an absolute high and inspired on several counts. Being a valued member of a gold-winning team that worked so well together, and was prepared to go to any lengths to ensure everything was done correctly, was an immense feeling. The tears rolling down my face as I held Corney while the National Anthem was played showed how much it all meant to me.

'I was privileged to be one of the eventing "gang" that went to watch the athletics in the Olympic Stadium before we all came home. We witnessed David Hemery breaking the world record and winning the gold medal for Great Britain in the 400m hurdles. We were absolutely hoarse by the end of it! From that day forward, I became a huge fan of the whole amazing experience of an Olympic Games. My ambition from then on was not just to ride at Badminton but also at the Olympics but, failing that, I was determined to take every opportunity to get there somehow in one capacity or another.'

There were several celebrations to which the whole British eventing squad was invited, the most memorable being at the Whitbread Rooms in the presence of Her Majesty Queen Elizabeth, the Queen Mother. Mike also had the chance to attend the live evening of what was then the 'Sportsview Personalities of the Year'. Surrounded by so many sporting personalities, Mike was amazed by the experience and was fascinated to see how the whole programme was put together for a television audience.

The Aussies, who had come away empty-handed from the equestrian side of the Games on this occasion, came back to Britain for their eleven-month quarantine period and were this time based at the home of Lord and Lady Vestey at Stowell Park. Bill Roycroft was back yet again because a number of his horses were in the team. This time it was his talented middle son, Wayne, who came with a young rider called Jim Scanlon, who both had the objective of competing at Badminton, particularly since Bill's great rival, Colonel Frank Weldon, was not only the director of the overall event but also the designer of the cross-country course.

> **Mike:** 'Socially either the boys would be down in our neck of the woods, or I'd be up their end, but this time it just wasn't quite so easy with a few more miles between us, so the drinking was restricted – but it didn't stop the great repartee between us.'

Jim and Wayne were involved in a significant milestone for Mike during Easter of 1969. It all started on the Thursday before Easter when Mike had a phone call from Raymond Brooks-Ward.

> **Mike:** 'Raymond asked me what I was doing on Easter Monday and I replied "Nothing planned". He went on to explain that he was supposed be commentating at the Old Berkshire Hunt Point-to-Point on Easter Monday but was now unavailable and asked if I would be interested in doing the job. I quickly replied that I'd only asked for some advice from him, and hadn't intended to be commentating on my own straightaway. "Not to worry Mike", he

said, "because on Easter Monday there are very few runners and it's quite an easy job." So I asked him "How do I go about it?" "Well," he said, "get the entries sent over to you immediately and over the holiday weekend sit on the loo and learn the colours. I promise faithfully, there won't be many runners and you'll be fine. Take a couple of mates with you, because they can note the fallers or any other action you don't happen to see and that's very helpful." Well, with considerable concern I reluctantly agreed and my Easter, as Raymond suggested, was spent on the loo learning the colours! So off I set with Wayne and Jim for the Old Berks Point-to-Point at Lockinge, near Wantage, which was a lovely venue that attracted big crowds but thankfully, as Raymond had predicted, very small numbers in each race.

'We arrived and were quickly introduced to all the officials including Len Caudwell, the chairman, a well-known figure in racing. He showed us all the facilities, including my commentary wagon, which was on the side of a good hill, giving us tremendous viewing. There were traditional straw bales to lean on and a head-microphone with which to do the commentary, with a switch just under it. So, I was ready and prepared. The first race, the Members', had just two runners, one set of colours black and red worn by John Wills, the other colours red and black worn by Richard Shepherd, two well-known riders in the point-to-point world. With just the two runners my "race readers" alongside me were rather gung-ho but the race went to plan, with all the phrases that I'd heard from the commentary of the great Peter O'Sullevan. All was going well until the last fence when I suddenly realised I had the runners the wrong way round – which was not a great start!

'The second race was going to be more complicated because there were five runners, so I spent time in the changing room making sure that I knew the colours belonging to each horse and arranged to meet my "race readers" on the wagon ready for the start. The boys, meanwhile, had discovered quite a few very good-looking girls whom they knew and so they were really rather laid-back about the start of the second. I already had my glasses up scanning the start when they returned and I asked them why they were late because the race was now over five minutes behind the scheduled time. Apparently the reason for the delay was that there was such a huge crowd that the Tote couldn't take the money quickly enough and so the start was put back. We had no communication with the officials and thus didn't know what was happening. So, as I leant against the bales, I said to Wayne and Jim, "Why don't they hurry up and start – the silly buggers". Now, anyone who has ever picked up a microphone, will know that there is often a short time-lag between you saying something and the actual words coming out over the public address system. You can imagine my horror as I heard "Why don't they hurry up and start – the silly buggers". coming across loud and clear to the listening public! In leaning against the bales I had inadvertently switched on the mike! However, I commentated on the race with the boys' help and I'm delighted to say this time we got it right. As you might imagine, the boys thought it was hilariously funny. I, however, was convinced it would be a very quick end to my commentary career. Amazingly enough Len Caudwell also thought it was hugely amusing and said he very much hoped I'd come back next year. You could have knocked me over with a feather!'

That was Mike's first professional commentary experience. He then joined the Jeanne Griffiths Agency, which looked after not only Raymond Brooks-Ward but also Tom Hudson and Noel Phillips Browne, who were the main names on the big County Show commentary circuit. Mike was hopeful that he might get the opportunity through the agency to stand in, particularly at some of the smaller shows, when they were short of commentators.

With the excitement of Mexico now behind him, it was time for Mike to settle down to work on the farm. All the investment injected into the two dairy herds of 180 cows in total was reaping dividends. Fewer acres were required for the same number of cows, which meant that land was freed for alternative use. Although it was traditionally a livestock farm, provided that several areas were drained properly, reasonable arable crops would grow. Mike's time at the Royal Agricultural College was helpful in his new job of drawing up a plan to introduce crops, which would require costing and implementing. There were several government-run schemes, providing grants to promote growth and improve efficiency within farming.

> **Mike:** 'So this was something I could get my teeth into and set up the future for when I took over from Dad.'

Despite his role on the farm, Mike still had time to foster his dreams in the eventing world, but he knew he had to apply himself if he were to be considered for national team selection. The Junior European Championships had been initiated at Eridge in Kent in 1967 by Colonel Babe Moseley. This competition was for riders eighteen years of age and under and was beginning to produce some exciting new talent.

> **Mike:** 'So there was no hanging around if we wanted to get somewhere. The likes of Richard Walker and Stuart Stevens were beginning to fly high, with Mark Phillips, Polly Hely-Hutchinson and Bridget Parker, all pupils of Bertie Hill, catching the eyes of the selectors for the senior team. There was also a young Hugh Thomas beginning to make his mark with some promising horses being trained by Brian Crago, an Aussie gold medallist from Rome in 1960. So the competition was definitely getting stronger.'

During the planning stage of the 1969 eventing season, all Mike's hopes were still pinned on the seven-year-old Farmer Giles. As a big and backward young horse, Giles had been taken slowly, but had been placed a couple of times in novice competitions and been given showjumping experience at some local shows by Australian showjumper Toots Murcheson.

Mike: 'I had discussed Giles with Richard Meade and he suggested I took him to Dick Stillwell, a successful showjumper who had helped Richard regularly with Barberry. Dick used athletic exercises to develop horses' technique and these were also helpful for improving the rider's judgement to a fence, and I certainly needed that! The plan was to begin with some novice classes prior to competing at intermediate level, with the aim of a first three-day event in the autumn, hopefully at Michael Foljambe's lovely home at Osberton in Nottinghamshire, an ideal first three-day event for a young horse. We always had our eye out for another horse so Giles didn't have all the pressure on him but nothing came along, prospects being either too expensive or not what fitted the bill.'

Having had a few effective lessons with Dick Stillwell at his Berkshire base, Mike and Giles tackled a number of novice events in the spring season. (In those days the season ran from mid-March to mid-May followed by a summer break, when the ground was deemed too hard for eventing. The autumn season started again in early August and continued until mid-October. It would be another ten years before the demand for continuous eventing meant that the season ran from March to October without a break, as it still does today.) Bertie Hill's early assessment of Giles was proving correct, with top placings at Kinlet in Shropshire (including jumping over a spectator who walked out in front of a cross-country fence as they were about to take off!) and Everdon in Northamptonshire, always regarded as having a difficult cross-country course.

Tidworth, by Salisbury Plain, was held in early May every year and would have been regarded as an intermediate three-day event by today's standards. It was considered a good pointer for future star horses and riders and ran a section as the final trial for the Junior European team selection.

Mike: 'Mary Macdonnell and I rode in our first Badminton together in 1964 and she rode Kilmacthomas as an individual[1] in the Moscow European Championships of 1965. It was a great start for her and, to follow on from Kilmacthomas, she had bought from the showjumper, Ted Edgar, a new horse called Skyborn by a popular sire of event horses called Little Cloud. Things did not go well for her at Tidworth and although the horse was qualified for Burghley that year she decided that Skyborn was not the horse for her. So I got a call asking if I would like to try him and see whether I would like to ride him at Burghley that September.

'You can guess the answer! Skyborn was soon down at Slads Farm and, with two horses in prospect for the season, we advertised for some live-in help at the stables. Jane Robson, a Canadian girl, who was doing polo ponies locally, came to work for us for several seasons and continues to keep in touch.'

Although Skyborn was not the best mover, he had an adequate temperament, albeit rather strong and a decent jump. Soon Mike and Skyborn were off to Dick Stillwell for an assessment and came back with several exercises to try to improve the overall picture. Dick, an expert in his field, also advised a change of bit. There was only time for two practice events if the horse was to be a starter at Burghley.

Mike: 'Riding another horse was exactly the sort of opportunity I was looking for, so we had an easy outing around our local event at Dauntsey Park and then took the long trip to Eridge in Kent, where the final trial was for team selection for the Europeans at Haras du Pin in France. Frankly, if we couldn't jump around, there

---

1   Generally a team of four and two individual riders represent each country in a championship.

was no point going to Burghley, but Skyborn came up trumps in both the showjumping and cross-country, so we decided to take our chance at Burghley because, even if we finished close to the bottom of the dressage, it would still be great experience.'

The British team were unable to compete at Burghley because it was only a few weeks before the championships, but they did win the European team title and Mary Gordon-Watson, reunited with Cornishman, won the individual title. Mark Phillips on Rock On and eighteen-year-old Richard Walker, on his Badminton winner, Pasha, made their debuts as individuals.

The European results in France created much press interest because of a new type of fence called the Normandy Bank. This entailed jumping over a ditch onto a bank and then bouncing straight over a set of rails with a maximum drop of 1.80m on the landing side. Mark Phillips on Rock On jumped it all in one in Haras du Pin, which was possibly a heart-stopping moment for all concerned!

Mike: 'There was nothing like that on the Burghley course, thank goodness, but the undulating terrain of the venue increased its difficulty. The course included all the well-known fences such as Capability's Cutting, The Dairy Farm and The Trout Hatchery and was a big test for us. I really had no knowledge of how Skyborn would last the trip or jump some of the more technical questions, but I did know he had plenty of scope. The dressage was better than expected but we were still well down the field. However, in those days, if you had no penalties on either roads and tracks or steeplechase and did a fast, clear cross-country round, you could make up a considerable number of places and that's exactly what happened. In all the cross-country rounds I have ridden, I have had very few that improved more and more the further we went. Once our confidence was up and running, we were able to up a relentless pace. Skyborn was a natural jumper (as he also showed in the showjumping phase, even with me on board!) but

Dick Stillwell had wrought some excellent improvement. Totally unexpectedly, we finished second to my Mexico colleague, Gill Watson, who received her just rewards by taking the Burghley title on the Olympic reserve horse Shaitan, with Irishman Mark Darley, who won Badminton in 1962 on Emily Little, in third place. Could this be the horse I'd been looking for to give Farmer Giles as much time as he wanted to mature to his best? Mary Mac, as we knew her, was absolutely thrilled and had already said I could keep the ride for next year.'

What had initially seemed set to be a quiet year of competition was now beginning to look very interesting because, a few weeks after Burghley, Giles completed his first three-day event at Osberton. It was perfect for that stage of his career and he coped easily, demonstrating how genuine he was. The dressage and the cross-country were as good as Mike could have wished for and he was well in contention before the final phase. However, the demands of the speed and endurance took their toll for the final day's showjumping and Giles was somewhat weary.

Mike: 'He felt just like the proverbial car with a flat tyre and, as a result, had three fences down. Despite that, we came home elated from that event with a sound young horse who still looked a real prospect for the future.

'Looking back, we could probably have been accused of being greedy. There was a new event in Holland in a place called Deurne, which was directed by Hendrick Wiegersma's father, who was not only the local doctor but was also very respected in the horse world. Lorna Sutherland (later Clarke), another top-class prospect who won Burghley in 1967 on Popadom and was a pupil of the brilliant trainer, Captain Eddy Goldman, asked whether I would join her and Edwin Atkinson in going to that first three-day event in Holland. The only horse I could take was Skyborn, who had come out of Burghley kicking and squealing so, after much deliberation, we decided it would give us further experience, especially if we were looking to the future and a possible team scenario. It was a real adventure because we had no chef d'équipe, didn't really know where we were going, or what to expect when we got there. We thought we might even have to do the washing up if it all got too expensive!'

It was certainly eventing from a different era and, being a first-time event, there were certain teething problems, but the camaraderie was superb throughout. The roads and tracks phases, mostly through woodland, were poorly signed and, with no knowledge of the area, it was evident that it would be easy for riders to lose their way:

Mike: 'If we did get lost we could neither understand nor speak the language to ask directions! Despite our fears, we all had good rides and gained experience of riding in woods. You think you are going faster than you really are as the trees fly past.'

The English contingent all ended up with time faults, but Skyborn still managed to finish second to Mike's fellow dairy farmer Gerrit Lozeman, whose daughter Alice rides for the Netherlands today. More importantly, Skyborn had done his rating no harm at all and came home safe and sound.

Mike: 'I had hoped that the ride on Skyborn might help my cause in trying to obtain some future outside rides and give me more experience for my long-term Olympic dream. Although that never happened it was a catalyst for more Olympic involvement for me that I could have ever dreamed of having. I never did get to see Raymond at work at the Bath and West Show but I did find myself on a growing number of occasions being called in as a substitute for the "big names" when they couldn't attend the smaller shows. I also enjoyed three years of race-reading for the Old Berks Point-to-Point before it clashed with an eventing commitment that I couldn't afford to miss. I must confess that I didn't see my career being involved with race-reading because it was a real skill that I lacked, but it was a great experience even in those early days!'

The year 1969 turned out to be a big step forward on several fronts for Mike and made him ponder what might unfold in the years ahead. Early in 1970 Colonel Bill Lithgow rang him, asking if he would accompany the team to the World Championships in Punchestown in September of that year, to help behind the scenes as he had done on previous occasions.

Mike: 'I didn't dare say "no" even if I was dreaming of getting into the squad myself.'

Badminton's cross-country course was developing each year. Colonel Frank Weldon, as course designer, was introducing new, enterprising fences developed from ideas he had seen used elsewhere in the world. There was no doubt that the new fence for 1970 would be the Normandy Bank. Colonel Frank's stated belief in course designing was to frighten the rider but not the horse, which he had an uncanny knack of achieving. He initiated the idea of creating areas with a series of interesting fences in close proximity, so people could see more action from the same place. Perhaps more importantly, fewer cameras were required to provide increased and improved television coverage. Such siting made the sport more accessible for the vast assembled crowds on the cross-country course and brought more of the drama of the course into focus, highlighting the skills and bravery of horse and rider. This, together with the fact that the Royal Family could be seen mingling with the crowds and enjoying every minute, helped make Badminton a big social occasion, which was reputed to attract a quarter of a million people over the three days.

Mike: 'Skyborn was scheduled for Badminton so we decided to take him down to Bertie's so we could practise over his Normandy Bank, which Bertie had made down on the river flats. No one was sure how the fence would jump after Haras du Pin. We all rode down there to see it and it was the ugliest fence I'd ever seen. It looked enormous so in fact the practice session was put off until we'd all built up some confidence to have a go! The day came and actually everybody was very quiet at breakfast that morning, but about four of us were destined to give it a try. We all voted that local boy Stuart Stevens should be the first to have a go. The river flat was the best part of a mile long and Stuart, riding the diminutive Benson, went to the far end to get up speed because Bertie had advised us to go quicker than we felt comfortable with, in order to have enough energy on the bank to bounce out over the rails. Well, Stuart came steaming up the marsh but about three strides out the horse was starting to doubt what he was being asked. They both slid straight into the ditch, which was so deep that we couldn't see Stuart or his horse. Luckily, Stuart and the horse were none the worse for the attempt. When they eventually climbed out and we realised there were no injuries, we all began to see the funny side – but we did wonder what Benson was going to think of the real thing! That fence was never ever attempted again and so how we were going to jump the real thing at Badminton would remain a mystery until we got there!

'I firmly believe that the cross-country course that Colonel Frank set that year put Badminton on the map as the unofficial World Championship. It became the one competition at which every rider, from wherever in the world, aspired to ride, and wanted to be able to say that they had been there at least once in their career. It did look very daunting that year, especially with the new loop incorporating the enormous copy of the Normandy Bank, which was followed by a sharp turn to what became known as the famous Ski Jump. If you jumped from the top to the bottom of the latter (and you shouldn't but some did) it was over two metres down. It really was a case of frightening the riders but (if you rode boldly enough) not the horses.

'It was a great competition that put some new horse and rider combinations on the map, but at the same time caused plenty of trouble – particularly at the Normandy Bank. I still remember jumping it and genuinely feeling that I was simply flying because of the length of time we were in the air over the drop off the bank. It was fine if you jumped it well, but much more scary if you didn't.'

Bertie Hill was producing some lovely horses, but was at the end of his competition career, so Mark Phillips was given the ride on a lovely grey called Chicago. Stuart Stevens rode at his first Badminton on the diminutive but powerful Benson. He also rode an exciting young prospect called Classic Chips whose half-brother, Demi Douzaine, was the ride of ex-Beaufort Pony Club member Toby Sturgis, another star produced at Rapscott.

Chicago and Benson both performed well enough to be on the long list for the World Championships at Punchestown that autumn. They were joined by Richard Meade, who won on The Poacher, Mary Gordon-Watson, reigning European Champion on The Cornishman, and Lorna Sutherland on the very popular and consistent coloured horse, Popadom. Skyborn was brilliant on the cross-country and, despite a disappointing showjumping round, still finished in the top twelve.

Mike: 'It was a memorable moment for me to win my first treasured silver replica of the Whitbread Trophy; an award for finishing in the top twelve. I couldn't help but notice a very stylish nineteen-year-old lady, a pupil of Captain Goldman, riding a horse called Mooncoin, who finished tenth at their first attempt and very much caught the eye of several, not just me![2] Moreover, you can imagine my excitement when I received a phone call from the chairman of selectors. Skyborn had gone well enough at

---

2   This was Angela Sowden who two years later would become Mrs Tucker!

Badminton for us to be added to the bottom of the selected long list. It was a huge thrill.

'The week after Badminton I had another phone call, which this time was from Derek Allhusen. Bez Thomas, his rider, had been having difficulty with a young home-bred horse out of his good mare Laurien. The horse was entered for Tidworth three-day event but had started to have a few refusals with Bez and so I was asked whether I would take the ride. There was no time for a practice competition and only two weeks in which to try to get to know the horse and have some schooling sessions. There was no doubt he wasn't in love with cross-country. New surroundings and a couple of spins jumping round the farm led by another horse seemed to revive his enthusiasm so I felt we should take our chance. He was a lovely type of horse, with good movement and a more than capable jump if he chose to use it. The freshening up proved to have worked and he duly did the business by winning his section. Derek Allhusen was over the moon. Sadly, the horse's enthusiasm didn't last long. When he came back into work after a short break he soon reverted to his old tricks. Disappointingly, he was returned to Derek's lovely home in Norfolk, but riding him had been good experience for me.'

Mike's disappointments continued. Skyborn, being long-listed, was invited to compete in a dressage competition at the Royal International Horse Show as part of the squad monitoring.

Mike: 'When we arrived, we discovered to our horror that Skyborn was lame when he came off the horsebox and so took no further part. Things were really not going well, but we did have one final string to our bow for 1970 and that was Farmer Giles. He had progressed well through the intermediate classes and was being targeted for the second holding of the Dutch three-day event at Deurne, which we had so enjoyed the first year. This time there would be many more British entries. It wasn't an ideal competition for my long-striding young horse because of the wooded areas of the cross-country but it would be a good test of control and discipline.'

By that stage, Mike had a good team at home so the work could continue with Giles while he was at Punchestown with the eventing team. It is crucial to have reliable and capable help, especially with a horse that has to have important work prior to a three-day event.

The squad for the World Championships was to meet at Burghley and travel out immediately afterwards.

Mike: 'I went there to meet up with everybody and get into team mode. The team tack room that I was allocated included Lorna and the young rider Angela Sowden, already at her second Burghley with her good grey, Mooncoin. I'd had a number of girl friends over the years from my Young Farmer days and the eventing world but nothing serious. However, this young lady from East Bridgford in Nottinghamshire had really bowled me over!'

As a consequence, the conversation between Mark Phillips and Mike in the car on the way from Burghley to Punchestown did not wholly concern the results at Burghley or what might happen at the World Championship in Ireland! In addition to Mike's thoughts about Angela:

Mike: 'Mark had developed a friendship with Princess Anne as she was becoming more involved in the sport. With a team of talented horses and with the coaching skills of Alison Oliver, the Princess showed she would be capable of achieving great things. Without doubt, there was a flush of young talent that could only bring the sport more into the public eye, which was potentially exciting news.'

The famous racecourse at Punchestown is surrounded by wonderful natural countryside. Although the venue had hosted a European Championship in 1967, this was its first World Championships and it was set out to be a real test.

Mike: 'Once again my job was to liaise between the team management, the riders and the grooms and hopefully ensure that everything ran as smoothly as possible for the riders in particular.'

The Irish, who were defending the title they had won four years earlier at Burghley, had the famous foxhunting man Thady Ryan as chef d'équipe, and the Americans had the successful French rider Jack Le Goff, who had moved to the United States. The British Team under Colonel Bill Lithgow had been unbeaten since 1967 and was looking for a first World title.

Mike: 'It looked a challenging task, with a long and demanding cross-country course including one or two controversial fences. Some fences involved typical natural Irish "razor" banks, which are very narrow across the top, which few horses would have encountered. One fence that caused considerable discussion and apprehension was a wide oxer with a significant drop on landing, approached from a short turn between bushes. It was considered that a drop behind an oxer was a conflict of ideas, because a horse doesn't naturally jump out over a drop. This proved to be the case and the fence was the cause of numerous falls, some of which were quite dramatic. In those days, fences were not removed from a course even if they were causing excess trouble. Mark and Chicago jumped right into the middle of the oxer and came out between the two rails, which meant he hadn't gone through the necessary flags. So Mark had to jump back on, turn around and try it again. Fortunately, the horse was brave and jumped it successfully at the second attempt. It was just as well because Stuart Stevens and Benson retired on the cross-country and Mark's score with Chicago was crucial to get a team score. Lorna and Popadom was another partnership that came to grief at the drop oxer but brilliant clear rounds by Mary and Corney and Richard on The Poacher put Britain in the lead, with the Americans the only other team to complete. Like Mexico, it was another dramatic cross-country day that frankly wasn't in the interests of the sport, but Britain went on to win the team World title with Mary and Richard winning individual gold and silver medals and Jimmy Wofford for America, on the exhausted ex-Irish horse Kilkenny, who had to be virtually carried round the showjumping, hung on to bronze.[3] I had been kept extremely busy, but ultimately it was all worthwhile. It was another huge learning curve for the sport, even if some of it wasn't what we wanted to see in future competitions.

'We were due to pack up and leave for home with the horses on the Monday evening boat. However, Thady Ryan had offered anyone who fancied it an early morning's hunting with his wonderful Scarteen pack before we left later that day. Four of us took up the offer. We all rode hirelings and I had my first taste of banks, ditches, scrambling through hedges – you name it; we did it all! The cry of his hounds was superb and it was a sad moment when he blew for home at around ten o'clock but my horse, who had been spooky but honest, was really quite tired. I asked the kind person who took the horse from me when we returned to the transport, "How old is the horse?" and nearly fainted when he said, "Well now, I'd say he'd be three years old and backed about a month"!

'There was plenty of chat on the way home about that morning and I suspect it couldn't happen anywhere other than Ireland. So,

---

3   Jimmy met Mike at Tweseldown in 1968, where they argued about the respective merits of British and American beer. This formed the basis of a lifelong friendship, which Jimmy recollected with both humour and compassion in a letter of sympathy to Angela following Mike's death.

it was "Home James" and back to pick up where we had left off with Giles's preparation for Deurne.'

On returning home, Mike was delighted with Giles's fitness and progress and had just one more outing at Wylye before preparing to leave for Holland two weeks later. Wylye was well run by Lord and Lady Hugh Russell and was establishing itself as a popular international three-day event.

Mike: 'The plan was just to do the dressage phase of the competition, but then ask for permission to do some fast work with Giles up the surrounding steep hills. We were all scared of Rosemary Russell and I feared she wouldn't allow it, but not only did she agree, she also said I could use some of her schooling fences as well. It proved a great preparation for our trip and we were all set for Farmer Giles's biggest test yet.'

Farmer Giles, now an eight-year-old, was the first horse that Mike had produced from a two-year-old. Compared to the more Thoroughbred types Mike had competed at this level, Giles's temperament was by far the easiest. He was by the Thoroughbred, Little Cloud, out of a part-bred Cleveland Bay mare. Cleveland Bays are mostly associated with driving, although there have been some good sport horses from the breed. Giles's dam also produced Shaitan on whom Gill Watson won Burghley, and Viscount, a top horse ridden by Lars Sederholm. The Swedish-born Lars was not only a high-level event rider himself but, through his Waterstock Training Centre, where he was supported by his wife Diana, he became one of the most influential trainers of successful riders in all disciplines.

Mike: 'So there was quite a bit of interest in this young horse, especially as Dad had bought him for two hundred and fifty guineas which, even in those days, was not much money for an event horse!

'Gail had done a wonderful job on my horses throughout that season but was due to leave us in September, so I asked Angela Sowden if she would help me with Giles in Holland. She agreed and so we set off to Deurne at least pre-armed about what to expect, with a bigger and more competitive international field than the previous year.'

As is often the case in October, the trip across the Channel was delayed by bad weather, but they arrived in plenty of time for the start of the competition and, once again, were made to feel very welcome. There were very few changes from the previous year. The competition was to be moved to Boekelo the following year because the many trees made it too difficult for the crowds to enjoy the spectacle of the cross-country.

Mike: 'It was great to have Angela there because we could discuss the course together and I could benefit from an experienced pair of eyes to watch and comment during the various warm-ups.'

Despite never having previously experienced crowds, Giles lived up to all hopes and finished in the top ten.

Mike: 'He coped well with the twisty, wooded cross-country and finished with a clear round in the showjumping, which was pretty unusual for me and, most important of all, he was now qualified to compete at the "local gymkhana"[4] in Spring 1971.'

Giles had earned a well-deserved break before he was brought back into work at Christmas to prepare for Mike's fourth attempt at Badminton.

Mike: 'I would be competing against my very hardworking and successful groom from Deurne when that time came.'

---

4   As Mike referred to Badminton.

Meanwhile on the home front:

Mike: 'Home was becoming more like a hotel, with all the visitors whose hospitality I'd enjoyed on my trips overseas arriving on our doorstep – Mum actually loved it! In fact, when we got back from Holland, Roger Haller, who had been on the same Pony Club exchange as me in 1965, was over from the States looking for horses with Bertie Hill, and found one called Golden Griffin who he really liked and bought. Then Aussie Peter Winton arrived on the doorstep with his new bride Vicki to catch up with all the news and teach his wife how to cut the butter![5]

'That winter I was making regular trips up the old "Fosse" to near Newark where the Sowdens lived and Angela was making trips down to Gloucestershire. Her Mum, Lorna, was the horse enthusiast, had hunted all her life and was very supportive of her daughter's talents and dedication. Father Basil was an estate agent with Turner, Fletcher and Essex in Nottingham and both had worked hard to give their daughter every chance to succeed, supporting her training with Eddy Goldman and Yvonne Nelson – a talented teacher who formed an Equestrian School, later called the Fortune Centre for Riding Therapy, down in the New Forest. I was always made to feel very welcome at the Sowden home and enjoyed plenty of laughs and leg-pulling from Angela, her parents and her sister Felicity too.

'During the winter of 1970/1971 we made plans for our campaigns. Angela decided to spend some time with Molly Sivewright at Talland (who also still kept an eye on my dressage) and I planned to spend time with Dick Stilwell to work on my showjumping. The idea was to have at least two outings before Badminton, with a final run at the popular Brigstock Trials in Northamptonshire, which always provided a testing cross-country

---

5   A reference to the Tucker family's butter-cutting rituals, as described in Chapter Two.

course as an ideal preparation for those aiming for the "big one". The April date of Badminton meant that earlier competitions could be threatened by bad weather, so Tweseldown and an excellent event put on by the Wookeys at Rushall were alternative choices.

'The spring preparation went well and we arrived at Brigstock, where the world and its wife would be putting the final touches to their mounts, on target. Most of Giles's gallops were done on the estate at Chavenage, a short box drive from home, where there were some good hills, but this would be the first time that Giles's fitness and stamina would be put to the test this season.'

A few weeks before Badminton, Mike had a phone call from Lorna Sutherland. At that time, Lorna had a base at Bucklebury for her team of horses, which saved her hours of driving backwards and forwards to and from her home in Scotland. Lorna was riding another of Derek Allhusen's young horses out of his mare Laurien, called Laurieston.

Mike: 'Lorna was not finding him easy, as he was extremely sensitive and strong and she told me I would be getting a phone call to see whether I would take the ride. The call came and I agreed to have the horse at home straight after Badminton. I would see how things went, with a possible target of Tidworth in mid-May.'

Angela was having her second ride at Badminton on Mooncoin. She had already completed two double clears at Burghley on him, the first in 1969 when she also competed in the Pony Club Team Showjumping on a different horse; a record that's never been equalled.

Mike: 'There was plenty of local interest in the field including Mark Phillips on Great Ovation, known as "Cheers". Aunt Flavia Phillips had a great eye for finding young horses and this was probably her most outstanding; a find from up in the Heythrop hunting country. He'd been produced slowly and because Chicago was sold to Germany after the 1970 World Championships, it had to be his turn.

'The going was good, the weather fine and there was plenty of incentive to "go for it", with an eye on the European Championships at Burghley that autumn. We had a great support team and there was keen competition between the young riders who had been part of the Junior European teams, namely Angela and Stuart Stevens on Classic Chips, who were 1968 team-mates at Craon, France. Bertie Hill was extremely busy with all those who had been through the "Rapscott Finishing School".

'Typical of the spirit within the sport in those days, there was a tremendous camaraderie between us all and everyone would help each other when it was needed, but when it was you and your horse in competition, it was all systems go! Both Mooncoin and Farmer Giles had done good tests (Tucker was beginning to "do" dressage) and were up in the top third. We both followed up with fast clear rounds throughout the speed and endurance phases. Mark and "Cheers" set the pace; Princess Anne had gone really well on Doublet, much to the joy of the crowd, and Debbie West and Stuart Stevens gave eye-catching performances too. Much to our delight, Mooncoin and Giles had jumped their way into the top eight of the leader board. There were no dramas for the leading combinations at the final horse inspection, leading to a nail-biting final jumping phase. Angela had been a very successful junior showjumper so she knew her game when it came to this phase and I was aware that I had to pull out all the stops to beat her. For about the only time ever, I managed to remain in my overnight place and stay just above Angela and we finished sixth and seventh. Princess Anne thrilled the huge crowd by finishing fifth on Doublet, who was bred by Her Majesty the Queen to be a polo pony but looked a very exciting prospect. Mark, on Great Ovation, won the first of his four consecutive Badminton wins. Giles was one of my easiest rides ever at Badminton and oozed class right from the start. Even Dad had to have a celebratory drink when we got home.'

There was little time for celebration, however, as attention was turned to the horses going to Tidworth, and the arrival of Laurieston. The handsome horse duly turned up and it was soon apparent that he would be a difficult type to relax. He was good-looking and athletic, with loads of presence but not very big.

Mike: 'We spent our first few days just trying to settle him and I had lessons booked with Dick Stillwell, who had worked with Major Derek Allhusen and his horses for a number of seasons. There was absolutely no doubt that Laurieston was extremely talented if you could find the key to him, but we didn't have long before the popular Sherborne event in Dorset, in which he was entered as a warm-up for Tidworth. It was not a good start. The cross-country had already started before Laurieston did his dressage test and once he heard the speakers, he immediately tensed up and just would not settle. The judge's horn went for the start of my test, I trotted in and tried to halt, whereupon Laurieston reared straight up and I slipped gracefully off the back over his tail! I did manage to keep hold of him and so stood to attention, took my hat off to the judge and marched out, much to everyone's amusement!'

It was back to the drawing board. This involved time spent quietly trotting around on a loose rein before gently taking up a contact and asking Laurieston to work. Derek and Lorna were most helpful and, bit by bit, progress was made – but there were only ten days before Tidworth and his work was far from established. Luckily there were small crowds at Tidworth and, compared to events such as Badminton, the atmosphere would hopefully be peaceful.

Mike: 'We managed to find some quiet areas of the polo fields where we could give him plenty of work and he did settle down to do a reasonably decent dressage test. With luck nothing would prove too difficult for him on the cross-country, and this turned out to be the case. To my amazement we managed to do exactly what Derek had wanted and he completed an excellent clear jumping round for me to win my second consecutive Tidworth title, which I would not have believed possible after the débâcle at Sherborne! Angela hadn't seen him at his worst so she wondered what all the fuss was about.'

There was a busy autumn ahead because both Mooncoin and Giles had been short-listed for the European Championships at Burghley in early September and Laurieston and Mike, together with Mark, Lorna and Michael Moffett had been chosen to go to the Olympic 'test' event in Munich later that September.

Mike was kept busy with commentary jobs from the Jeanne Griffiths Agency. These included Market Deeping Country Show in Lincolnshire in June and Burley-on-the-Hill Show, in Rutland, run by Robin Leyland over the second May Bank Holiday. The stunning house at Burley offered a wonderful backdrop to where the Pony Club Championships were once held. This commentary job started 1971 and it was where Mike first saw the young Whitaker boys (John and Michael) and Geoff Billington in action, and introduced him to the best jumping he had encountered thus far. Trevor Banks brought his good horses to jump there and Malcolm Pyrah was on home territory, so top-quality riding abounded.

Over the winter, Angela and Mike had discussed getting engaged and had made the decision that Angela's father, Basil, should be officially asked for his daughter's hand in marriage when Mike stayed for the Market Deeping Show that June. Angela's family had moved a few hundred yards up the road from the White House in Newton to a lovely cottage, with several acres, where Basil had built a stable yard from where his daughter could compete.

Mike: 'Having returned from the show, I nervously cornered Basil and asked him if I could have his daughter's hand in marriage. His first expression was one of exasperation because he'd spent money on the new stable yard when it wasn't going to be used! But it was all in fun and both Basil and Lorna were overjoyed that I was taking their lovely daughter off their hands. They were a trifle worried, however, when we said we hoped to get married on the first of January 1972 in approximately six months' time. We wanted to have an Australian-type wedding (late in the day and already dressed for dancing) that we suggested might be a white tie occasion, as late as regulations would allow in the evening. I think my parents had been expecting news on this subject for several weeks so they weren't surprised when I rang them to tell them we were engaged. George Weldon, who – although he'd given up riding – had remained a close mate ever since Pony Club days, was to be best man, with Roger Alexander and Mark Phillips two of the groomsmen – although I wasn't sure they would succeed in getting me to the church!'

With all that excitement over, it was down to business with the horses. The final trial for team selection was once again at the Abergavennys' estate at Eridge Park in mid-August. Laurieston stayed with Mike to allow more time for them to bond. Mike was as spoilt as ever; with the farm well-staffed thanks to his parents, he was able to continue preparing his horses from Slads, although with the wedding in sight, plans had to be made for living arrangements and stabling for all their horses.

Both questions were resolved quickly. A delightful cottage was up for rent in the middle of the Estcourt Estate about a mile from Slads and a good mile from any public highway. The old cart-horse stables at Church Farm had the scope to be made into decent competition stables, so Lionel and Ann Green, who came from the Lumb family up in Nottinghamshire, were employed to set up and run the stable yard, which had to be ready for use before the turn of the year.

Mike: 'That summer flew by but all the work necessary for the European Championships had gone to plan. Angela and I did our preparations at our own home bases and set off independently (fortunately as it happens), to what was going to be a very competitive final trial at Eridge. We had done no more than arrive at the venue and let the ramp down when Giles gave a number of coughs right in front of Peter Scott-Dunn, the team vet. There could have been no worse place to take a possibly infectious horse, with all the potential team and eight individual horses stabled together for the final workout. There was only one answer and that was for a distraught me to get the hell out of Eridge and go home as soon and as quickly as possible.'

On the way home Mike summoned Jeffrey Brain to come immediately to see the horse. It was confirmed that Giles had been suffering from a mild infection. The response to the treatment he was given would clarify what could happen next. Giles responded quickly, stopped coughing and was soon bouncing about again. Although he had been withdrawn from the European Championships as a 'nominated individual', should the veterinary surgeon pronounce him fit to run, he could compete as one of six extra individuals allotted to the host nation. Giles's blood tests and heart checks were fine both before and after a final check gallop. After considerable discussion of the possible risks, Mike decided to take his chance as an individual at Burghley and joined the other eleven.

Angela and Mooncoin had performed well at Eridge. She and Princess Anne on Doublet were selected as individuals and the team consisted of Richard Meade, Mark Phillips, Mary Gordon-Watson and first-timer Debbie West on Baccarat. It was a strong group of riders that boded well for the future of the British sport, all of whom got on well together.

Mike: 'The dressage went well for Britain and for Angela and I, who both did close to our personal bests. The course was of true championship proportions, offering plenty of places to make mistakes but, with full concentration, we felt it was all possible, especially with the going being perfect.

'A huge crowd had come to watch the Princess in her first championship, with many of them in good voice! There were more spectators on the steeplechase than I'd ever seen before. I set off with Giles feeling fine. We trotted round the roads and tracks and out of the woods onto the golf course for the steeplechase. I had a really classy ride, hitting all the check times easily until suddenly, as I passed through the finishing flags, he stumbled and kept on stumbling until he went down, never to get up again. He had suffered a heart attack, giving me an easy fall, but I was totally devastated and didn't know what to do or where to go. Suddenly I was surrounded by people, with Bertie Hill and Dick Stillwell being the first I recognised who came to comfort me. They had a job to lead me away because I didn't want to leave my beloved friend. The rest of the day was an absolute haze. My parents were there and were as shocked as I was at what had happened. Of course I needed to support Angela and had to pull myself together, so I didn't in any way give her negative vibes before her ride, which I didn't find easy.

'The day was a good one not only for the British team, but also for Princess Anne, who led after cross-country and went on to win, and Angela who jumped her third clear cross-country round in three attempts and was among the élite of Europe on the scoreboard. I am ashamed to say I found it difficult to take much interest in the competition on the final day, despite a British clean sweep of all medals. I did realise that I needed to get back on track and start focusing on the trip to Munich with Laurieston, which was only a short time away. How lucky I was that I had something else to focus on and help forget the awful loss of Giles. It was a huge lesson about life in general that one has to face from time to time.'

Mike was thrilled that Angela agreed to accompany him to Munich as groom for Laurieston. All the four riders and grooms knew each other well, and Colonel Bill Lithgow was chef d'équipe, so it promised to be fun as well as an informative trip with the Munich Olympics in mind. Ford of Britain had given the British Show Jumping Association [as it was then known] and the British Horse Society two new horseboxes to help transport teams around Europe.

Mike: 'Those in our group were to be the first drivers of these boxes transporting horses, food etc. down to Southern Germany. It would entail miles of autobahn driving. I'm not sure that the authorities knew what risks they were taking in putting us lot in charge of driving these brand-new vehicles, although Lorna of course had probably done more lorry driving than all the rest of us put together. We got down there without incident, thankfully.

'The facilities were good in general, although I do remember that, because of a shortage of practice jumps, Mike Moffett and Demerara took to jumping the picnic tables in the park, which was very much frowned upon but at least gave us some more fences to jump! It was also the October Beer Festival in Munich, which did threaten to be a slight distraction, particularly as there were some great German Oompah bands playing and I had set my heart on conducting one – and succeeded! Quite rightly the chef d'équipe curtailed that exercise rather quickly and it was brought under control.'

Not every country brought horses to Munich to try out the facilities, but Jack Le Goff had brought over two of his young stars.

Mike: 'Bruce Davidson, who was really setting the American eventing scene on fire, came with my old mate Roger Haller to have a look. They were both aiming to spend time with Lord and Lady Hugh Russell, training at Wylye the following winter.'

The cross-country was quite undulating and long, and had a significant bounce fence at the top of a steep incline that required respect. The Allhusens had come to watch Laurieston and were happy with his dressage test.

Mike: 'By cross-country Laurieston was on form and was looking to go considerably faster than I was planning. On the steeplechase he was strong and it wouldn't have been a pretty sight and the same could be said of parts of the cross-country, particularly where I needed to anchor him before combination fences. Although he jumped clear, and was quite fast too, he finished tired because of the constant fighting to go faster. He looked a weary horse that evening and the groom had quite a late night attending to him! He perked up next morning and jumped well enough to finish in third place. The rest of our squad had decent rides and a great deal was gleaned for what to expect next year, which was the purpose of the mission. Disappointments were to follow for me when Derek explained afterwards that he was going to take the horse home on his return for Richard Meade to try. Frustrating and disappointing though it was, when I analysed it, I couldn't argue with Derek's decision and of course Meade was to work his magic a year later and that made the decision totally justified.

'It had been a turbulent year to say the least and I have reflected on many occasions since about the decision to run Giles at Burghley. It was our decision and no one else's but, having been given a clean bill of health by the vet, we thought all would be well. If that sort of situation were ever to arise again, there would be no discussion and, whoever the horse in question, he would be turned out to rest and recuperate. It was a very hard lesson to learn with a most genuine and generous horse.'

CHAPTER EIGHT

New Life Together

The 'event' of the year was yet to come, and it was time for the planning of the wedding, which was to be held at five-thirty on the first of January 1972 at Shelford Church, with the reception at the Sowdens' home near Newark.

Mike: 'There had been a few pre-wedding parties: one with my Young Farmer friends, which proved a real test of stamina down near home, and then one where we were staying in Ratcliffe, the night before the wedding, which totally blew any idea of going hunting on the morning of the wedding! Roger Haller had come over from the States and so with Mark Phillips, Frank Weldon and company there was a very long, rowdy and "different" game of cards, which brought about several red faces and considerable complaints from Mother a few rooms down the corridor!'

A bus was organised to come from Gloucestershire full of family and friends. It was to be a great gathering of both families, as well as a *Who's Who* from the eventing world.

Mike: 'The church service was truly memorable in the lovely Shelford Church, with some gusty singing followed by the splendid reception including dinner, dancing and speeches and everyone getting on so well. To add to the tremendous generosity of both Angela's parents and mine, Dad made me a full partner in the farm, which was a wonderful surprise. It was a night that both of us remember and treasure to this day and set us up for a wonderful life together.

'We flew off to Tenerife for our honeymoon, which was warm and relaxing but, with the sort of lives we were both used to leading, we soon yearned to get back and set up in our new home together at Walnut Cottage with all our horses at Church Farm.'

Mike's grandmother was still alive and living on her own at Church Farm and, thanks to the help of her family, continued to enjoy her life there. She died in December 1972 aged ninety-five. She left a lovely house, but one that required considerable refurbishment and modernisation. Fortunately, arrangements had been made earlier for the house and farm to stay in the family, and these had passed on to Mike's father when grandmother's husband died nineteen years earlier. She was certainly a strong and hard-working lady, and was a great example to the rest of the family.

Marriage, joyous as it proved to be, inevitably brought with it significant changes.

Mike: 'In my mind, our wedding changed the focus of my responsibilities. Having come back from Mexico in 1968 with the burning ambition to compete at the Olympics for the best part of the four years that had passed, I had chased that dream. However, I had come to realise what a tough task it was and although I hoped I could continue trying, I needed to concentrate on making the farm work for the family and perhaps also earn some income from the equestrian world when I could. Although I was only earning a small amount from commentating, I did wonder whether that could grow. I was doing some three or four events a year on the commentary side for the agency and was getting back good reports of my work. At the same time, I was being asked to do more and more cross-country commentary, which didn't pay, but was excellent practice.

'Angela and I discussed whether I should try to ride Mooncoin. Angela had developed him into a reliable top horse through her undoubted all-round skills, whereas I normally gained my occasional successful placings through my speed and cross-country riding skills. We had tried a first effort at the Midland Bank Championships in Cirencester Park the previous autumn. Alas, it ended in disaster by me missing my stride at the very first fence and going "splat".

'Despite some highs, 1971 had been a year to forget riding-wise and it was time to move on. I had no horses in the pipeline to event and although I had offers of a few rides, I decided to have one further go with Mooncoin at Badminton, with which of course, I had a love affair! Thanks to Angela's great help, Mooncoin and I began to enjoy more of a rapport and as the spring went on, I think it got even better. We won't talk too much about the dressage because with me wasn't as good as it was with the "Boss". What's more, I had a terrible habit of nodding my head in the trot, which quickly got me the nickname of "Noddy"!'

Frank Weldon produced the usual big track at Badminton, which that year headed out in the direction of Huntsman's Close. There was a big drop out of the small copse, after which there was a quick turn to a set of rails followed by the familiar Elephant Trap.

Mike: 'I was busy concentrating on turning to the rails after the drop when Mooncoin pecked on landing and I slipped out of the side door as neat as a whistle! I quickly hopped back on board, which you could do in those days, and re-established a decent rhythm, only to get stopped on course behind the arena. We eventually got going again and I had a great ride home, especially over the big fences along the Vicarage Ditch, but it was all too late by then. But at least we got round and I received my fifth Badminton plaque for completing the competition. Those plaques sit on the mantelpiece today, providing some very happy memories. One of the other highlights of that Badminton was witnessing that all the hard work put in by Richard with Laurieston was really paying off. Richard had taken him slowly over a good number of cross-country courses during the build-up and the horse's jumping had greatly improved. There were definite glimpses of a real Olympic medal horse in the making, which was as exciting to me as it was to the selectors.'

One of Mike's biggest steps forward in the commentary field was in 1972, at the Great Yorkshire Show. It was one of the biggest agricultural shows in the country but clashed with the start of the July Hickstead meeting. Noel Phillips Browne was lead public address commentator at both, with Raymond Brooks-Ward and Dorian Williams who did the television commentary at Hickstead.

Mike: 'I had never worked live with Noel, but was asked to spend the first day with him, work with him on the second day and then do the final day on my own. Noel's library of competitors and horses had to be seen to be believed. I had heard Raymond talking about it and it was every bit as good as he had said – and no computers in those days!

'Major Reg Whitehead was also on the arena team with Julian Davey and showjumping ace, Alan Oliver, who was helping Reg with course design. They were all a wonderful help to me in getting to know everybody. That same team, led by Reg, was responsible for putting on top-class jumping at a number of the big County Shows, so it was a very good one for me to be associated with. For many, the Great Yorkshire was the best showground in the country and, with Noel as my mentor, I quickly found a way to do the job that seemed to work for the Yorkshire officials.

'By the time we got to the last day, I had found enough people to ask for help so I could do the job on my own. Angela and Mum-in-law had brought the caravan so I was able to do the necessary homework overnight. Although I was nervous, I felt reasonably confident that I could cope by the time we started on the final Thursday morning.

'The Yorkshire spectators love their showjumping and it is always one of the best jumping shows on our calendar. It was the famous Cock o' the North day and it also happened to be one of the final trials for the Munich Olympics. What made me very nervous was that Bob Hanson, the famous owner of horses such as O'Malley and a big sponsor of the show, was sitting alongside me. Harvey Smith, Malcolm Pyrah and David Broome were all through to the final jump-off and it was a thriller. I think David Broome won it, but what delighted me was when Bob Hanson and, a bit later, Trevor Banks came up and said "well done". That meant so much to me. I have only missed two Yorkshire Shows since 1972 and to this day, I believe it was this occasion that properly started my commentary career.

'Meanwhile, Mooncoin had a smile back on his face because he was back with his "Mum", seemingly none the worse from my attempts on him, and they were setting their sights on Burghley.'

During that time, Solihull Riding Club had organised a day trip to fly out to Munich for the Olympic cross-country action. With an inside interest of the British team, Mike and some of his local friends spent a long but interesting day as spectators. As is invariably the case, when one is used to seeing things from the inside, it's never as good simply to watch. However, the fact that the team performed so well to clinch the gold medal, and Richard Meade on Laurieston won individual gold, it was special to be there, even as an onlooker and at least congratulations could be passed on, if only from behind a wire fence.

Mike: 'I had some fun that year competing on a few novices, although none were stars of the future, but actually did more cross-country commentary and was really enjoying the experience. The great thing about having ridden around some of the courses was that I am sure I was able to deliver a more knowledgeable and interesting commentary.

'Although we didn't know it at the time, Mooncoin, as he was affectionately known, carried another important passenger at Burghley because it was confirmed soon after the event that Angela was expecting Emma.[1] It certainly didn't deter either of them, because they completed their third clear cross-country round in a row and their third top ten placing, having finished eighth in the Europeans in 1971 and sixth at Burghley in 1972 behind Janet Hodgson on Larkspur, which was some record.'

The Midland Bank Championships at Cirencester Park that autumn was used as an opportunity to celebrate Britain's great success at the Munich Games. For the first time, they were to be covered on BBC television and the producer, Alan Mouncer, was then one of the legendary producers of sport. Laurence and Jane Rook threw a splendid celebratory party at their home, Beverston Castle, just outside Tetbury. Included in the extensive eventing guest list was the BBC production team, many of whom had

---

1   Angela recalled: 'Burghley used to be a happy time because of the memories of when I first met Mike in the tackroom there. We used to stay in our lorry, which had living – a far cry from when Mike used to go off eventing in his trailer in the early days! It was at Burghley in 1972 that I couldn't understand why I was feeling so sick in the mornings because I was not normally that nervous and only afterwards discovered that I had ridden round when I was expecting Emma!'

been part of the coverage from Munich – the Olympics where the fateful terrorist raid occurred, that Raymond Brooks-Ward was involved in.[2]

> **Mike:** 'Raymond was kind enough to introduce Angela and me to some of the production team during the evening, including Alan, who invited us to look round the television scanner and see how it all worked before the competition got under way.'

Mike had been asked to be part of the cross-country public address team consisting of several people rotating commentary with periods of rest because of the pressure they were under. This was intensified by providing running provisional scores to add to the interest, and keeping the leaderboard up to date as the competition unfolded.

> **Mike:** 'I made sure I wasn't late for the appointment to see the scanner as it was the hub of where the production happens and where the programme is put together. From there, the producer sets up the cameramen to whatever picture he wants and then picks the appropriate ones to go out on air from a huge bank of screens. The sound and recording engineers are all linked so the producer can communicate with everyone to put the programme together. I had never seen this before and I was spellbound but had one more place to visit, which was the commentary area. *[This was where each commentator would be handed a headset on which the*

---

2   Brooks-Ward was interviewing HRH Princess Anne in the Olympic Village when news came that the Israeli athletes had been taken hostage by the Black September Group (in what is now known as The Munich Massacre) and that the hostages were being taken to the main airport – which is where the bulk of the journalists headed. However, all BBC commentators in those days had individual drivers and Brooks-Ward's was a young German Army corporal. Over his military radio the driver learned that the hostages were, in fact, taken to Fürstenfeldbruck, a NATO airbase. Brooks-Ward's journalist training kicked in and, along with David Coleman, he went there immediately. For thirty-six hours the two men broadcast to the BBC network – and saw the helicopter explode. Nick Brooks-Ward, Raymond's son, said that when his father returned from Munich he never talked to anyone about the incident – apart from Mike Tucker.

producer could be heard, talking as required, to the cameramen and any of the crew. The producer was also able to inform each commentator where he was going with the pictures and when he was coming to them. There was a huge amount on which to concentrate and absorb, particularly in the early days, when a course could have two scanners, giving two sets of pictures from different areas of the course so, for the commentator, it was important to identify each horse and rider on the correct part of the course.]

Mike: 'When we were in the commentary box, they were rehearsing the cameras for the next day's production, so Alan encouraged me to pick up the mike and have a go. Interestingly, it was a bit like "rubbing your tummy and patting your head" when you were commentating on the pictures, whilst listening in your headset to the producer talking to his camera crew or even directing you. It required plenty of concentration, but I found it fascinating.'

On the topic of his recent marriage, Mike said:

'Married life at Walnut Cottage was wonderful. We would often see foxes and deer ambling past the kitchen French window and although we were out in the country we had family living within a mile of us. It was no more than a mile to Tetbury as the crow flies, but two miles by car. My family only ever had one dog and the terrible wrench for us all when it went missing, never to be seen again, meant we never got another. The Sowdens, on the other hand, always had dogs and were never without them, so when Robin Gundry offered us a lovely brindle and white Lurcher as a wedding present, we both agreed we would love to have it. Even as a pup, it found jumping easy and we called it Dikler after the very good steeplechaser who was also a very good jumper.

'With the expected birth getting ever closer, we agreed to ask Jane Bullen if she could come for two or three weeks to help Angela get into a routine. Jane had trained in nursing and was called by the press "The Galloping Nurse" when she rode at Mexico. To our great joy, it fitted into her schedule and she agreed to come. The baby was due in early May and Angela was set to go to Malmesbury Hospital when the time came. The dairy was kept pretty empty so I wasn't too tied to milking, but there was a new horse trial on the ninth of May being put on by Polly Hely-Hutchinson and Bridget Parker, two good friends for many years, at which I had agreed to help. It was called Farleigh and was held on Polly's parents' land just the other side of Bath. Bridget, Polly and her husband-to-be, Hamish (parents of Alec, the technical delegate, at the London Olympics) and I had all been pupils together with Bertie Hill. We had many, many funny moments and Hamish's laugh was exactly like Basil Brush, which meant you could always tell where he was and roughly what trouble he was in!

'Sod's Law really did exist, because I had already gone to Farleigh when things began to happen, so my dear Mum sprang into action and took Angela to hospital. Before you could say "Jack Robinson" she was ringing me to say we had a baby daughter and all was well. I was on the receiving end of a lot of teasing about being at Farleigh rather than by my wife's side, but I had permission to leave earlier in the afternoon than planned and set off for Malmesbury Hospital. Mother and daughter were glowing and my own Mum had done a great job in telling everybody who should be told! That all happened on the ninth of May and the family had to cope with mother and baby when they came home until Jane arrived on the twentieth. However, wild horses couldn't keep the grannies away!

'Angela coped really well and with Jane around we had lots of laughs together, with an odd flood or two with all the washing that was going on. However, the highlight of Jane's two weeks' stay was when Captain Mark walked in unannounced to tell us the tremendous news that he had just become engaged to

Princess Anne and was likely to get married later in the year. The problem was, we only had some pretty old sherry to celebrate the moment but that didn't stop us, although next morning, the head was not in great shape!

'The season of 1973 had a totally new perspective with baby Emma on the scene. We had a new girl helping in the yard who lived with us, called Jane Evans. She was a tremendous worker and was with us for two years and, on and off, for even longer than that. There is a funny story concerning her. We had the occasional hunter livery in the yard and there was one grey cob who no one wanted to ride, but Jane normally got lumbered! We would usually jump most of the way round our farm when we were out on exercise but this grey was not the most athletic of jumpers. One day, Jane had ridden the horse out but about an hour later, she strolled back into the yard to pick up a saw. She had attempted to jump a post and rail, and the cob had straddled it and got stuck. So Jane walked the two miles to collect a saw and was then going back so she could get the cob off again. He was still there when we got back and we managed the escape quite easily, but she was never allowed to forget it and didn't go jumping on exercise again. Despite all that, she was an immense asset to our yard, especially with Angela very much occupied with young Emma, and was the greatest fun.'

Angela still had Mooncoin to get her back into the swing of eventing and her target was to get to Burghley for the fifth consecutive time. Mike was riding a novice for June Warren on the suggestion of Alan Oliver. The horse was a great jumper but it was questionable whether his temperament would be good enough.

Mike: 'The horse did make progress but was never quite steady enough, particularly since the standard of competition was getting better and better. I'd got a reputation for riding big horses (perhaps

Above: Loading the horses at London Airport prior to the 1968 Mexico Olympics.

Left: Mexico cross-country.

Below left: The first water jump on the Mexico cross-country course before the water level rose to almost the height of the fence.

Below: Sergeant Ben Jones on The Poacher at the final fence of the Mexico cross-country – note no hat!

Above: The British 1968 Olympic gold-medal winning three-day event team *(left to right)* Major Derek Allhusen, Jane Bullen, Richard Meade, Sergeant Ben Jones. [Courtesy of The Associated Press Ltd]

Below: Skyborn second at Burghley, 1969. [Photographer: Findlay Davidson]

Top: Angela on Mooncoin and Mike on Farmer Giles during a lap of honour at Badminton, 1971.

Above: Mike and Laurieston having a sticky moment at the water jump on the steeplechase phase of the Munich Test Event in 1971. Richard Meade rode the horse to Olympic individual and team gold in 1972. [Photographer Hugo Czerny]

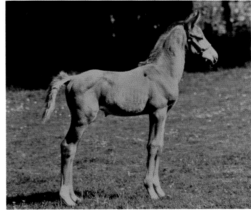

Far left: Mike and Angela newly engaged. [Photographer: Findlay Davidson]

Above: Dalwhinnie at Boekelo, 1981 – note the fence construction with no safety features.

Right: General Bugle, home-bred, orphaned at ten days and hand-reared.

Below: General Bugle – an anxious moment when winning the Novice Championships at Locko, 1981.

Below right: General Bugle showing his scope and class at Badminton, 1983.

Far left: A proud moment – Badminton 1983, Mike seventh on Dalwhinnie and second on General Bugle.

Above: Mike on Ben Wyvis walking around the collecting ring with HRH Princess Anne on Arthur of Troy prior to the showjumping at Ledyard, 1975.

Right: A small royal fan of General Bugle – a very young Zara Phillips. [Photographer: Srdja Djukanovic]

Below: Her Majesty the Queen presenting second prize to Mike at Badminton, 1983. [Courtesy of Kit Houghton]

Above: A young Mike interviewing David and Lucinda Green at Gatcombe. [Courtesy of Kit Houghton]

Left: Warming up the audience at the Royal Windsor Horse Show.

not so surprising as I was small myself!) which had come mostly from riding Farmer Giles and probably as a result, I got a call from our close mates, Polly and Hamish Lochore, wondering whether I might like to ride a big horse of theirs called Ben Wyvis. He wasn't an oil painting but had an enormous stride matched by a very big jump, which would perhaps suit my style of enjoying going on long strides – probably too many! We took him on in the spring of 1973 and I found him a very willing and able partner who made good progress through the season. Although he didn't win a decent class, he actually qualified for Badminton the following spring.

'The farm was going well but we were always looking at ways we could improve productivity, particularly on the dairy side. We looked mostly at things like improving the veterinary side of the calving index so we could have a regular calf per year. We depended greatly on two very loyal, local families to do much of the work although year on year, mostly because of mechanisation, we were gradually reducing the part-time labour force. The Sparrowhawk family had been part of Long Newnton village for several generations already. One of our tractor drivers from that family, John, had a daughter who would come to the farm on a regular basis to see the animals, in particular the horses, and Jane Evans was great at getting her involved.

'It was autumn when we returned to full swing although Burghley didn't quite turn out as we had hoped for Angela. She was unseated at the Waterloo Rails to break her great run at that event, but was then chosen to go to a new event in Hamilton, Massachusetts, called Ledyard. It was run by a new rising star in the sport called Neil Ayer, who went on to design the Los Angeles Olympic course in 1984 and the World Championships in Gawler, South Australia in 1986. The Americans were paying to fly out horses from Ireland and France as well as Britain to this stunning site which, being in the midst of the autumn colours, was at its spectacular best.'

As reported in *The Chronicle of the Horse*:

'Neil Ayer, for whom the USEA Head-quarters in Leesburg, Virginia are named, almost single-handedly ushered in the golden era of American three-day eventing by gathering at one time, in one place, the very top riders, judges, horses, and eventing enthusiasts from around the world.

From Thursday, Oct. 18, through Sunday, Oct. 21, 1973, Neil and Helen Ayer's Ledyard Farm, in Hamilton, Mass., became the focal point for eventing in the United States and around the world. The afterglow from that weekend has lasted all these intervening years.

There was one Canadian, three from Ireland and three from France, but the country that came "loaded for bear" was England, with the current gold medalists from both the World Championships and Olympics on their squad, plus winners and top finishers at both Badminton and Burghley among their thirteen riders.

The advanced division entries were a similar *Who's Who* of riders from that era, especially the British, who sent World Champion Mary Gordon-Watson on World Champion Cornishman V; Bar Hammond on Eagle Rock, just second that year at Badminton; Chris Collins, fresh from winning the Swedish Grand National Steeplechase; Badminton winner Lorna Sutherland; Merlin Meakin on Lynette, just fourth at Badminton; Diana Thorne, just second at Burghley to Capt. Mark Phillips on Maid Marion; Olympic gold medalist Richard Meade on Minuet; Angela Tucker, Olympic Team gold medalist, riding Mooncoin; and finally the eventual winner, Sue Hatherley riding Harley.'

Not for the first time when Mike had flown with horses, he experienced an anxious moment when an Irish horse misbehaved so badly that the Captain took the decision to turn around over Ireland, fly back to London, drop off the horse and set off again. Angela, meanwhile, had been offered a lift to Heathrow in Colonel Moseley's Bentley to join up with the riders to fly out, so she set off in considerably more comfort. Despite the delay, the horses arrived at Ledyard fit and healthy, which was just as well because the cross-country course, although beautifully presented, was in fact quite tough.

Mike: 'The set-up was great, with a lovely hotel close to the venue where we all stayed. Our American hosts provided grooms for each of the overseas riders so I was totally spoilt, particularly as a number of the officials I had met on the 1965 Pony Club exchange were also officials there.

'The Americans under Jack le Goff were making striking progress, especially with the young guns like Bruce Davidson, Tad Coffin and Roger Haller challenging the experience of the likes of Mike Plumb and Jimmy Wofford. The competition promised to be strong, with Mark spearheading the British challenge, having just won Burghley on Maid Marion. Having recently won both Badminton and Burghley, it was reported that Phillips could ride a dining room table and still win!

'The British team vet, Peter Scott-Dunn, was brought out, which was just as well because there was a very talkative parrot in the hotel lobby that had a habit of waking up early and making a lot of noise. One morning, there was an announcement over the hotel tannoy asking if Mr Scott-Dunn would come to reception to treat the parrot because someone had taken a pot-shot at it and it required treatment. The vet was not amused but the parrot did recover!

'It was an excellent competition but not even Phillips with his wedding less than a month away could defeat the Americans, although Angela on Mooncoin proved that her fall at Burghley was no more than a blip to finish in eighth position. The Americans were generous hosts and several of us joined Neil Ayer, the master and huntsman of the pack kennelled on site, for some early morning hunting in probably the most colourful hunting country I had ever seen and finished a tremendous week in some style.

(Two years later, owing to the cancellation of Badminton in 1975, another British squad went over to compete in the Ledyard three-day event. The riders included Mike on Ben Wyvis, who finished fifth and Sue Hatherley on Harley, who finished second to Bruce Davidson on Golden Griffin. Of the others, Lucinda Green on Wideawake was eighth, HRH Princess Anne on Arthur of Troy tenth, while Mark Phillips on Laureate experienced some difficulties on the cross-country. One of the abiding memories seems to be that they all stayed in a lovely house with a swimming pool. Apparently everyone ended up being thrown in; a game initiated, unsurprisingly, by Mike and Mark!)

To revert to the earlier visit, Mike recalled that:

'Granny Tucker had looked after Emma while we were away and had spoilt her rotten to the extent that there wasn't an overwhelming welcome from her when we did get home. My Mum became known as "Sweetie Granny" and because Lorna (Angela's mother) had two terriers, one called Pepi, she was known as "Pepi Granny".

'The year 1973 finished in unbelievable style with the wedding of Mark to Princess Anne on the fourteenth of November in Westminster Abbey. I was honoured to be an usher, along with a number of Mark's army colleagues as well as some from our memorable Pony Club days. We had a briefing on our task in the Abbey the day beforehand, so we organised a restaurant for that evening which was a fantastic mixture of friends from the length and breadth of the country, all in good form for this special occasion. We were particularly spoilt because childhood friend Roger Alexander (William's brother), was in the hotel trade and at that time was one of the senior managers of the nearby Kensington Garden Hotel and was able to set us up in style. It was a dreamy couple of days and we had to pinch ourselves to believe it was actually happening to us. Our ushers' task wasn't too taxing and I think we put everyone in their right seats. The Abbey was brimming with dignitaries from around the world as well as plenty of familiar faces from home and the world of eventing. The singing and music were out of this world and something to be remembered forever.

'The day was far from over for us when the service finished because Polly and Hamish Lochore and Angela and I had been invited to the wedding breakfast at Buckingham Palace afterwards. We had agreed to meet up straight after the service to find the organised transport that was to take us up Pall Mall and through the famous gates into the inner quadrangle of the Palace. There were just fifteen tables and we soon realised when we saw the table plan, just how privileged we were to be included. The bride and groom's families took centre stage, with the dignitaries and members of the Royal Family both from home and abroad spread around the state room. It was hard to take it all in and it was truly a day never to be forgotten. It was the talk of many a dinner party for quite a while afterwards!'

The previous chapter was completed using material recorded by Mike just before he died. It was just after writing out Mike's recollections of the happy period following his marriage to Angela and the birth of his daughter, Emma, that Emma rang me with the sad news of his sudden death. With Mike no longer available to contribute personally to this biography it has, as mentioned in the Preface, been necessary to adjust its original structure in order to complete it as a tribute to him. To this end, I have used information kindly supplied by Angela, Emma and Andrew (Mike and Angela's two children) augmented by the recollections and anecdotes freely and willingly supplied by Mike's friends and colleagues from his many walks of life.

CHAPTER NINE

Dalwhinnie and Bugle

Angela and Emma Tucker supplied the information for this chapter. Angela explained: 'Dalwhinnie was owned by Juliet Arden. He was given to her as a four-year-old in exchange for a mare who couldn't be kept sound enough to event. The mare was taken to Gordon Giddings's stud to be covered but instead Juliet came home with an unbroken chestnut gelding by Darialatan out of the same dam as Warrior (winner of Burghley with Jane Bullen in 1976).'

As a young horse, Dalwhinnie was quite naughty and international dressage judge Isabel Reid was witness to him bucking off Juliet on more than one occasion. It was at that point she suggested the horse should be sent to the Tuckers for further education. Mike and Angela decided that the horse needed 'entertainment', which he enjoyed by being well hunted by Mike with the Beaufort and then commencing his eventing career. He soon showed promise and, although not over-talented in his natural movement, his genuine nature and desire to please overcame his limitations. In the end Mike found him a very easy horse to ride and always snaffle-mouthed. He soon progressed up the ranks, finishing sixteenth at Boekelo in 1981, in the same placing at Badminton in 1982 and seventh at Burghley that same season. The following year, he acted as pathfinder for

Mike at Badminton when he gave invaluable insight into how the course would ride for Mike on his second ride, General Bugle. The two horses finished second (General Bugle) and seventh (Dalwhinnie), which Mike admitted was the highlight of his riding career. Sadly, after Badminton, Dalwhinnie had heat in a leg and was retired from top-level competition, but he carried on after a lengthy rest as a perfect schoolmaster for a young rider, Tor King.

General Bugle, foaled in 1975, was by Spartan General, also the sire of Spartan Missile (second in the 1981 Grand National under John Thorne, behind Bob Champion and Aldaniti), out of a mare called Bugle March. She had won the Tidworth event and was owned by naval officer Edwin Atkinson. While he was away at sea he had lent the mare to the Tuckers for breeding. Bugle was only ten days old when disaster struck and the mare died of 'retained cleanse'. The Tuckers were strongly advised to find a surrogate mare but, in the interim, Bugle had readily accepted a teat and bucket. However, this was indeed a labour of love because he had to be fed five or six times a day. Mike was out of the country at the time, so it befell Angela to make the mile trip from their home at the time, Walnut Cottage, to Church Farm. She made the journey in the car with a precariously balanced bucket of milk both very late at night and very early in the morning. She recalled: 'It was so spooky going to feed Bugle in the middle of the night. I also remember one time, a full bucket of milk tipping over in my car and having to go back and fetch another one.' I don't doubt the smell stayed in the car for a very long time!

Being hand-reared meant that Bugle was inevitably cheeky and precocious. He was sent off to Willie Donaldson as a three-year-old and was long-reined and broken in the traditional manner. Angela did much of Bugle's early schooling because Mike was busy on the farm. She said: 'On one occasion – he must have been a five-year-old – I had decided it was time he learned some simple lateral movements. I was schooling him in our manège which was down by the orchard and was open-sided. Well, Bugle decided it wasn't for him and he tried to sweep me off under the branches! He wasn't the most straightforward horse and used to "ponce" his way round the dressage but invariably got good marks. Comparing the two, Bugle had so much presence and natural talent, but Dalwinnie made up for his lack of expressive movement by having a heart as big as himself and was so consistent and such a fun horse because both Mike and I rode him.'

Bugle rose up the eventing ranks with consummate ease, but Mike always wanted to run him in the Foxhunters' Steeplechase at Aintree, so he was sent into training with David Nicholson and finished fourth in a chase at Stratford, ridden by Richard Dunwoody. Unfortunately, he had heat in a leg afterwards so this was his only run over fences. In 1981, as a six-year-old, the powerful, long-striding Bugle won what was then the Midland Bank Novice Championships at Locko Park but not, according to Mike, without anxious moments. In fact Mike's daughter Emma, recalled: 'I remember watching video of Dad on Bugle at Locko winning the Novice Championships and jumping the string at the end (Bugle ran away with Dad)!'

Bugle competed in his first international event in Germany as a seven-year-old. He was always very bold and over-jumped at a sunken road, tripping up the step on the far side, which was an inauspicious start to his international career. The following spring, he was taken to Brigstock for the traditional pre-Badminton run, which again did not go according to plan. Bugle was very strong across country and gave Mike a difficult ride, so it was a dilemma whether it would be wise to run him at Badminton. Maybe he should be given another year to mature? However, the decision was made to run him since he was fit and sound and Mike decided he would use a gag instead of a snaffle for the cross-country. Angela said: 'We had five horses in the yard heading for Badminton, but two went lame and I had a fall, which put me out, so it ended up with just Mike and his two horses as runners.'

Bugle gave Mike the greatest thrill by finishing second to Lucinda Green on Regal Realm, with the ever-consistent Dalwhinnie in seventh place. What a proud moment for the Tuckers! Emma said: 'I remember watching Dad ride the cross-country on Dalwhinnie and Bugle at Badminton in

1983. I was very nervous watching on the close-circuit monitor in the phase D box. Dalwhinnie went down on his knees at the Footbridge. It was a very proud moment when Dad was second on Bugle. Bugle was really a family pet as Mum and Dad bred him.'

The fact that Mike incurred two penalties in the dressage for 'error of course' by either doing sitting trot when he should have been rising, or the other way round, was no doubt something that needled him for many years, because without those penalties, he would have won. But never one to dwell on mishaps, Mike put that behind him and remained delighted with how his two horses had performed.

In the aftermath of Mike's death, I discovered a recollection he had recorded of this event:

> **Mike:** 'The biggest highlight for me as a competitor here has to be when I finished runner-up back in 1983 riding my home-bred General Bugle. Frustratingly, if I hadn't gone wrong in the dressage, I would have won, but then there's never any shame in losing to Lucinda Green. He was very green but he got better the further round the course we went. It was a busy day for me. I rode Bugle and Dalwhinnie, and then commentated on the partnership that denied me the trophy, Lucinda on Regal Realm.
>
> 'What made Badminton particularly memorable was that it was one of the last years that Her Majesty the Queen presented the prizes. The 10th Duke of Beaufort, known as "Master" knew Bugle well from the hunting field and ensured that the Queen got to meet him. That moment, and Master's enthusiasm for the horse, was very special.'

Bugle was over 17hh and suffered from persistent leg trouble. He ran only twice in 1984, and was withdrawn from Badminton after the cross-country, again with heat in a leg. He ran in several one-day events in the 1985 season, with several placings, and was selected for the European team in Frauenfeld but sadly he had heat in a leg after his final canter out there and had to be withdrawn. It was a huge disappointment.

The year1986 was a very wet spring and the going at Badminton was more reminiscent of a ploughed field than a cross-country course. Frank Weldon announced on the Friday night that 'Badminton would go ahead whatever', much to the horror of many of us who were having their first ride there! I had asked Mike to walk me round the course and he was hugely supportive and helpful. All I yearned for was one of those silver horses for being in the top twelve placings, and the universal advice was to go for a slow, safe clear round, which is exactly what I did on Marsh Heron and finished in eighth place at the end of a competition full of attrition. Poor Mike ended up in the bottom of the Vicarage Vee with Bugle and incurred 80 penalties, however, he still completed for his twelfth Badminton – no mean feat. Despite his disappointment, he was thrilled that I had achieved my ambition, for which I credit him entirely.

Mike was becoming more and more in demand for commentating at that time. He therefore decided that it was time for him to hang up his boots as a competitor, but not before he and Bugle had ended the season on a high note by finishing seventh at Burghley.

Angela took over the ride on Bugle and was one of a few riders invited to compete at Ridgewood in Canada with him, all paid for by sponsorship organised by the Canadians. Mike was invited out as commentator but grooms' expenses were not covered. Fortunately, Mike Petre, their old friend who still lived in Canada, was able to organise a groom for Angela, much to her relief. Bugle did his usual good test and was up with the leaders after dressage. Angela recalled: 'Bruce Davidson had two horses in the competition and I so wanted to beat him! On the chase, Bugle stumbled in a groundhog hole which, although it had been filled, was still very soft. In retrospect I think that's where he may have aggravated his leg but he seemed fine at the time.

'I remember sitting in the ten-minute box, hoping that Mike would come and brief me on how the course was riding, but he didn't appear and there I was with a groom I didn't know. Anyway, I played safe and went one long way near home, so finished with a clear and just a few time faults.

We were lying second after cross-country, with Bruce in first and third. The veterinary inspection was a bit 'touch and go' for us, but we scraped through. Sadly, Bugle stopped at the third fence in the showjumping – possibly he was feeling his leg – so we went down to third and Bruce was first and second. That was the last time Bugle ran. We managed to keep him sound enough for a bit of hunting but in the end he had colic and we had to have him put down. He was a great horse – a really old-fashioned type.'

CHAPTER TEN

Commentating — Mike on the Mike

In his eulogy to Mike, **William Alexander**, Mike's childhood friend, recalled: 'In the mid 1950s Michael's eye was drawn to horses, and his grandfather, Ted Jones of Didmarton, was a tenant of a Badminton farm. This meant that he supplied a wagon plus straw bales for the south end of the showjumping arena at the three-day event. Mike, Roger and I would cycle over to Badminton very early on showjumping Saturday, lock our bikes to the fence at the top of Kennels Drive and bag the wagon for our families. One day, Mike leapt off the wagon and flashed a piece of paper and pen in the face of a distinguished gentleman who happened to be passing. He duly got the autograph of Dorian Williams, which I think started his fascination with commentating.'

It was many years later, in 1977, that Mike actually started commentating for the BBC, but for nearly a decade he combined this with riding at the top level. Once he had retired from competitive riding in 1986 he was able to concentrate fully on his new career and discovered his true forte as a commentator. He quickly became established as the familiar voice over the loudspeaker at competitions, and his informative commentary was enjoyed by millions on both BBC and Sky television.

At Mike's family funeral, I and my husband **Malcolm** gave a joint eulogy where we acknowledged: 'As if Mike's achievements as a rider and international official were not enough, most would remember Mike as the voice of BBC equestrianism. He took over as main commentator on the sudden death of Raymond Brooks-Ward in 1992, going on to be principal commentator at six Olympic Games. His deep knowledge and warm, charismatic style of delivery introduced the sport to a much wider audience.'

When I asked people who had worked with Mike, either as fellow commentators or on the production side of the media, if they would provide some reminiscences of their time working with him, they were fulsome in their praise. A number who had worked with him over long periods provided personal 'histories' of their working partnerships, explaining various aspects of the evolution of equestrian broadcasting and recording the challenges that sometimes had to be overcome.

BBC producer **Jim Reside** provided the history of how Mike's broadcasting career began. 'Recollections of Mike Tucker are fairly easy to recall. His charismatic personality saw to that. But here is my take on how we met – and how he started a new career behind the microphone.

'Cast your mind back to the long hot summer of 1976. Drought conditions and very hard ground everywhere. I was an assistant producer of limited experience at BBC Sport, working on the Saturday afternoon programme *Grandstand*. The programme editor dispatched me to Goodwood to film the horse trials that would feature in the following weekend's programme. That week the Prime Minister James Callaghan had appointed Denis Howell as "Drought Supremo". Predictably, the heavens opened immediately – and suddenly wellies were the order of the day at Goodwood.

'And so it was that I stood soaked to the skin, wishing I was somewhere else, as the riders conducted their cross-country course inspection. I needed cheering up. Into view came a seemingly effervescent chap wearing a fedora.

"Who's that?" I asked.

"Ah, that's Michael Tucker, one of eventing's larger-than-life characters", I was told. Needing an authoritative view on the course and conditions I nervously approached him.

"Hello Mr Tucker. Sorry to interrupt – but I'm Jim Reside of BBC Sport and wondered if you'd consider doing an interview on camera for *Grandstand?*"

"Certainly my dear chap. Please call me Michael – and where would you like me to stand?" If only all sports stars were as user-friendly. I duly cheered up.

'Two years later, with the Badminton and Burghley Horse Trials annually on the BBC calendar, *Grandstand* was encouraged to televise the 1978 Midland Bank Horse Trials at Locko Park, particularly as they were part of the selection process for the forthcoming World Championships in Kentucky – and so all the top riders would be competing, including Captain Mark Phillips and Princess Anne. The dressage was on Friday, but Saturday afternoon would feature live coverage of both the cross-country and showjumping phases. Who would produce this multi-camera outside broadcast for the BBC?

'The senior producer of the BBC's equestrian coverage was in Aachen for the European Showjumping Championships and had taken the senior commentator, Dorian Williams, with him. And so the very unexpected call came to yours truly – toddle off up to Derbyshire and plan for live coverage throughout the afternoon. "Oh yes, Dorian Williams will be in Aachen so you'll need to find a co-commentator with Raymond Brooks-Ward." Okay. Who would know about eventing who wouldn't be competing at Locko Park? And quite simply that is how Mike Tucker's broadcasting career began. We both learned a lot!

'I was a relatively junior producer and wanted to make my mark as an outside broadcast director of imagination. So new camera angles were examined and debated but, as a former cameraman, I knew the one angle missing from equestrian television coverage in the 1970s was a rider's-eye view of the cross-country. Digital TV signals and miniature cameras were still years away. And yet … I had seen a shoulder harness for a small television camera at the BBC's special-effects department. I use the word "small" advisedly. Compared to today's digital "point-of-view" cameras, these analogue cameras now seem the size of double-decker buses – and probably weighed as much when strapped on one's shoulder!

'However, we're talking Michael Tucker here. And the challenge was acknowledged – and accepted. So, on the Friday, he strapped on this contraption, mounted up – with some difficulty I seem to recall – and then proceeded to jump two of the cross-country fences with this camera and video recorder sitting like a parrot on his shoulder. Word spread amongst the riders and many turned up to watch this courageous demonstration of horsemanship. And so we played this segment into the broadcast just before live coverage of the cross-country, which also proved to be Mike Tucker's first live commentary for the BBC in a broadcasting career lasting the best part of forty years.

'The Midland Bank Horse Trials were televised from Locko Park for a further seven years before moving under a different sponsor to Gatcombe Park, where they remain to this day. I moved on too – to producing the BBC's Formula One coverage. Murray Walker had to put up with my demanding and impatient voice in his headphones, as Mike Tucker had done so willingly every year at Locko Park. Mike went on to voice all of the BBC's equestrian programming – from duckings in the lake at Badminton to the pinnacle, British Olympic success and gold medal ceremonies.

'Moist-eyed memories that will never die.'

Nick Brooks-Ward, a son of Raymond's and now, thanks to Mike, recognised as a leading equestrian commentator, explained how Mike combined what he had learned from Raymond and Dorian Williams with his own expertise and style to bring something new to commentary on equestrian sport. 'There is no doubt that Mike was the next generation of commentators – when my Dad started he was trained by Richard Dimbleby and was very much in the BBC genre. In those days the stars were David Coleman, Des Lynam, Harry Carpenter, Dan Maskell, Dickie Davies, Richie Benaud, Brian Johnston and of course Dorian Williams –

all with wonderful knowledge and mellifluous voices – but Mike was one of the first of the new mould of broadcasters who had actually competed successfully and so brought a different set of skills to the commentary box, using inside knowledge and expertise to bring a whole new depth of knowledge to the sport. Yes, there were expert summarisers, like Stephen Hadley and Brendan Foster – but there had been very few athletes turned broadcasters – now it is the norm – Boris Becker, Steve Cram and Mike Atherton to name a few.

'But there is no doubt that Mike learned from my Dad and Dorian that research was everything – no matter how much you did there was always more to do. Mike was taught that for every hour of broadcast you needed to do four hours of research – no mean feat when you consider that, when commentating at Badminton or Burghley on cross-country day, you would often be in the commentary position for eight hours and then go and do the edited version for the following day's *Grandstand* after the cross-country had finished.'

Hugh Thomas, director of Badminton Horse Trials, has a number of memories of the many times he spent with Mike in the commentary box. 'I spent several years sharing commentary positions with Mike – both public address and TV. I think he started TV just a bit before me but we did eventing, team chasing at Hickstead and showjumping together until I stopped when I took over Badminton in 1989. We were the juniors to, at first, Dorian Williams and then Raymond Brooks-Ward. Gradually I moved towards presenting and Mike specialised in commentary. Funnily enough, he was never completely comfortable in front of the camera, but totally in command behind the microphone.

'On TV there are a few special occasions I remember. We were at Locko Park for the Midland Bank Championships and he was riding General Bugle. He rode the course a few minutes before the start and I commentated – as a camera check – he got totally run away with and couldn't pull up at the end and jumped the string at the end of the course! There is a tape of this somewhere which he used to show friends.

'Also at Locko, he and I were left in charge one year because Raymond was unwell. Jim Reside was the producer. We ended exactly on time and then heard the dreaded words from BBC London: "Hello Locko – we will be with you for another ten minutes!" Nothing recorded, totally live. I flannelled for a bit while Mike went off to find someone to interview – I was reduced to commentating on him walking back across the main arena with some poor rider dragooned into interview action. I was never more relieved than to hand over to him to do the actual interview!

'Public address with Mike was always fraught with danger! He liked nothing better than winding up his friends – though please note always in a generous way.

'For several years in the 1980s Mike and I ran or helped to run events on the same weekend. His (Tetbury) was on the Saturday, mine (Rotherfield Park) on the Sunday. We each rode at the other event – and also commentated. My great advantage was that his came first – so I could take the piss out of him – however, he had the opportunity to come to us the next day and say whatever he liked, safe for at least another year.

'One year at Rotherfield we hosted a *Jim'll Fix It* programme – or slice thereof – for the BBC. The young girl for whom it was being fixed wanted to meet some event riders and learn about cross-country riding, so I recruited Tucker to come on his Badminton horse Dalwhinnie to be filmed jumping a few fences. We decided on the Water – a decent enough obstacle, but at what would now be called intermediate or two-star level. Cameras ready, action – two refusals and then a fall from the maestro. He eventually succeeded in jumping the obstacle, but the editing for the finished programme must have been substantial!'

Giles Rowsell was another event rider and co-commentator at horse trials: 'I originally met Tucks as an event rider but we began commentating as, at that time, the commentating was dire and we were determined to improve things.' However, he said, 'While we tried to make things more professional we always had a huge amount of fun – sometimes too much!

'My very first recollection of commentating with Mike was when we were at Downlands Horse Trials when control was operated by Norman Patrick who masterminded the Prince Philip Cup Mounted Games.

He invented the first "trotter board" to follow horses around the cross-country course. It consisted of a piece of white Formica on which he had drawn lines to produce squares with a number in each. Pieces of paper with a number on each represented the horses and it worked fine until somebody walked into the tiny commentary box and all the pieces of paper blew away!

'Despite his attention to detail, he never really minded getting names wrong. A good example would be Vittoria Panizon who, for years, he insisted on calling Victoria. After several years he got it right but then began pronouncing her surname as if it were some kind of loo cleaner!

'Bramham was always a very special event for us, with the Lane Fox hospitality being legendary and the world being put to rights into the early hours, helped by quite a bit of liquid inspiration. After a day's commentary Tucks was always very generous, producing large quantities of Pimm's, but it took us several years to discover that he would collect up empty Pimm's jugs, claim the ten-pound deposits and so "buy" us so much Pimm's!

'Also at Bramham there was a legendary story of how Patrick Conolly-Carew shattered the "thunder box" – absolutely true, but there was always a suspicion that somebody else staying in the house might possibly have had a hand in its collapse. Mike was always thinking of some joke that he could play on someone.'

'My last "event" with him was a double act for children and parents of the RA Pony Club. We had not prepared anything but just winged it, bouncing ideas and stories off each other. We certainly enjoyed it and I think the audience did as well! It was a bit like the double act cross-country commentating, almost telepathically, knowing what the other was going to say and bouncing remarks back and forth. Even our wives enjoyed the evening, although they had heard similar stuff for years!'

My husband **Malcolm** had been a friend of Mike's since 1966 and commentated at major horse trials and championships both at home and abroad. He had this to say: 'Among Mike's many other qualities, he was an excellent problem-solver and a first-class teacher – I was fortunate enough to experience examples of both these attributes.

'I spent twenty enjoyable years behind the mike at Badminton on cross-country day, and the early ones were alongside Mike before he moved on to the BBC. As any commentator will testify, long hold-ups on cross-country day are a nightmare. We all prepare for it beforehand with important sections of the programme to be reproduced over the air, as well as a host of "thank-yous" and future events to be announced. However, for a long hold-up, this is never enough and although "silence is golden", long periods of PA silence can kill an atmosphere and add to the public's fears that a major catastrophe has occurred.

'During one long break in the 1980s, with vast sections of the programme reproduced, Mike jumped to his feet with a roving mike, grabbed a radio and said "Keep waffling for a bit longer, Wol, and I'll find a rider." Within minutes, over the radio came his chirpy voice "Okay, you can shut up now, I've got Toddy", referring to Mark Todd, who had just gone clear. Mike then conducted a really informative in-depth interview with Mark, full of interesting facts as to how the course rode, striding in the combinations etcetera, laced with the usual trademark humour. Simple, and possibly obvious, but it took Mike, the problem-solver, to "invent" the system, which is now commonplace among PA cross-country teams, and is as appreciated by the eventing public now as it was on its inaugural day over thirty years ago at Badminton.

'Although I had done a fair bit of low-grade broadcasting, I had never previously done "blind" commentary with no TV screen before me when Mike asked me to comment on some military displays at Olympia that he was broadcasting live for a non-BBC outside broadcast. Although he and I were rarely serious together for more than five minutes in the fifty-odd years that I knew him, this was different. He took on a completely different persona as he immersed himself in what was going on in the arena and coaxed me through my role, asking all the right questions and leading me to the right comments of explanation. Above all, he gave me huge confidence to express myself and reproduce all my experience of seven years' mounted duty. He was, in short, an utter professional and got the best out of yet another rookie!'

Lorna Clarke, an ex-international event rider, commentated on the cross-country for the BBC alongside Mike for many years. As Lorna Sutherland, she and Bill Roycroft from Australia (with whom Mike stayed on his trip there) are the only two people to have ridden three horses round Badminton in one day. She recalls some wonderful anecdotes from her days spent in the commentary box with Mike: 'As a commentator, Mike had huge knowledge of the sport, not only from his own eventing experience but through his many years of course building, being a technical delegate, being on endless committees, running his own horse trials, etc. As a result, he built up a huge number of eventing contacts and friends with whom he used to stay, and he got to know the personal "non-eventing" side of many riders as well as their professional side and was therefore able to make his commentary much more interesting. This also brought a more human level to the riders (who perhaps often seem élitist) for those watching at home, as he knew how many kids they had or when they last crashed their car or recently got divorced or whatever.

'I fell into commentating by chance more than anything else. I was doing a course walk at Luhmühlen in Germany as I wasn't riding at the event and Raymond Brooks-Ward asked me whether, if I was doing nothing else, I would come and say a few words in the commentary box during the cross-country. This I did and stood behind Mike and Raymond watching the close-circuit monitor, which was quite fun. After that Johnnie Watherston, the BBC producer, asked me to do a bit at Badminton, although I was still riding in those days, and that was how it all started for me, with Mike showing me the ropes and bringing me in as we went along. After Raymond Brooks-Ward died in 1992 Mike became the lead commentator and I was what is called a "colour commentator"; he would introduce and set up the programme and get the whole thing on the road and then refer over to me for technical input as to why a horse fell at the last fence or why one was covered in grease, and so on. He did this part too, sometimes, and if he made the odd technical mistake or got it wrong it was great fun to pick him up on it and correct it … I have to say he never got upset when I did this; he took it all in his stride!

'Mike loved his job and we did three Olympic Games and many European and World Championships together, plus the major home events such as Badminton, Burghley and Gatcombe. I think one of the main highlights when we were working together must have been when Zara Phillips won first the European Championships at Blenheim and then the Worlds in Aachen. His excitement and enthusiasm were unbounded and it was obvious to all how genuinely thrilled he was.'

(At this point, I am pleased to be able to add **Zara's** own tribute to Mike: 'Mr T has always been a great influence and part of my life, whether it was as a neighbour, friend of the family, person to respect on a horse, someone to follow on the hunting field or the voice of my career. You always knew it was a top-class event when Mr T was commentating. If you could hear his voice it meant that there was a serious challenge ahead of you. I was very honoured to have him commentate on my World Championship individual gold and his voice will forever ring in my ears as the Voice of Eventing.')

Lorna continued: 'People often think being a commentator is "oh very smart" and living the high life – well believe me, it is not! Usually Mike and I were stuck in a portable garden-shed-type hut with two chairs and two TV monitors where we could see nothing of what was going on outside at all! Mike would have hundreds of notes spread out everywhere; we each had a set of earphones and a lip mike and there we would sit for five or six hours, and this summed up our glamorous days out at the famous events!

'I remember at one European Championships when, regardless of the weather, we were put in a small tent in a wood with the standard two chairs (in this case foldable) and two monitors on uneven ground.

'Then in Achselschwang in Bavaria we were in what I call a commentator or judge's truck with windows looking out over a small part of the cross-country in the middle of nowhere. This was fine, except that the TV output was going down the tube to London several hours after the cross-country had finished and while we were waiting to commentate, darkness fell and the wagon had no lights other than the TV monitors, which was fine for me as I only had to talk about what I saw on the screen, whereas poor Mike had a terrible time trying to read his notes and starting lists, using a torch to identify each rider, their results up to this point and any other relevant information he had on them and making it sound as though it was happening "live". Not an easy task – however, it was the European Championships and the British were doing rather well so you are supposed to get these things right!

'Mostly we did not cover the dressage phase of the three-day events (other than a quick summary of the highlights before showing the cross-country live). However, this all changed with the introduction of the "red button". This now meant that people could press the red button on their TV remote and get almost the whole event from start to finish. A great invention I'm sure, but it meant that Mike and I had to commentate, albeit in a much more relaxed fashion, over two days of often very mediocre dressage tests for the first phase of the event, which can become a little tedious!

'Our nearest nightmare came at the Sydney Olympics. All had gone well throughout the event and we were pretty happy about it as Mike rounded off after the showjumping phase and medal presentations. We were just packing up our paperwork when someone from a foreign TV crew sitting behind us said "Mike, you got the results wrong!" At first it seemed impossible, but then looking at their paperwork and the main scoreboard in the arena, reality dawned – we had got it wrong. Once again this would probably not have been too serious for me, but for Mike it could have been a disaster – the BBC are proud of their record in sport and their high standards. I can only guess how they would have reacted to a major mistake like this at the Olympics.

'What could we do? Then someone mentioned that there had been a little outdoor BBC TV crew in the car park some time ago; if they hadn't left, they might be able to help us. I have never seen Mike, and our producer Dennis Kelly, run so fast – and in the Sydney heat! We tore out of the grounds and searched the car park to find the TV van as it was about to pull out. We screamed the situation at them and they were wonderful.

Fortunately (although the TV was going out live) there is a slight delay before it goes down the line to London and that was our saving grace, along with the two BBC guys. They got out huge cable reels for us to sit on, a mini table to put the monitor on, connected it all up and gave us a mike between us. They picked up the end of the showjumping as it was going out live at home, wiped our original commentary and let us commentate over the last couple of horses and the medal ceremony again. *They* deserved a medal (or several) I am not sure to this day if they ever realised how indebted we were; they saved us from disaster and I'm sure Mike was eternally grateful.'

Tina Cook who, like Mike and Lorna before her, has combined a long and successful career in eventing with commentating, offered her heartfelt recollections of time spent in Mike's company: 'I am writing this with real emotion of losing a friend and mentor in my life and I will miss him greatly. Mike reminded me so much of my beloved late father, Josh Gifford, who was fun, kind and had such strong old-fashioned moral values of respect in his manner and dress. "Please and thank you cost nothing, but mean so much." He was straight-talking but also wanted to encourage the young to find enjoyment in a sport he so loved.

'I was first given the opportunity to work with the microphone at the 2000 Sydney Olympics when I was reserve for the British eventing team and was wandering around feeling frustrated and needing something to do. Mike bravely put my name forward to do some radio work with Lee Mackenzie. I loved it and Mike must have seen some potential in me and put my name forward. I have pushed for every opportunity to work in the business since. I feel privileged and lucky to have had the opportunity of sitting next to him in the commentary box, learning and being guided by him. As a competitor he could understand the competitive mind and relay that through his commentary and, as I am still competing, he always wanted my opinions to keep up to date on the modern view of the sport.

'More recently, at the Rio Olympics, I worked alongside Jonathan Agnew for Radio 5 Live. BBC and Radio 5 were seated in very close proximity, spending two weeks together working, but also having fun going out and enjoying the local hospitality in the evenings. With Mike in his Team GB baseball cap, he was looking like the true English gent.

'In 2017 Mike asked me to come up for a fundraising evening for his local church. I agreed as long as my daughter Isabelle and I could go out hunting with the Beaufort the following day. I arrived with a horse, a pony and two children and had a wonderful couple of days of Tucker family hospitality.

'We will miss him as a man, as well as The Voice.'

Another rider who worked on commentary with Mike is **Judy Harvey**, a Fellow of the British Horse Society and an FEI international dressage judge, rider and trainer. Judy acted as Mike's dressage expert on many occasions and was privileged to share magical moments with him during the London Olympics. She first met Mike when experiencing a mix-up as a competitor: 'My first encounter with Mike was at the Brightwell's Auction Challenge at Addington. I was competing two horses. Mike was doing the commentary and playing our CDs; it was dressage to music. For my first ride the wrong CD came on. I gesticulated at the commentary box that the CD was for my other horse. They gesticulated back that they had two CDs and they were both the same. I was adamant that they were wrong and got off my horse and went up to the commentary box. It then dawned on me that I had left the other CD in my car CD player. Mike enjoyed teasing me about that for years!

'I first did commentary with Mike at the Europeans at Windsor. It was the era of Totilas and a magical performance. I then did Olympia with him a couple of times and was over the moon to be asked to do the London Olympics. Mike was so kind and helpful, showing me the ropes. Our commentary position was exposed to the elements and we got soaked and baked. The sessions were long and there was no time to get food. Having starved on the first day, Mike was very happy when my husband brought us sandwiches on Day Two. We had a memorable dinner up in Blackheath where we were staying; Pippa Funnell was with us too and we drank *caipirinhas* in anticipation of Rio. We all went out on the heath to watch Usain Bolt win the hundred metres. There were crowds of Jamaicans and we all shouted ourselves hoarse screaming Bolt home.

'When our dressage team won gold Mike took off his headphones and belted out *God Save the Queen* at the top of his voice. When Charlotte won gold Pippa Funnell and I were in pieces, so Mike passed us the loo roll to dry our tears, while he continued to bring the viewers at home all the emotion and atmosphere.

'When the BBC decided not to take me to Rio, it was Mike who first rang me. He knew how gutted I would be and, ever the gentleman, told me how disappointed he was.

'We did many shows together – he put up with a bit of stick from the dressage community, but I knew how brilliant he was at bringing excitement and passion to the viewer at home.

'He was a true gentleman and he loved his job.'

BBC producers **Johnnie and Wendy Watherston** had this to say about Mike's time as a commentator for the network, and his ability to deal with the complexities that were often part of the process. 'When Mike started commentating, he was working alongside Raymond Brooks-Ward and learned how TV equestrian coverage worked, but when he took over as lead commentator, he was hit with a whole new set of complexities. He was now responsible for so much more than just giving an expert view on what was happening on the screen, but also setting the scene, updating the competition, doing interviews, filling in if there was a delay and working to strict timings when coming off air, running in recorded segments or replays. All this had to be done listening to talkback from Johnnie and me, the art being to filter out our instructions being given to other members of the broadcast team, whilst picking up those that were specific to him – and talking sense at the same time!

'The most difficult thing to cover is the cross-country phase of an event – there may be four horses on the course at the same time and editorially it is necessary to switch quickly from one to another, meaning Mike had to instantly pick up and identify the new horse and rider, where they were on the course and how they were going. Although he would be guided on talkback, graphics could not always keep up and he had to be very quick to adjust to the situation as well as keeping a rapport with a fellow commentator throughout what was a very long day!

'Although there were probably times when Mike cursed our voices in his ear, he may have missed them when working abroad on events like the Olympic Games and other championships. There, he was totally dependent on the pictures provided by the host broadcaster; he never knew who the next competitor shown would be, where they were, or if they had a problem somewhere on the course.

'Sometimes replays were put in without warning, sometimes showing the same action twice (I'm sure in error!) but all things that could make a commentator look stupid. At one World Games the commentary box for the cross-country was positioned away from the start/finish area and, with poor graphics, no computer scoring and no running time clock, commentary was very difficult – in fact the only footage of the eventual gold medallist was one slow motion of the horse going through a combination, which was played in later. Now, with improved computer scoring and timing, the job has got marginally easier.

'Although at events Mike was liable to be wearing several hats, he was a wonderful team member, popular with all his colleagues, always enthusiastic and brilliant at conveying the excitement and emotion of a competition, whether it be the "diggy dogs" at Olympia or an Olympic gold medal in sight.'

Simon Brooks-Ward, director of the Olympia Show, reiterated Mike's overall qualities as a commentator, and made particular reference to his performances at that venue: 'For over twenty years, Mike Tucker was the senior commentator at Olympia, The London International Horse Show and The Royal Windsor Horse Show, taking over from Tom Hudson.

'He brought his own fruity and individual style to the commentary box. The wonderful thing about Mike was that he always appeared to be enjoying himself and this came through the microphone to the audience, who responded in kind. You knew that, with Mike on the mike, there was a person who could react to any situation and bring the right tone to whatever was going on in the ring.

'At Olympia, it was the dog agility that brought out the Doctor Dolittle in him. He would always express himself as though the dog was talking, speeding up the comments for the Jack Russell and sounding slow and ponderous for the Great Dane. It was always a tour de force and one of the reasons why this competition is still as popular as ever at the show.

'In one morning production meeting I suggested that it would be good if a commentator could do a course walk of the new indoor driving competition and explain the nuances to an uneducated public. Mike got carried away ... instead of a course walk it became a course run. In and round the driving obstacles he went in ever-decreasing circles (to this day I am unsure in what direction). And then he came to the bridge, which he made a dash across – twice. Red-faced and out of breath he limped through the finish to tumultuous applause.'

Gerry Morrison, a BBC TV producer and director who worked closely with Mike over the years recalled: 'My earliest recollection of Mike was in the mid-1980s when Mike assisted Raymond Brooks-Ward in the BBC commentator's box at Badminton. He was very much the commentator debutant in those days. I was a BBC graphics operator back then, and Mike always struck me as a jovial but knowledgeable expert with a great voice for equestrian sport. It was obvious that his first-hand experience of eventing opened up a new perspective on one of the great sporting events. At that stage, I had no idea that I would be lucky enough to rise through the ranks to be the BBC TV director for equestrianism.

'One of the most vivid memories I have of Mike at first hand was at Aachen for the 2006 World Equestrian Games. Together we walked around the cross-country course and he explained the likely routes that each horse might take. I always find when looking at the fences first-hand that the obstacles seem enormous – far bigger than they seem on TV. Mike however, explained that though challenging, the fences would prove a straightforward test for the competitors. He was right ... it was a masterclass for a new TV producer from one of the best in the business.

'I was the world feed TV director for the Olympic Games in both London and Rio, and Mike provided the sound track for some of British equestrianism's finest moments. Success for the GB team in dressage, eventing and showjumping across both Games provided great memories for me, and obviously for the British viewing public. I don't tire of reliving the gold medals for Charlotte Dujardin and Nick Skelton, with Mike's voice describing the action.

'Mike was also synonymous with the Christmas Show at Olympia. If not down in the arena describing the action at first hand, he would be the BBC viewers' link to this most festive of shows. My children (when they were younger), would always ask, "Who is the man who always tells the audience they're not cheering when the dogs are on the agility course?" (Example: "*Boys and girls, in four days it will be Christmas Day, and you're not cheering …*")

'He was always referred to thereafter as "You're not cheering!"

'Mike was a great friend and colleague. Always available for a friendly chat, always approachable if any potential problems needed ironing out. Someone whose opinion was most eagerly sought, someone whose voice conveyed so much. He is already most sorely missed by all his family, friends and colleagues.'

Chris Lewis, BBC equestrian producer of the London and Rio Olympic Games, also has many fond memories of working with Mike: 'Barcelona 1992 and the last day of equestrian events, the showjumping final, took place in a monsoon-like thunderstorm. That was the day I was introduced to Mike Tucker who, despite the appalling conditions, was his usual jovial and warm-hearted self. He was second commentator to Raymond Brooks-Ward and what a double act that was. I was producing the fast response unit that usually managed to rush in for coffee break and we were doing a quick story at the venue. Our paths did not cross again until 1999, when BBC Sport decided, in its wisdom, that I would produce the European Showjumping Championships at Hickstead as host broadcaster. Up until then my equestrian expertise and experience had been limited to riding a hand-led donkey on Hunstanton beach. The result was that my skill in covering a "leg at each corner" was almost non-existent. As a consequence, I started planning camera positions with little thought for the horse or rider. Michael, instead of laughing, supported a number of my suggestions and even helped present this to the FEI, the governing body. He guided me through this baptism with humour, and unselfish kindness, which laid the foundation of a warm and close friendship.

'In the Athens Olympics in 2004, the BBC equestrian team, Michael, Lorna Clarke, Stephen Hadley and I, were billeted in an army officers' training camp and we each had our own separate cabins. Room service came every morning to clean the rooms and on the second day there was a knock on the door and a female voice called "housekeeper". I opened the door to the vision of Mike wearing a cap and an apron (if he had shorts on underneath I could not tell) and holding a duster and bucket. Behind him were the girls, giggling.

'During those same Games Michael decided it was time for me to learn how to assess and add up the scoring in dressage. He stressed how important total accuracy was and how much he relied upon this. After the twelfth competitor I was still working out the score for the sixth, to the sound of Mike tut-tutting. When the day's competition finished I looked up to see that Michael had been doing it on the side as he had done for years and this was a total wind-up.

'Later I was in the privileged position of producing the equestrian competition for both the London and Rio Olympics for the Olympic Broadcasting Service. At the end of every day Michael would be standing outside the control vehicle in the compound full of praise and support. There were times when it was needed.'

Another BBC producer, who joined Mike's team in 2003, was **Michael Cole**, who provided further evidence of the high regard that everyone had for Mike. 'When I was first assigned to work on Badminton Horse Trials in 2003 I was far from expert about equestrian sport. I had worked on a fair amount as part of the general duties of an assistant producer on the BBC's *Grandstand* programme, but now I was to be programme editor. In theory I was responsible for determining the editorial line of our coverage – who we featured in the preview, which horses we showed during cross-country, how we would hopefully manage to miss nothing even when there were four horses on the course, four miles to cover and around fifteen cameras at our disposal. Luckily I was working with Chris Lewis as senior producer and Mike Tucker as lead commentator. "You'll like Mike," Chris told me, "he's tremendously welcoming and will really help you get up to speed."

'Chris could not have summarised Mike better. I'd met Tucks briefly at the Sydney Olympics but we didn't really know each other well. The way BBC Sport worked, Mike would have met dozens of junior producers over the years at big events, but would work more closely with the producers at the domestic events the BBC covered – the equestrian "experts" so to speak. Now I was one of them, and more than a little apprehensive.

'But from the first time we got together to discuss Badminton 2003, Mike could not have been more helpful in investing me with at least some of that expertise. He was so open to a newcomer. Never for a moment did it feel like an imposition that the BBC had sent him someone who didn't know eventing in real depth. Quite the opposite. He seemed genuinely excited to be welcoming someone new into his world. He knew how much fun I was about to have. He introduced me to so many people in the eventing world. Sometimes it was because he thought they would be helpful in my education, but more often it was just because he thought we would get on and enjoy each other's company.

'That was typical of Tucks. He was a facilitator and social secretary too, making sure that everyone had a good time and enjoyed being involved in the sport he loved so much. The net result was that, very soon, I felt much more comfortable with the task ahead of me. He'd helped me become much more knowledgeable very quickly and also made me realise that I was part of his team now and it was a big team with lots of friendly faces, always ready to help.

'For the first days of the London Olympics in 2012 I was lucky enough to be sent to Greenwich to be the commentary box producer with Ian Stark and Mike during the eventing competition. At big international events such as the Olympics, BBC Sport doesn't produce the TV pictures, but instead takes the pictures delivered by the host broadcaster. We were lucky enough to know that, in London, this job was in the hands of our former BBC colleagues, Chris Lewis and Gerry Morrison, working for the host broadcaster, but it meant that my job was the best seat in the house and relatively simple, essentially being an extra pair of hands, eyes and ears for Ian and Mike – simple in theory.

'In practice the London weather meant that our open-air commentary position was somewhat exposed. In bright sun it became hard to actually see what was on the TV screen – not ideal for commentary. So the first job was to build some kind of makeshift protection using cardboard boxes and plastic filing trays. This basically did the job, but it did mean that instead of enjoying the majestic views across Greenwich Park, we were huddled under our cardboard shelter, eyes glued to the TV.

'But Tucks also needed to keep an eye on the scores for each movement in dressage, which were only available on the electronic scoreboards in the arena. So every few moments he would pop up his head from under the cover to look at the latest news from the judges. He reminded me a little of the meerkats from BBC Natural History unit's popular programme of the time, up on his hind legs looking for information.

'As well as bright sun we also had torrential rain to cope with. It came on strong just as Tina Cook came into the arena for her dressage test, from what I remember. So plastic covers were quickly draped over our commentary position. The technical team don't like the equipment to get wet if possible, but aren't so worried about commentators and producers. We are supposed to be waterproof. But overall the two days of eventing dressage were quite an experience, sending us back to the hotel completely drenched but also with sunburn. A typical British summer.

'Through the years working with Mike, I also came to realise how appreciated he was by the BBC audience. Many commentators get to work for BBC Sport, but very few of them become the voice of their sport. Tucks was undoubtedly the voice of equestrian sport. He worked hard to make sure that his commentary was accessible for the wider audience that comes to BBC for its sport coverage. It's a tricky balance to deliver commentary that opens the sport up to the general viewer but doesn't patronise the expert audience. When a commentator is right at the heart of the sport they can sometimes be tempted to commentate for their friends and fellow experts. In other words they ignore the wider audience but can be sure they won't have an awkward moment at a dinner party trying to defend the need to make the commentary accessible. Not Mike. He knew that his biggest job was to make sure that he worked hard for all the audiences. As a result, when big moments came along – such as Zara Phillips's World Title in 2006, or the downpour of gold medals in London and Rio – Tucks's commentary brought the sport to life for the big event viewers.

'In the era of social media and internet forums, sometimes that approach means that the dedicated audience don't necessarily appreciate the more accessible commentary. That's a shame, but at BBC Sport we didn't worry too much if a chatroom criticised Mike – we knew we had the right person for the big occasion. And personally, when I met people on holiday or at other sporting events and told them I produced the equestrian coverage for BBC, invariably they would say something along the lines of, "I like that bloke who does the commentary. It sounds like a big event when I hear him." They wouldn't necessarily know that his name was Mike Tucker, but he made them enjoy the sport they were watching and, in the end, that's what matters.'

Liz Thorburn worked with Mike for a number of years and was BBC TV's equestrian producer from 2013–17. Reflecting on her long association with him, she said 'Working with Mike at BBC Sport for the best part of twenty years, I only ever saw and heard him live life to the full and in perpetual good spirits. A wonderful colleague, it was a joy to work and spend downtime with him – impeccable manners, incredibly modest, empathetic, a true professional, thorough mentor, willing to share wisdom and advice – he was so much fun and had a great sense humour! I never heard him complain, and drama and ego were non-existent. He was at his best when commentating on purely live coverage. He wasn't so keen when he had to factor in commentating for highlights at the same time as that, naturally, does interrupt the flow of speech. However, although reluctant at first, he did embrace my "training" methods – consisting, mainly, of pointing at post-it notes stuck in front of him with instructions such as "clean in", "clean out", "ident", "wrap!". I also could sometimes speak to him on talkback but he could turn me down, so occasionally I had to resort to the odd poke on the arm! I never did get him out of the habit of saying "of course" though and, annoyingly, despite knowing I'm an owl not a lark, he never did get out of the habit of phoning me at the crack of dawn! (We'd often joke about that.)

'In the BBC commentary box, Mike's position was always to sit on the left with his co-commentators to his right. On multiple occasions, using his wisdom, he identified and helped recruit co-commentators – the BBC regulars and the occasional guest ones – he then mentored and supported them, not just when they were in the box with him, but all year round he'd have chats and maintain contact. His advice was never forced and everyone welcomed it, and treated him with huge respect and appreciation. He had an exceptionally good relationship with whomever was in the commentary box with him and was very generous and inclusive, allowing others plenty of time to speak but also ensuring that commentary was kept on track and relevant. The atmosphere in there, no matter what we were covering or the conditions, was always upbeat, calm (high excitement at medal stages excepted!) and very pleasant. We never failed to operate as a team – no one even considered bringing in an ego; it was the kind of place where that thought would never have occurred to anyone.

'Socially, he was so much fun too and, again, the team spirit was high (even when our medal prospects had failed us!).'

Liz has considerable experience of the varying conditions that can confront commentators and production staff, and kindly provided her recollections of some major events. She explained: 'All the three established BBC annual events – Badminton, Burghley and Olympia – run like clockwork so there, at least, we were protected, with cover over our heads, proper seats to sit on and a decent view, plus technical experts were on hand to support/fix issues. The same could not be said for some of the foreign events we covered! Hours and hours and hours, hot/cold/windy, open-air or shoe-horned into a commentary box no bigger than a hamster cage and/or sat on ridiculously uncomfortable seats with sporadic/non-existent technical support, an obscured view, plus lack of toilet facilities, food and water was not unusual. Mike never ever complained. He reminds me of a Scottish expression: "Och wheesht and get oan wae it" – Mike never failed to do that!

'At the 2013 European and Showjumping Championships in Herning, Denmark, the commentary box was in a football stadium. Commentary dropped off-air quite a few times and it took a while before the Danes realised it was down to Mike accidentally kicking the plug out of the socket – although I blame them for rigging it badly in the first place! Our motel was in the middle of nowhere, about an hour's drive there and back every day and with no food available anywhere when we returned after our long days. Mike never complained and was always still raring to go every morning.

'In the same year the European Eventing Championships were held at Malmö, Sweden, and the Swedes had organised this one very well and, as our hotel was in the heart of Malmö, everything was easy and within walking distance. We enjoyed this trip a lot! However, the following year's World Equestrian Games at Caen, in France, was rather different. This was an "eventful" trip – disorganisation was rife. At the cross-country, in the pouring rain, we couldn't park anywhere near and had to wade through thick, gloopy mud to get to the worst commentary box ever! There were tiny football stadium-style seats – sixteen of them all joined together – the BBC had four seats in the middle, the backs of which reached to just below the waist, offering no support whatsoever – incredibly uncomfortable especially considering we were to be in them for six continuous hours minimum. Mike and Ian brought their hotel pillows with them to sit on just to try and ease the pain. There was only a narrow shelf in front of us where the monitor showing the coverage was placed, but it was so high that a crick in the neck was unavoidable and there was nowhere to put any notes. As the day wore on, the temperature got colder and colder and, with no walls, the wind whipped through tunnel-like. The worst was still to come though – GB's Harry Meade, in second place, was not covered by the French TV director and yet Mike still managed to keep the viewer up to date with commentary purely by catching glimpses of Harry in the distance through the trees and the rain. Then Sandra Auffarth, the current leader, was the last competitor to go on the course – thus a crucial round and exciting times. The commentary was reaching a crescendo when, without warning, the commentary box collapsed, a massive crack sounded and Mike, Ian, Andy (soundman) and I were catapulted backwards with such force that we were lying on our backs with our legs and feet straight up in the air! This didn't just disrupt the BBC commentary, but all the other broadcasters, as the crack was so loud and then the hilarity at what happened too great! Many of them stood up to take photos of us. Strangely, although the seats were joined together, none of the four seats to our right or the eight seats to our left were affected. Typically, Mike was the first to recover – if you listen back to it, all you can hear is a bit of kerfuffle, a pause and then Mike picks up saying "I've got to tell you our commentary box has just collapsed, we're all on our backs and the producer's got her legs in the air, which is a bit of a worry" – and then he just carries on commentating on Sandra Auffarth! Meantime, poor Andy's trying to get up and examine his bruises and Ian and I are just crying with laughter. Whenever Ian tries to pick up with commentary he just loses it and laughter takes over, but Mike just steps in and carries on regardless – I don't think there is any other commentator past, present, future who would ever have been/ will be so stoic!

'The showjumping and dressage were in the Caen football stadium, where facilities were not great. Only one toilet and a large queue are not helpful during live broadcasting, where time is unforgiving. Although this was not as bad as the toilets at Le Pin. There Ian Stark ate a dodgy burger the night before cross-country and I recall Mike pointing him in the direction of the toilets calmly describing them: "They're over there but they're a bit rural." In truth, they were horrendous – a hole dug in the ground with a makeshift wooden seat on top and only a scoop of sawdust for a flush!

'Unfortunately, as GB were expected to progress in the showjumping, the round where the entire GB team exited was not covered live by us, but knowing that the GB audience would want to see the GB riders we had to think of something. With Mike's help I selected several riders from that round and then I negotiated a deal to buy the pictures from the host broadcaster. Ollie (BBC self-shoot journalist/reporter) and Andy then rigged up a makeshift commentary box in Ollie's hotel bedroom and we recorded this round "as live" at seven in the morning before we all went off to work again. Watching the highlights, the viewers would never have known, although what the hotel guests in the nearby rooms thought at being woken up by Mike's and Ian's words of wisdom I dread to think (the two of them weren't exactly quiet when they were in front of a mike!)

'We had one day off during this event and Mike, Graeme (cameraman) and I spent a very pleasant day in nearby Bayeux, queuing to see the Tapestry, wandering around the town and cathedral and visiting the World War Two museum.

'The 2015 European Showjumping and Dressage Championships took place in Aachen, Germany. This was a fun trip, but our accommodation in an industrial estate looked, smelt and felt like a youth hostel, with only a vending machine for catering (breakfast excepted). The town was reachable by taxi, though, and we enjoyed some fine evenings out. This was where we introduced Mike to *caipirinhas*. I have photo of him with his first – served in a pint glass with a tree sticking out of it! He loved the drink and the pints slipped down easily; the strength of the alcohol disguised in the sweet taste. The stadium was fantastic but the commentary box was the smallest I've ever seen – Mike and his co-commentator sat, elbows in, squished between the walls and I had to stand outside on an upturned bucket peering over their shoulders. The beams supporting the stadium roof also obstructed the view. Did Mike complain? Not a bit of it!

'At the 2015 European Eventing Championships at Blair Atholl, Scotland, we had mud and freezing conditions on cross-country day, but it was a wonderful trip. Ian Stark was course designer so Tina Cook and Harry Meade joined Mike in the commentary box for this one. Mike guided them and all were totally at ease and enjoyed themselves.

'The 2016 Olympic Games in Rio, Brazil, was the best of all the trips! What a team! As usual, we worked and socialised together and, as this was the Olympics, we had the radio team alongside us – Jonathan Agnew (Aggers) and Tina Cook.

'The trip didn't start so well for Mike – his luggage got stuck in Madrid and he had to wear the same clothes for four days, although I think he managed to borrow the "essentials" from Ian Stark. He was elated when his suitcase finally arrived on the day we all walked the cross-country course and he was delighted, showing off his fresh clothes, although Aggers proclaimed: "I can't believe you actually waited for *these*, I'd have claimed the insurance myself!" It was the first time, I'd ever seen Mike "goldfishing" and then speechless, but he did laugh!

'On day one, we were commentating on the dressage phase of the eventing and, during a break between the afternoon sessions, I was sitting beside Mike and Ian in the commentary box, catching up on emails. I read one that said there had been a shooting at a press centre in the Deodoro area, so I exclaimed "Wait until you hear what's happened" (told them) – "I wonder where it was?" (There were eleven sports in the Deodoro area.) Mike's matter-of-fact response was "We know, we were there." I couldn't believe it and pressed him for the details. Apparently the bullet had come through the roof with a bang and ricocheted off the floor only a few feet from them. "I can't believe you went out to lunch, almost got shot and didn't think to tell me!" Mike just shrugged and said "But we're fine … you might want to check with Graeme [cameraman] though, he was only a couple of yards away and looked a bit shaken." That was the day I told Mike "I've always said you were bombproof, today you've proved it!"'

Although Mike may have been bombproof, he was clearly not coffee-proof. Liz recalled the day when, with only seconds until the start of live commentary, Mike managed to spill his coffee over himself and the commentary box equipment. 'It was a real team effort to rescue the situation, dry it all off but we still picked up right on time – phew!' **Jonathan Agnew**, present in his radio role at the time, also recalled this incident and observed that 'fortunately, order was restored and Mike went on, as usual, to produce many hours of engaging, informative commentary'.

Liz's closing recollections of the Rio Games emphasised the camaraderie between those covering the various sporting disciplines, with Mike typically at the heart of things. 'Although the entire BBC team was spread around Rio in different accommodation, most of the other sport commentary and presenting teams were staying in our hotel. The hotel bar in the evenings became a pre-dinner hub where it was lovely to have equestrian meets athletics meets hockey meets rugby, etcetera. A lovely Italian restaurant was just a short walk away and we ate there regularly. One evening, we introduced Mike to Mexican food and *margaritas* – which went down almost as well as the *caipirinhas*! The beach was also just a short walk away and the last few days we'd have a race with the cycling team to see who would get first to a little beach bar we'd adopted. We'd all have a laugh and put the world to rights over several *caipirinhas*, which, of course, tasted so much better in their home country! On the final night after Nick Skelton won gold we were down there as usual celebrating. There was a makeshift karaoke (a tiny tin bucket – previously holding napkins – acted as a great speaker when an iPhone playing music was placed in it). Mike, Andy Austin, Tina Cook and the cycling team including Chris Hoy were all singing their hearts out, not a care in the world!'

Mike's passion and versatility as a commentator were widely respected. **Alice Plunkett** remarked that 'Mike's passion and enthusiasm, whether at the county show showing me the class of Red Devons, racing when he was stewarding at Cheltenham, or at Olympia doing the Shetland Grand National was amazing. The last job he agreed to do with me was very special. I felt really strongly that we, as a country, weren't appreciative enough of the extraordinary quartet of horses we had from the different disciplines, so set about getting them together. Thus, in April 2017 Big Star, Valegro, Chilli Morning and Sprinter Sacre walked into the paddock at Cheltenham together, with Mike compèring. It was a hugely emotional and special moment and one I will treasure. As I went to thank Mike he stopped me and thanked me. No one else could have been more perfect to give the day gravitas and meaning than Mike but, even after all the successes and triumphs he had been involved with over so many years, these wonderful horses still really moved him. He just loved the best of horse sport and it loved him.'

In his eulogy at Mike's memorial, **Nick Brooks-Ward** also referred to Mike's versatility and touched upon his knowledge of the world of cattle breeding. 'For so many of us his electric commentaries were the signature of Mike – and he could turn his attention to talking about literally anything – from dog agility at Crufts, six Olympic Games, the Royal Bath and West and the Great Yorkshire for over forty years to the Pony Club Championships – there was nothing that he couldn't turn his hand to, with brilliance, empathy, knowledge and timing.

'But for me his finest times on the microphone were his Burke Trophy parade commentaries in the heyday of the Royal Show – this was Mike at his finest – notes about over forty breeds of cattle spread far and wide (he was never the tidiest in the box!), over four hundred of the world's finest cattle parading in front of him and he would never draw breath for over an hour and a half, imparting his knowledge and experience to a packed audience of over ten thousand like-minded people – this was quite simply the best you could ever hear. And when the judge slapped the rump of the winning breed the excitement in Mike's voice would ripple around the audience and there would be a huge cheer – to achieve that in a cattle parade is a true sign of brilliance.'

Despite Mike's undoubted knowledge of cattle breeding, long-time friend **Tim Harding's** recollection of his first meeting with Mike was memorable for a slippage in *species* recognition.

'It was in 1981 that I first met up with our dear friend Mike. I was fortunate to be leading my cow Crichel Aline 177 Ex as grand champion in the Holsteins. She had been champion at numerous shows, from the North West Dairy Show to Bath and West, and was renowned throughout the breed. She was also unbeaten in 1984, and thus well-known. Mike was doing the commentary at the Royal Cornwall and I repeat this in his words: "Leading the champion Holstein is that well-known breeder,

Tim Harding with his exquisite Crichel Aline 177 Ex, looking a picture. She is by that well-known *stallion* Grove Starlite Ex." I creased myself laughing and never allowed him to forget it whenever I saw him in the eventing and cattle world. To be fair, I think it was his first Grand Parade commentary, but not his last!

'What a man and what a friend. They don't make them like that now.'

Another contributor who made reference to the Royal Show was **Major Chris Tar**, former Commanding Officer of the King's Troop RHA, and steward at many of the top shows, including chief steward of the main ring on the Sunday of Burghley Horse Trials and chief steward at Olympia. Whilst admiring Mike's expertise, he couldn't resist indulging in the sort of wind-up that Mike himself was not averse to pulling. 'At the Royal Show, the most impressive arena display was the cattle parade in the grand ring. This included cattle from all the beef breeds and all dairy breeds: a very impressive and prestigious display of UK and Continental cattle.

'I was a main ring steward and was involved in marshalling the various breeds around the ring and lining them up for the presentation of the championship trophy. Mike always sat at a six-foot table ringside, from where he would deliver his extensive knowledge on all of the breeds to an attentive audience. His commentary was very professional and non-stop as each breed passed his table. I decided to write a note and place it in front of him during his commentary. The note said: "Mike if you were a beef breed you would be a Dexter." This caused Mike to choke over his commentary, which created an uncharacteristic and noticeable pause in an otherwise faultless delivery. I hope the public did not notice. Mike was red in the face and stumbled verbally back into his stride.'

Giles Rowsell, along with other colleagues, was another who hatched a plot to distract Mike with the written word in revenge for various past pranks. At the time, Giles was cross-country controller at the Atlanta Games. 'One memento from the past lives in the Tuckers' dining room at Church Farm. At the Atlanta Olympics 1996, we spotted a sign in a restaurant that said "Takeaway Tucker Available". This was too good a slogan to resist, but despite being a rather moderate restaurant, we had to eat there three times before they would agree to let us have it. The plan was to produce it at a critical commentary moment. With the aid of Mike's fellow BBC commentator, Lorna Clarke, I crawled along the row in front of where Tucks was commentating and, on her instruction, I raised it in the gap between his two screens whilst he was waxing lyrical on pure dressage (hardly his forte), but to our disappointment he continued as though nothing had happened – ever the true professional!'

Chris Tar supplied further evidence of times when Mike's professionalism was challenged – perhaps, in these cases, to more effect: 'On another occasion at the Royal Show the guest military band was the Wellington Police Pipe Band from New Zealand. Mike struggled to announce the band for its main ring performance twice every day. He would announce the band as: "Ladies and gentlemen we are very pleased to welcome our guest band from New Zealand – the *Wellington Pice Polipe Band* !" The next performance it would be the "*Wellington Peep Polite Band*", or the "*Wellington Polipe Pice Band*" and so on. He got it right for their last performance.

'One year at Olympia a well-known main ring celebrity decided she had taken a fancy to Mike and wanted his body, or so Mike thought. Whilst flattered initially, Mike realised that this was a serious threat. He therefore planned his escape and fled back to the hotel at speed, hotly followed by said lady. So flustered was he by his pursuer that, in order not to be followed any further and in his panic-stricken state, he ran up the down escalator and almost fell flat on his face – but managed to escape. The lady in question settled for another well-known commentator who sadly is also no longer with us.'

One incident I learned of highlights Mike's versatility as a commentator, the ease which he established true and lasting friendships, and his facility for indulging his sense of humour – although, on this occasion, the "biter" got "bit". **John Peacock**, chairman of the Shire Horse Society, told me: 'I have known Mike since he started commentating at the Shire Horse Show forty years ago. For the last twenty or so years my wife Betty and I had become good friends with Mike and his family. We have spent some fantastic times in his company, not only at shows but shooting weekends at Church Farm where Mike would be the perfect host all day but never picked up a gun. As well as all his fun-making he could also be a very serious person with whom one could have a deep conversation: he was always ready to offer good advice but never afraid to ask for your opinion in return. A good friend whom Betty and I will miss more than words can say.

'One occasion that we always laughed about with Mike, was the heavy horse pairs obstacle driving class at the East of England Show some twenty-five years ago. It was the last class of the day and I was one of the drivers walking the course. Mike was really playing to the crowds and giving all the drivers some stick with his mickey-taking. On returning to the collecting ring we asked the stewards to try to get him out of the commentary box for the presentation of awards after the class. Arrangements were made for our grooms to stand fast with the horses and, as the last rosette was presented, four or five of us got down from the box and, before he realised what was happening, we had caught him and, with one person on each leg and arm, we carried him to the water jump and dumped him in. His only worry was that someone took the microphone so it wouldn't get wet. He took it all in very good spirit and carried on commentating to the end. Luckily the sponsor of the class, who happened to be the managing director of the Swallow Hotel where Mike was staying, also saw the funny side of it all and arranged for Mike's clothes to be cleaned, washed and pressed ready for the next day's showing.'

Another soaking that Mike endured was a testament to his professionalism but, according to **Giles Rowsell**, undeserved and less amusing for him. 'Tucks has talked about the sheer joy of London 2012, but left out how the huge thunderstorm that occurred in the middle of Tina Cook's dressage test caused the competition to be suspended. Although our commentary tower had taken a direct hit, at least we were dry – he was out in an open stand getting absolutely drowned and, despite our many calls of how sorry we felt for him, he could not see the funny side.

Several hours later, when we had retired to the pub just outside the main gates of Greenwich Park he was still wet through and insisted on several medicinal whisky macs.'

During the many years spent travelling around various shows and events, it is not surprising that Mike was sometimes party to not so amusing incidents. One that perhaps falls into the latter category was recounted by **Mike Bullen**, brother of Jennie and Jane, well-known for his years with Pedens, when he would arrange for horses to be transported all around the world, and as a steward for many years at top shows. 'The first year of The Horse of the Year Show at NEC Birmingham in 2002, Mike had his car packed for the weekend with items including his dinner jacket, competition notes and so on in preparation for commentating. *En route*, he stopped at a garage to fill his car with fuel and, when going to pay, he left his key in the ignition. He returned to where his car had been just in time to see it being driven rapidly up the road by someone else! There was a taxi at the garage where he had been refuelling, so Mike took it to the NEC, cursing at the price.

'Being Mike he managed to commentate from memory without any of his notes. Once over the first annoyance, he reacted light-heartedly to a lot of leg-pulling in the bar of the hotel where everyone stayed for the show. We don't think he ever got his car back – which was probably no loss with it being a farmer's car – neither did he ever see his clothes again.'

On the occasions when Mike retained possession of his vehicle, he still had to deal with the practicalities of getting home safely, often after a very long and arduous day's work. His family commented: 'We were always worried when Mike drove back late from a show because he tended to get rather sleepy. He found the best way to stay awake was to sing along to Abba at full volume! We went all together as a family to see *Mamma Mia* and Mike loved every moment of it. The Carpenters and Neil Diamond were also among his favourites.'

Of course, Mike being Mike and equestrian sport being what it is, there were the inevitable quirky moments around the commentary itself. **Elizabeth Inman**, director of Burghley, recalled a couple. In the first:

'Mike was introducing Tiny Clapham as she entered the arena. He tried to say "Here is a lady who has had a lot of success" but he, uncharacteristically, stumbled on his words and said "she has had a lot of sex". Poor Tiny, you could see her shoulders shaking with laughter as she tried to continue with her dressage test.' She continued: 'One of Mike's challenges was trying to be sure which rider had started their test if the number could not be seen. On one occasion a male rider was in and the entry list was being scanned to identify him. Mike said "It must be X as he is wearing a Swedish cap." Someone retorted "He'd look pretty silly if he came from Holland" (as in wearing a Dutch cap). Mike had to turn off the mike as it took a while until composure returned.'

The late, great Peter O'Sullevan had a reputation for remaining icy calm when calling home one of his own horses to win a major race but, for Mike, commentating on his own wife required at least a veiled hint of the 'hurry ups'. **Angela** told me: 'I remember one time when Mike was commentating and I was riding Good Value at Burghley (this was the horse on whom I had previously led the dressage at Badminton but then I fell off cross-country!). As I was turning back to come home down Winners' Avenue, I heard his voice over the loudspeaker saying "Angela Tucker and Good Value have jumped Centaur's Leap and are coming back down the Avenue" and I then heard him say "And now hopefully she'll pick up the pace as she turns towards home." This was in the hope that I would put my foot down!'

I was also told a funny story by **HRH The Princess Royal**, which she described as the commentator's curse! 'I was riding at Knowlton Horse Trials many years ago on a mare called Mantilla. I was galloping across a field when I heard Mike over the loudspeaker say something like "And Princess Anne is going very well …" At which point the mare stopped dead, with no fence in sight, right underneath the telegraph pole with the loudspeaker on it. It was right in the middle of nowhere and so I don't think there was anyone there to see me shaking my fist at the speaker, shouting "Oh shut up Tucker!"

'On a different topic,' she added, 'in recent years, I saw more of

Mike at agricultural shows than at equestrian events. He had such a vast knowledge about cattle, being a dairyman, and interestingly enough our conversations were more about livestock than horses.'

For all his energy and enthusiasm, Mike had always been a realist. **Michael Cole** recalled: 'Over the years when I was at the BBC, Mike had always asked me to let him know if I ever I thought he was "past it", as he bluntly put it. I'm glad to say that I never felt that time had come. I left BBC Sport after the London Olympics and I was pleased that my successors felt the same. So, on he continued to Rio. And as a freelance producer I continued to work with him at Badminton each year and sometimes at Olympia or Global Champions Tour events.

'But Mike had always been clear to me about one thing. He thought that commentating on an Olympic sport for the BBC was a pleasure but also a responsibility, which should be taken seriously. If a commentator wasn't sure that they wanted to do a full four-year cycle through to the next Olympics, they probably should get out soon enough to let their successor have a good run up to the Games. Ahead of Rio he told me he thought the time might be approaching to have a good think about the future, and after Rio he had made up his mind. The success of the GB team, led by Nick Skelton and Charlotte Dujardin, would be hard to beat, but also he said that the demands of the non-stop commentary on the red button were considerable and he had decided the time was right to hang up the BBC microphone.

'I think he probably got the timing perfect. It must be tempting to keep going when you are still doing a good job, but as the legendary commentator on football – and many other sports too – Barry Davies said when he gave up *Match of the Day*, "I'd rather have people asking why I'm leaving, than wondering why I'm still here." By the time Tucks stopped working for BBC TV Sport, only Barry Davies and John Motson had been commentating for them for longer.

'He had many other things to concentrate upon in his life – above all his family, growing with grandchildren he loved so much – and he was happy with the timing that would let someone else have a good run in to

Tokyo for the BBC. In that context it seems all the sadder that he didn't enjoy many more years of his semi-retirement. Of course, with Tucks it would never be a full retirement. There was so much to do, so many people to help. He wouldn't have had it in his nature to be selfish, but I expected that the years after his BBC retirement in 2017 would at least see him have a bit more time to devote to himself, Angela and the family. Life's just not fair sometimes, is it?

'Mike decided to put down his BBC microphone for the final time at Badminton in 2017. Of all the events he worked on, it was the closest to him – personally as well as geographically. The "local gymkhana" as he often called it. The BBC and everyone who worked with Mike were determined to make a bit of a fuss of him. Needless to say, that meant he had quite a lot of people queuing up to say thanks to him.

'Paying tribute to Tucks on air was relatively straightforward. Clare Balding recorded a lovely interview with Mike and we dredged the archive for pictures of him in his competitive prime – on General Bugle coming second behind Lucinda at Badminton. The reaction from the viewers was tremendous. Their messages made it clear that they were sorry to see him go.

'More tricky was working out how his friends on the commentary and production team could say thanks and make a little presentation. Could we take him and Angela out for dinner during Badminton perhaps? "That would be lovely", Mike said, but he was concerned that they had quite a lot of friends staying or visiting during the event. It would be a bit rude to leave them to their own devices, he felt. Having been to Church Farm a few times over the years during Badminton, I understood his point. But despite having a houseful already, Angela and Mike threw open their doors and said the BBC team must come over too. And so we did, as always welcomed into the warmth of Tucks's extended circle, with guests seated at every available position in a variety of rooms.

'The BBC's director of sport, Barbara Slater, who produced Badminton herself for a few years, came up with the idea of getting a special front page of the *Radio Times* made and framed, paying tribute to Mike. It was a lovely idea and his BBC producer in Rio and at so many other events, Liz Thorburn, made a great job of having it designed and produced.

'It was a lovely evening. Mike seemed really touched to have so many of his telly friends mixing with his wider circle. He didn't need to work at being the centre of attention. People naturally gravitated to Mike because we all knew we would have fun together. That came across in his commentary and was a huge benefit to the BBC and its viewers for more than four decades.'

Malcolm and I would always stay with Mike and Angela for Badminton and we felt honoured and privileged to be part of that BBC farewell evening. It was a moving occasion and despite the cheery laughter during speeches from both Michael Cole and Mike himself, there was a definite feeling of genuine sadness that an era was now over.

One thing that became very apparent when looking through the contributions to this chapter was the number of times that Mike's colleagues mentioned how helpful and supportive he had been to them. **Michael Cole** took the time to explain that 'The world of TV sport – like many parts of the media – is not exclusively made up of selfless individuals who are delighted to see their colleagues thrive. There is quite a lot of rivalry at times. "I succeed if he fails", can sometimes be the attitude. That wasn't the way with Mike. I'm sure a lot of that is down to the welcome he himself got from Raymond Brooks-Ward and Dorian Williams when, as a rider in the 1970s, he would get off his horse and head straight to the commentary box. But it is also completely in keeping with how he lived the rest of his life.

'So whenever I suggested we should see if X or Y fancied doing a spell in the commentary box, not only was he not worried that the new person might be a rival, but he positively welcomed them to the team. He would do all the "heavy lifting" of listening to the constant information in his ear from the director and me, leaving the new commentator free to watch the pictures and offer their insight. But rather than waiting for my suggestions, more often it was Mike ringing me to say that there was someone he thought would be really good to use on the team. He was generous to a fault. 'And when it came to the Olympics, often BBC radio would send a very good broadcaster to cover the equestrian sport, but not necessarily one who was steeped in equestrian sport. Mike was always their first port of call, offering advice, expertise and introductions to help them have a great Olympics. Unsurprisingly they all remained good friends when they had moved back to their week-to-week duties on football, cricket or rugby.'

My husband **Malcolm** backed up **Michael's** sentiments when he observed: 'All his protégés have testified to Mike's caring and helpful approach when they, as rookies, joined him in the BBC commentary box to add their contributions to those of Mike as anchorman for the production.'

With that in mind, the following is a selection of some of the final recollections of some of the people who expressed special gratitude to Mike for his help and support.

Nick Brooks–Ward recalled how encouraging Mike was to him as he began his own career in commentary: 'To me, he gave so much – with his knowledge and support. There were some commentators who didn't want this young upstart to come and play on their wicket – but Mike was different. Always encouraging, supporting and guiding and sometimes criticising – but never with malice – always with positivity.

'His first advice was at Olympia in 2000. I was a young upstart and had been given the opportunity to join the commentary team – he never stopped helping me then and right up until he died. I distinctly remember on the last night of that Olympia, after I had commentated on my first ever five-star Grand Prix and Mike had just finished television – he was on his way home to act as field master of the Beaufort the following day, and he came and found me and said "You're on your way now and I am going to help you get there, just like your father did for me" – and he never stopped!

'To make that case even stronger, we were at Windsor Horse Trials in 2004 and I had just been contacted by ATHOC (the Athens Olympic Games Committee) to be the lead commentator at that year's Olympic Games. They weren't paying that much money and it would have meant four weeks away from home – even more difficult as Di and I had an eighteen-month-old baby at home. I asked Mike what I should do – he told me there and then that I had to jump at the opportunity as offers like that will only come around once in a lifetime, and that I would meet people who would influence my life whom I would never have the opportunity to meet if I didn't go. That was the sagest piece of advice I have ever received and he was, as usual, a hundred per cent correct.

'Another great moment was in 2006. We were sitting in the commentary box at the Royal Show and we were commentating on the British National Championships in front of a packed audience – and the announcement was being made as to who was being awarded the 2012 Olympic Games. There was a big screen in the bottom of the grand ring and we went live to Lausanne. Guy Williams, who went on to be crowned National Champion, came into the ring with Hamlet – and they stood stock still in front of the screen. As we all remember, it was touch and go between us and Paris and when the moment came and Jacques Rogge announced "London" there was a huge cheer from the crowd, Guy Williams punched the air and Mike and I hugged each other. Mike turned to me and said "Well Nicko – I guess we will have to go on for another six years."

'He thought about retiring after London, at that stage, but I am absolutely positive that after the tremendous success of all the equestrian disciplines in London he decided to carry on – and the pinnacle was of course Big Star and Nick Skelton in Rio 2016 – as ever his sense of timing was impeccable.

'I can honestly say that since my father died in 1992, there is nobody who has helped, guided and supported me in all my walks of life more than Mike. He taught me to be humble, to take the punches and the criticism, to be with people from all walks of life and to strive to be the best that I could be. He was always there – impossible to get hold of straight away at times as he was so busy – but my word he never once let me down.'

Harry Meade, son of the late Richard Meade, is another rider who has, in recent years, combined a successful eventing career with TV commentary. He said: 'I had no idea what to expect on my first live session. To my surprise there was no form of briefing or instruction, it was simply a case of arriving five minutes before we – Mike, Ian Stark and I – were due to go live, sit down, switch on the microphones and get going.

'I was here entirely thanks to Mike. In 2014 I was asked to provide commentary for the Official Badminton DVD. Recording it was great fun but I never imagined it would be something I'd do again.

'The following spring I received an unexpected phone call from the BBC, asking me to be part of the broadcast team at Badminton that year; it transpired that Angela had watched the DVD and suggested to Mike that he listen to the commentary. After doing so he had contacted the BBC suggesting I be given a chance at the real thing.

'Although I'd heard Mike's commentary all my life, witnessing it for real made me appreciate the ingredients that made him the best in the business. His voice was the ideal pitch for recordings, but with it he could set the tone of the programme, lowering it and slowing the rhythm during a moment of suspense and then raising the tempo and volume like a conductor does an orchestra when the action was building to a crescendo.

'During the sessions Mike was very supportive; he gave me time to find my feet and eased me in with leading questions. As the lead commentator, his role was to hold the programme together, but also to allow the "expert", whomever his co-commentator was, to provide an in-depth analysis. Of course Mike's experience as a competitor meant he was able to perform the role of either lead or expert, but he was able to underplay his knowledge and set up Ian and me to respond.

'The thing that most impressed me was his mental fitness. The level of concentration was draining and in the lulls of the action, when I – and presumably the audience – might have lost focus, Mike was able to recap the day's action, turning up the octane and, like any great storyteller, re-engage the listeners' interest.

'As things started to gel, we became a trio who clearly enjoyed each other's humour and could bounce off one another. It didn't take long for Mike's gentle questioning to become increasingly leading statements, said with a twinkle in his eye and followed by long pauses. Knowing he was setting me, the junior in the room, up for a fall and with Ian sitting between us and also silently nodding and grinning, I willingly played the new boy and gathered up as much rope as they could hand me with which to metaphorically hang myself, at which point Mike swiftly played the elder statesman, publicly bringing me back into line, but visibly delighted with the entertainment.

'Together we had such fun; the friendship, humour and shared appreciation of the traditions of the sport, the virtues of the old-fashioned event horse and the principles of correct cross-country riding meant it really felt like three friends privately chatting through the action in the pub, with the audience eavesdropping on the conversation.

'This way of operating was down to Mike's charisma and the result was a cohesive, fun-filled and passionate debate – the polar opposite to a formulaic performance where each individual operates in isolation from each other. His passion and ability to put even the most nervous interviewees at ease meant that dialogues were seamlessly natural. His experience and strength of character led to a universal respect for him, ensuring the team was always kept in order.

'He was greatly encouraging of the young, but never patronising. Maybe the longevity of his career had allowed him to observe the stars of each era in their former lives as relative unknowns.

'Mike was always generous to the connections of competitors, giving the breeders, owners and grooms a plug whenever he could. He always saw things in a positive light and could report a controversial situation with great diplomacy.

'After that first Badminton commentary, we went on to work together at the next two Burghleys, the 2015 European Championship at Blair Castle and two more Badmintons, including his swansong in 2017, which marked his retirement.

'The trips further afield allowed time to catch up and, over a drink, we regularly dissected the current state of the sport, its general health and likely future direction, as well as the prospects of the British teams. His passionate concern and long history made him a sage tutor and counsellor.

'His final Badminton was unsurprisingly moving. In the closing moments he eloquently thanked the audience and the BBC for so many years of experiences and memories; that much-loved voice quivered and his eyes misted as he signed off for the final time. We turned off the mikes and Ian and I thanked him for what he had given the sport and each of us.

'After the end of the season, at our yard Christmas party, I was grateful to be able to tell Mike how much I had appreciated his support and generous encouragement, and how inspiring it was to have hung on to his coat-tails for the latter part of his career. It was the last time we saw each other.

'For many of us his will always be the voice of equestrian sport, delivered with utter professionalism and a gentle scattering of well-judged humour. But I will remember Mike beyond his commentary – as a stalwart servant to the sport; he gave so much back to the equestrian world through course design, officiating, event organising and the many committees on which he sat to help steer the sport, both internationally and domestically, on a steady course. For that he is an example that I hope I and other riders of my generation can strive to follow.'

Jonathan Agnew, who is primarily known as a voice from the world of cricket, had this to say of his sudden launch into the world of equestrian commentary: 'During the period leading up to the Rio Olympics, it was proposed that I should take a detour from the world of cricket commentary into what was, for me at the time, an unexplored world of equestrian sport. By way of preparation, I spent some two years walking with Mike around various courses – Badminton, Burghley and elsewhere – with a view to familiarising myself with as many of the technical details and rules as I could absorb. Throughout this time, Mike was incredibly kind and helpful and it was a great pleasure for me, in due course, to work with him at the Olympic Games, him on TV and me on radio.' He added: 'One evening, towards the end of the Games, as we were walking back from the restaurant, he confided in me that he thought this might be an appropriate time at which to "draw stumps" on his long career. The fact that he chose to use his recollections of these Games as the introductory chapter to this book seems to me entirely fitting and I will always treasure the time spent working with him.'

Clare Balding, who has become one of the UK's best-known presenters of a variety of sports, summed up her working relationship with Mike, and her thoughts about him overall, in these terms: 'Mike was always incredibly modest about his own achievements as a rider, but his bravery and enthusiasm over big fences translated to his commentary style. He was always upbeat, positive and full of energy. I first heard his voice when I was a child at Olympia and immediately got caught up in the excitement of the event – whether it was a valuable Grand Prix, the dog agility or the Shetland Pony Grand National, Mike could make it sound as if it mattered more than anything.

'I first worked alongside him at the Olympics in Atlanta, where I was a very green radio reporter. He was so supportive and encouraging, making sure I had all the information I needed and introducing me to key people behind the scenes. When I started presenting the coverage at Badminton, I had no idea how to take talkback from the director, how to talk to time, or cope with the complicated art of slotting in live interviews while there were still riders on the course who might be approaching a vital fence. I am sure I messed it up more than I got it right, but Mike only ever offered me confidence-boosting words of wisdom.

'Years spent on the circuit sleeping in the horsebox had prepared him for the most basic of accommodation and, believe me, it is never very glamorous working abroad for the BBC. At the World Equestrian Games in Normandy in 2014, we were staying in a trucker's motel, and in Aachen the following year one of the taxi drivers who had taken us into town queried the safety of the hotel in the suburbs where we were based. Mike never dreamt of complaining – as long as he had a bed, he was fine.

'In Athens in 2004 we had quite a story brewing at the eventing because Nick Skelton (who had been watching from the stands) alerted me to the fact that Bettina Hoy had gone through the start twice as she began her showjumping round. I ran into the press office to find Mike and tell him that there ought to be an objection. Angela was on the ground jury, which could have made it a little awkward, but he immediately went off to find out what he could, then came back to tell me that there was a big review in progress, but no one knew what the outcome might be.

"'I'm going live," I said, determined that eventing would be the big story on the six o'clock roundup of the Games. "Whatever they do, this is huge."'

'Mike looked at me with slight concern in his face. "Be careful," he said, "they won't necessarily make a decision today."

"'It's television" I replied, with a confidence borne of naivety. "We can say what's happening now and, if it changes, we'll change the story."

'Mike was right – it wasn't at all straightforward. Leslie Law finally heard that he had won the first individual gold in eventing for Great Britain in thirty-two years when he had returned home and was riding at a novice event in Solihull.

'I enjoyed many happy days working with Mike at Badminton, Burghley, Olympia, European Championships, World Championships and the Olympics. He was always full of energy, love for his sport and had an indefatigable enthusiasm for telling the story.

'Thankfully, his commentating career coincided with some of the great moments in equestrian sport – gold for Zara Phillips at the World Championships, gold for the showjumping team in London and the sudden rise in British dressage fortunes thanks to Charlotte Dujardin and Carl Hester, which gave him three gold medals to describe across London and Rio, before rounding off his Olympic Games commentary with a fairy-tale final individual gold medal for Nick Skelton.

'Mike timed his exit from the commentary box perfectly and I am just so sad that he didn't get long to enjoy his retirement. He would have been nothing but supportive to anyone taking over his microphone, as he had been throughout his career. He always came to meetings full of ideas and played a full part in the planning of who should feature in the highlights packages. How he fitted it all in with talking to every single person at every event we attended, I have no idea, but he was an inspiration in terms of working and making friends at the same time.'

CHAPTER ELEVEN

Official Roles – Course Design and Committees

Once Mike had made the decision to retire from active participation in competitive sport, he threw himself wholeheartedly into a variety of other activities and official duties. In addition to running Church Farm with the large dairy herd, and developing his role as a commentator, he also found time to pursue other avenues within the eventing world. Having sat on the Horse Trials Committee from 1974 to 1986, he then moved on to his role as an FEI official as course designer and technical delegate. (The latter is an independent expert whose role is to advise on the organisation of the whole event, especially the courses. Until the moment the competition starts, the technical director has sole authority and thereafter acts as an expert adviser to the ground jury and continues to assist both organisers and competitors.) These official capacities took him to many competitions and seminars around the world including New Zealand, America and Canada – the first-named being a country he was only too happy to revisit and offer advice on many occasions.

Mike's friend **Giles Rowsell**, a cross-country controller and commentator at many events both at home and abroad, explained that: 'His knowledge of the sport of eventing was second to none, which made him an excellent technical director, helping ground jury members in difficult situations and passing on advice at numerous eventing officials' courses at which he officiated. He had a big input into the sport in New Zealand and was honoured by the New Zealand governing body for his contribution to the training of cross-country course designers and officials.'

Mike's input to the development of eventing in New Zealand was explained further by representatives of that country. **Virginia Caro** and **Jennifer Millar**, an FEI official, offered their combined recollections of Mike's visits and influence.

Virginia recalled that: 'Mike came to New Zealand in 1980 at the invitation of the New Zealand Horse Society, as initiated by Boy Caro, who at that time was chairman of the Horse Trials Committee. Mike flew out immediately after Badminton, arriving on the ninth of May, and conducted eleven seminars throughout both the North and South Islands. He was eventing's first overseas expert, with a brief to advise on cross-country course design and cross-country riding, and all aspects of event administration. He was quoted as saying, "I had a brief visit here in 1967 and saw the New Zealand Pony Club Horse Trials Championships at Nelson, and was astounded at the high standard of cross-country riding."

'He visited again in 1983, thanks to the Olympic Solidarity Fund, and conducted thirteen seminars throughout the country from the second of November to the eighth of December, being joined by Angela for the last week. He attended the Horse Trials Committee meeting in Wellington on the fifteenth of November, where he advised that the grading system needed to be changed from wins to points, and recommended a sub-committee be formed to review the administration of horse trials, suggesting that the discipline should become autonomous so it could cope with development and ensure continued progress (as happened in 1984).'

Jennifer added: 'Mike was again of particular help when New Zealand had the Olympic Qualifying Trial for Los Angeles 1984, when he was able to advise the course builder on design to test the ability of both horse and rider.' [It seems that Mike's earlier advice about the grading system and the need for a sub-committee were acted upon, since Jennifer continued] 'A sub-committee was duly formed and New Zealand Horse Trials moved forward from then on.

'The Pony Club was very strong in New Zealand at this time and I was the course designer for the Pony Club Championships in 1984. I had previously travelled around the UK and Europe and had designed the cross-country with thoughts of what I had observed on my travels. I was forever grateful to Mike, who advised me and discussed the proposed course in 1983 with all the top Pony Club officials – who were not quite sure about some of the proposed jumps!

'Our paths crossed all over the world and I greatly enjoyed working with him. Particular memories include:

'The Seoul Olympics in 1988 was where he took me off jump judging and into the control centre. All forty of us helping to organise the Olympics stayed together in the one complex, where we spent our evenings discussing the sport, with Mike "The Imitator" taking off all our accents. He was an expert at this.

'Working with Mike at Windsor Horse Trials, where we all stayed in the jockey's quarters at Ascot – the cheapest accommodation in the area, with the Pony Club catering.

'Mike surprising us when we were canal boating in Wales. We had a message to pull up at the next lock, where we were totally amazed to see Mike and Angela, who came on board for the night. Mike was going to show us how to drive the canal boat but after bumping into the banks as he tried to steer we all agreed he was much better on land.

'Kentucky after Rolex, where we were driven from Lexington to Cincinnati by limo, all relaxing and celebrating with champagne, including Mike and Angela who were cuddling in the back seat, thinking back to their courting days.

'Mike was at his best when there was a "hold" on course at Burghley in 1996 looking for anyone ("a dog will do") to interview to keep the crowd listening to the commentary.

'I remember he arranged to meet me off the plane at Heathrow and he arrived in his horsebox and tried to park in the car park outside the terminal. All I could hear was horns tooting. His comment when I jumped into the box was "Be quick – don't think I am supposed to be here."

'Mike told us he was writing an autobiography and commented that if Bruce, my husband, didn't behave himself he would be featured in the book. Mike and Bruce were forever in contact when New Zealand and England were playing cricket or rugby – and bets were always on.

'Mike was always a wonderful host with Angela at his side. Church Farm was our home away from home, especially at Badminton time. We will miss Mike – a true friend, not only to New Zealand but personally. It is hard to believe he will not be there if I go back to England.'

Virginia kindly sent me an article originally published in the NZ Horse Society Inc. Bulletin, March 1984, which is reproduced below:[1]

TUCKER ON EVENTING

Michael Tucker, international eventer (second and seventh at Badminton last year), commentator, course builder, organiser, on his second visit to New Zealand in just over three years, was as enthusiastic as ever about the eventing scene here.

He was impressed by the improvements he saw – better cross-country courses in many places, increased interest and wider knowledge from those attending his seminars, though numbers were slightly down on 1980 (possibly due to the different time of year, spring as opposed to autumn), and the advent of the spring season.

---

1   The terms DC and A1 mentioned in the sixth paragraph of the article are divisions within the New Zealand Pony Club.

However, there were words of warning too – we must learn to look after our good horses, to prepare and ride them properly, and he emphasised that the groundwork MUST be done first. How often do we have to be told that our dressage must improve if we are to foot it with the rest of the world?

Mike says he is not fond of dressage, nor naturally good at it ("with my short fat hairy legs!"), but realising the value of what he calls "circles and bumps", he works at it, knowing that one must be in the top half dozen after the dressage if one is going to win these days, and that one's jumping improves as a result too.

He says we will still need the opportunity for more experience, although there are more events being organised as the spring season gets established. He realises we do not have enough "silly buggers" on the ground organising, and while he perceived increased co-operation between Horse Society and Pony Club, he encouraged further liaison, to help overcome the shortage of manpower.

Making DC *[A New Zealand Division of the Pony Club]* and novice heights the same, and likewise A1 and intermediate heights, was a step in the right direction, and should make more courses available to both Pony Club and Horse Society.

A special word to competitors – saying "thank you" to those who put in the long hours may make them think that perhaps it was worthwhile after all. And Mike knows, he organises trials on his own property.

He feels very strongly that the grading system is holding horse trials back, especially in the South Island. He advocates a change from wins to points, so more horses upgrade. At present we have novices which should be intermediate, and intermediates which should be advanced. This has resulted in some cross-country courses becoming unnecessarily demanding, especially for novices.

He says that course designers must remember we "do it for fun", and endeavour to build courses that create confidence. Horses should be sent out to finish the course (at least 80% round, and 50% clear), and the attitude of "stopping them here" should be wiped out. Horses need to learn from fair fences.

Things Mike considers unfair are:

1. False ground lines (acceptable at advanced level only)
2. Bad distances
3. Too many drops
4. Landing into banks
5. Downhill spreads, which are "downright dangerous".

He says the first three or four fences should be give-aways, to get the horses going. They should have good ground lines, and be made of solid timber. Ditches, parallels, and ramps are not suitable.

But riders should take the time to warm up properly, and let the horse know he is going "up a cog". Riding should be forceful, but not fast. He points out that sitting forward puts weight on the forehand, so one should sit up when approaching the fence, and also over fences with drop landings, to prevent "exit via the front door" if the horse pecks on landing.

When walking the course, Mike recommends looking at it as a novice sees it; lining up the fences to save seconds and also save the horse. "Standing off" fences uses unnecessary energy, and risks making a mistake. If there is any danger of the horse hitting the fence, jump it straight so that if you get flipped out of the saddle there is still the neck in front of you, not Mother Earth.

Mike says time faults are OK, if you are educating a horse. Confidence must come before speed if you want a safe ride. He applauds the introduction of training level trials to allow green horses and riders to gain confidence before tackling the real thing.

On fence building, he remarked that the far side of ditches, drains etc, should not be revetted, so horses do not get hurt if they land against them. Stubb posts make an attractive and easy support for rails, and give a fence good perspective.

Both course builders and riders should remember that horses jump easily going uphill when their hocks are under them, but going downhill they are on their forehand and it is difficult for them.

And finally a word to technical delegates. Mike says they must "grade" courses, not just measure them to ensure they come within the legal limits. A novice dimension fence can be a difficult intermediate fence, if conditions of terrain, etc, make it so.

We are indeed lucky to have had the opportunity once again to learn from this remarkable man's very broad experience.

Jim Wright farms in the north of New Zealand's North Island and is a selector for the national team. He and his wife Beth were to become firm friends with the Tuckers. He recalled: 'I was first introduced to Mike when he visited New Zealand to take seminars at the time of the New Zealand National Trophy, being held at Te Kauwhata, Waikato. This would have been around 1980, I think. This visit played a key role in the evolution of eventing in New Zealand and was the start of a long and fruitful friendship. He helped put New Zealand on track for the success it was to have in future years and was a mentor in both course designing and administration.

'On a further visit to New Zealand for a meeting at Taupo, shortly after I had had a bad fall while out hunting and spent a couple of nights in hospital, Mike in passing, and out of the corner of his mouth, muttered "Could have been the wire, Jim." The timing was perfect.

'The World Championships were held in Gawler, Australia, 1986. New Zealand, not renowned for their dressage skills, were doing very well after dressage – in fact the team must have been well up the board and beating the UK. With the party well under way, I had a sudden thought – must ring Tucker to give him a progress report. His answer: "Didn't even know that you *******s knew how to spell the word dressage." This perhaps started all those after-hours calls!

'When I first started to travel as chairman of directors it was Mike who found me a home to stay at within the Tetbury area, and a car to get around in – more than once in fact. I was always made very welcome.

'At Badminton, having just got off the plane that morning, I was starting to walk the cross-country before the competition began and was deep in thought. A voice out of nowhere was heard: "Mr Jim Wright from New Zealand can be seen approaching jump six." He never missed an opportunity.

'Mike was a good friend, confidant, with a quick wit and a tremendous sense of humour. I had many long discussions with him on the sport and the people involved in it, both over the phone and face to face. It was not always easy being a selector when one cannot always be there. He was my eyes, and his in-depth, honest comments and advice were very valuable both to me and New Zealand.

'I have had the pleasure of hosting the Tuckers at our hill country farm many times, enjoying his company and his comments on New Zealand, farming, the equestrian world, hunting, and families. An honour and a privilege to have known him. He will be sadly missed.'

Top: The BBC team at the Athens Olympics: *(left to right back row)* Steve Hadley, Chris Lewis, Mike Tucker, Rishi Persad; *(left to right front row)* Lorna Clark, Angela Tucker, Ali Bruce-Ball.

Above: Mike with Ian Stark in Hong Kong, 2008 Olympics. [Courtesy of Kit Houghton]

Left: Mike with Nick Brooks-Ward in the commentary box at Olympia. [Courtesy of Kit Houghton]

Above: Mike checking out a water obstacle at the Rio Olympics, 2016

Below: The imposing arena at Greenwich, London Olympics, 2012. [Courtesy of Kit Houghton]

Left: Mike at the 1992 Barcelona Olympics with Wolfgang Feld, course designer.

Above: Mike testing the water at the Lion Bridge, Burghley 1997. [Courtesy of Kit Houghton]

Left: The final combination on the cross-country course at the World Equestrian Games, Jerez 2002. Called by Mike 'the most difficult task I ever had in cross-country design'.

Below: The technical delegates at the first four-star event at Lexington, 2004: *(left to right)* Mike Etherington-Smith, Mike Tucker, Barry Roycroft, Cara Whitham, Wayne Quarles.

Bottom: The élite of the international eventing officials meeting at Blenheim in 2004 for the first safety seminar ever, which was led by Mike.

Above: A presentation to Mike by Peter O'Sullevan in recognition of work done internationally on eventing safety.

Below: Presentation to Mike at Badminton 2017, on behalf of the UK major shows and events where Mike had commentated for television, to mark his retirement: *(left to right)* Lord Vestey, Mike, the Duchess of Cornwall, Hugh Thomas, Lizzie Bunn, Elizabeth Inman. [Courtesy of Kit Houghton]

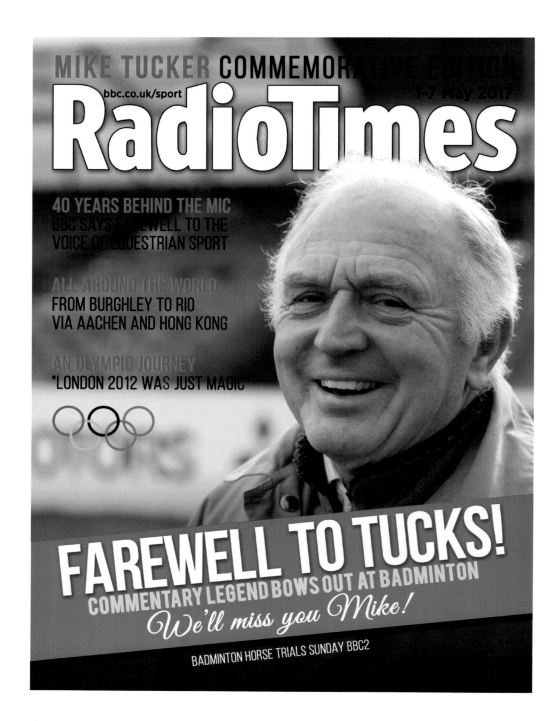

The BBC's director of sport, Barbara Slater, who produced Badminton herself for a few years, came up with the idea of getting a special front page of the *Radio Times* made and framed, paying tribute to Mike. It was a lovely idea and Liz Thorburn, his BBC producer in Rio and at so many other events, made a great job of having it designed and produced.

Top: A gathering of celebrities at Tetbury for the ride and drive challenge.

Above: Some of the ride and drive stars including HRH Princess Anne, Lucinda Green, Mark Todd and Richard Dunwoody, collecting for charity at Tetbury Horse Trials.

Left: A near miss!

Above: Mike on the grey D'Argent, as field master of the Beaufort.[© Bristol United Press]

Below: All Mike's family and grandchildren.

As was the case with his commentary work, in his official roles Mike was held in high regard by all those who worked alongside him and was generous in his willingness to help. **Mike Etherington-Smith**, who often worked alongside Mike, commented that 'On a professional note, Mike was undoubtedly the best technical delegate I have been fortunate enough to work with. Why I say best was that he made me, as a course designer, think and justify my plans. We worked together as technical delegate and course designer at many events, including at Fair Hill in the USA in 1989 where I was the technical delegate for a three-year stint and he was the course designer, and then for three years at Kentucky where our roles were reversed. We also worked together at Tetbury Horse Trials where I was technical adviser and he was organiser and course designer.'

Regarding Fair Hill, the following is an extract from an article by past executive director, **Charles T. Colgan**:

> In 1989 the organisers of the Chesterlands three-day event were looking for a new site for its CCI***. They were directed to Fair Hill and enlisted the aid of Trish Gilbert. When they saw the area of Fair Hill they knew its gently rolling terrain, meandering streams, and thick, lush turf made it the ideal venue for eventing.
>
> A Founder's Committee was formed and they secured the services of England's Michael Tucker, a world-renowned expert, to design a cross-country course that was worthy of its surroundings. Like a talented sculptor who "sees" the image within the marble, Tucker accepted the challenge. By blending the obstacles, the water, and the galloping lanes with the natural contours of the land, he produced a course that exceeded expectations. Mr duPont would have been proud.
>
> The first event was conducted in October 1989, and the CCI*** was won by Karen Lende [better

known today as Karen O'Connor] on Nos Ecus.

Tucker continued to apply his magical touch to Fair Hill for eight more years until, in 1999, he passed the reins to Derek di Grazia, a retired eventer who had won the third edition of the Fair Hill CCI*** in 1991.

Angela remembers: 'When we were on official duty at Fair Hill, when Mike was course designer and I was on the ground jury, it used to cause mirth when Mike would say to me on the radio "Darling, what do you want to do about …?" It was always made into a bit of a joke and I was known as "Madame President"! Of course, this would be considered conflict of interest nowadays!'

I also remember this particular trip so well! Malcolm, my husband, was invited to go as commentator for the inaugural running of Fair Hill and I accompanied him as 'assistant'. Mike was course designer and it promised to be an entertaining trip. (Our first task was helping to finish painting some of the cross-country fences under Trish's direction!) The competition was a huge success, and Mike's course rode well. On the Saturday night, there was a fancy dress party and somehow we were all kitted out in various outfits. Most appropriately, Tucks was dressed as a Friesian cow (I have no idea where it came from, although Katrin Norinder might have been responsible!) As ever, Mike threw himself enthusiastically and wholeheartedly into the role and we have a photo adorning the wall of our downstairs loo of Mike on hands and knees, mooing at the camera, accompanied by Malcolm wearing a borrowed Batman outfit, Katrin dressed as Minnie Mouse and me in something bizarre I'd cobbled together. It was a great party!

On the way home, Mike was on the same flight as us. We were extremely fortunate to be upgraded to club class, which we considered excellent news. When we had settled down into our seats, Malcolm announced that he would have one glass of champagne and then take a "sleeper". He put on his eyeshades and nodded off. Well, Tucks and

I thought that was far too boring, so we made the most of everything that was on offer. We started with champagne, then moved on to wine (with dinner of some description) and I rather think we even enjoyed a glass of port afterwards. The journey passed very quickly. It was towards the end that we began to feel a tad sleepy, and dropped off. We were all too soon woken by the 'ding-dong' heralding wake-up time. Malcolm removed his eyeshades, stretched and said he had slept really well and was ready for breakfast. Tucks and I, needless to say, felt absolutely terrible. We often laughed about it in later years but it didn't seem so funny just then!

One person with whom Mike had a long relationship, involving both of them in various official roles, was **Guiseppe della Chiesa**. During his eulogy at Mike's memorial service, **Giles Rowsell** recalled that 'One of Tucks's specialities was having his own names for some of his friends … Guiseppe della Chiesa from Italy was always greeted as "The big cheese" … followed by *"Voltare, cantare, one cornetto".*' The gentleman in question was an international event rider, is now a leading FEI official, and worked with Mike on numerous occasions. **Guiseppe** recalled how he first met Mike and how he subsequently worked with him in various official roles. 'If my memories are right I think I first met Mike when I was based in Great Britain competing with my horses in 1991/92. However, I may perhaps have met him even earlier when visiting for Badminton. We worked together at many events in different capacities and the following are the main ones I can remember.

'The first time it was the 1994 World Equestrian Games at Jerez de la Frontera, where Mike was course designer and I was assistant technical delegate to Guy Otheguy. We met again at the 1995 European Young Rider European Championships in Pratoni del Vivaro, where he was technical delegate and I was director of the event. I then asked him to be consultant to the Organising Committee of the 1998 World Equestrian Games in Pratoni del Vivaro, where again I was director for the eventing and driving competitions.

'Then, of course, there were the Olympics – Sydney, Athens, Hong

Kong, London, Rio. In all of them Mike was involved as a commentator and I was there in different capacities (international technical official, consultant to the Organising Committee, technical delegate, chairman of the FEI Eventing Committee) – but there was always time to have a beer together and "put the world to rights"!

'Also, he has been of tremendous support during my time as Badminton's course designer. This was not officially working together, but much more. He was a friend with deep knowledge about the sport, always ready with a word of advice or support. At the same time, being so close to Mike was not always that easy – the Friday evening at Church Farm was always something special … very special. It is to be noted that I had been there many times before and the main subject of the evening had always been the strongly opinionated comments about the course and especially the course designer and now – I was that man!

'During all these times together we got to know each other better and his help and guidance have been invaluable to me. I will never forget very late evenings with endless discussions regarding the sport, the future direction of eventing and clearly the governing body – the FEI! Talking about the FEI, it goes without saying that Mike was instrumental in my (initially very reluctant decision) to accept Hugh Thomas's request that I should serve on the FEI Eventing Committee. I can't say why, but Mike had a very strong belief that I was the right person for the position and he managed to convince me that I had a "moral obligation" to do something for the sport! (Clever man …!)

'I only understood much later why he was so keen to have me in the FEI. He finally had somebody to blame personally for all he didn't like in the direction of the sport! To be honest, we had many discussions on the evolution of the sport and if, at times, we might have had different approaches, Mike was very modern and pragmatic in his thinking and we always agreed that the sport we loved could have a future only if we were prepared to share, evolve, and even change something if necessary! Joking with Mike I would often tell him he was the most "international" British person I had ever met – he was easy, open-minded, great fun and had a special gift of being able to create a terrific team spirit wherever he was involved.

'Mike and Angela became real friends and we had memorable holidays together skiing in the Alps or exploring game reserves in South Africa. During these holidays the promise was that anything to do with horses and/or eventing would be banned from any conversation, but inevitably after a few days we regularly broke the promise and ended up discussing our beloved sport.

'Mike surely loved horses and cows and knew a lot about them, but mostly he loved people, of whom he had a great knowledge!

'Mike has been such a motivator and mentor for all the people who had the privilege to know him and/or work with him. He had the extraordinary ability to make everybody feel important, special, unique – and working with the team for the 1998 World Equestrian Games it was no different. Everybody adored him and the team spirit he managed to create on that occasion is probably one of the greatest lessons I will remember from him.'

Just as Mike and Guiseppe moved on from jumping courses to designing them, so did **Sue Benson,** formerly Hatherley, an international event rider who went on to become course designer at the London Olympics 2012. Sue explained how Mike's support helped her as she developed that role. 'I think I first met Mike when his wife, Angela, was competing at Ledyard Farm in Massachusetts USA in 1973. I was the new kid on the block then, but I soon felt part of "the team" as Mike's contagious desire for a party and a prank became the new normal. I remember him being such fun! The following year a British contingent, myself included, returned to America for a re-run and Mike was then a competitor. So, although we enjoyed a distant friendship, our paths only crossed at competitions. Later, when Mike retired from competition, he ran his own horse trials and designed the cross-country courses there. The Tetbury Horse Trials created a great awareness for me of Mike's designing skills, for they were exciting courses to ride – very imaginative and quite challenging. His designing career must have taken off from these early beginnings.

'I continued to compete right into the 1990s with notable achievements at three European Championships (gold and silver team medals) as well as wins at British Open and Novice Championships, and placings at Burghley and Badminton to add to that all-important early win in America in 1973. All this spanned nearly twenty-five years and by the time I had married, had two children and endured the inevitable ups and downs of the sport I was lurching towards retirement. In my heart I wanted to move on but I had become so entrenched in the habit of competing, and so loved my horses, that it was proving difficult to make the right move. This is where Mike came to my rescue. In conversation at some gathering in the early 1990s he must have asked me what plans I had for my future. I had, by then, spent several years writing articles for *Eventing* magazine (no longer in circulation), many of which were reviews of cross-country courses at the major events. The times I spent quizzing the designers and listening to their thoughts and interpretations regarding their designs fascinated me. So, when questioned by Mike, I replied that I would like to become a course designer. No more was said and the conversation melted into thin air. After all, it was just a fleeting notion on my part, at the time.

'In the spring of 1992 Mike made that first call, which was eventually to change the course of my life and give me an entire second career. Bicton Horse Trials in Devon was in the process of changing its organisation and officials. Mike suggested to them that they give me the task of designing all their courses – novice, intermediate and advanced. I remember him telling me that it would be a great event to start at because it couldn't get any worse than it was already! Nevertheless, in retrospect this was probably one challenge too far for me as a complete beginner. However, as a long-time top international competitor I was, in those days, regarded as well qualified. I remember Mike urging me to take on the task and promising to support me at every stage of the process. His belief in me was motivational, and he was true to his promise.

'On my first visit he took a whole day out of his busy schedule to walk the site with me and kick-start a few ideas – the process then continued without him and I messed up a couple of early designs. I would tell the builders what to build – in those days few fences were built as portables in a workshop – and then, when I arrived to view their handiwork, I would realise that what had looked good on paper was totally unjumpable in reality. Many posts went into the ground and came out again in that first year. During this process Mike returned a couple of time to view the "nearly finished" courses. I think my fences were probably rather "Pony Club" but he never made me feel inadequate or unqualified for the task, and his advice was always given with tact and humour. Looking back, I think he must have wondered what he had let himself (and me) in for. I had good ideas and knew my distances for related strides, but had no "feel" for where best to site them! After all, my whole riding career had been geared around jumping cross-country fences and I had not given much thought to why they were where they were!

'The competition, in that first year, has one stand-out memory. I thought I had done a great job and was waiting for the accolades, instead of which Andrew Nicholson (my hero of the next generation of riders) told me that he thought all three courses were "crap". I was humiliated, crushed and understandably upset, as my "high" turned to "low" in the blink of an eye. When Mike rang at the end of the weekend to ask how it had all gone I told him that Andrew had thought everything was crap so I was considering my resignation. Mike seemed dismayed and told me that he had never regarded me as a "quitter". I had wanted sympathy but received a sensible kicking instead. So I picked myself up, dusted myself down and worked hard on the following year's courses, hiring better builders and gaining a better understanding of what was required. I could not say I was a Mike Tucker prodigy. He had far too many other aspects to his life, but he listened and cared in a random conversation and then pointed me in a new direction. He supported me in that first year and then let me make the journey on my own, and I have never forgotten his kind and steady hand.

'More jobs came my way – Bramham, Gatcombe, Thirlestane, Boekelo in Holland – all top-end events, and then a breakthrough – the Pan American Games in Rio de Janeiro in 2007. Without qualified builders, and with most of my designs lost in translation, this was by far the hardest challenge of my career. By then I had long been on my own as a top designer – no Mike to help and support me, no one on the end of a telephone. I nearly walked out, but Mike's words echoed in my ears: "I never thought you were a quitter."

'Then, unbelievably, I was hired as the cross-country course designer for the London 2012 Olympic Games – the pinnacle of a career that was inspired some twenty years earlier by Mike Tucker. As the first horse entered the start box for that Olympic cross-country course I knew that Mike was in the BBC commentary box, waiting to tell the world how the competition would unfold – I can't imagine his thoughts, but I hoped he was proud of himself and me.'

Sue was not the only course designer at the London Olympics to benefit from Mike's support. **Nick Brooks-Ward** recalled: 'Perhaps my abiding memory of my travels abroad with Mike was to the World Cup Finals in Kuala Lumpur in 2006, run by an old friend in Peter Winton. It was the first time that Malaysia had hosted the World Cup Finals and at the same time the FEI General Assembly was being held there – so the great and the good of world horse sport were watching the Finals.

'London had just been awarded the Olympic Games for six years' time and there was a lot of talk at the finals that a foreign course designer was favourite to design the showjumping courses in London. In Mike's words that was unacceptable, as we had our own brilliant course designer in Bob Ellis. Mike gathered the troops – the first vice president of the FEI, the jumping director of the FEI and two bureau members – and invited them to my room. How kind, I thought. We opened a bottle of Chivas and chatted gently and the conversation became more fluid as the bottle went down. Then Mike struck the killer blow: "Why won't you consider Bob Ellis as the designer for London?" There was a lot of huffing and puffing – not enough experience, never designed a major championships, not known enough around the world, etcetera. – but that didn't stop him. He kept on saying that perhaps the FEI should appoint him to some more championships, and so on, and so on.

'As we all know, Bob and his team designed the showjumping courses for London and they are now recognised as the best showjumping courses at a major championships ever – Mike sowed the seeds that night.'

Course design ideally requires a good deal of time in which to assess the terrain thoroughly and make detailed plans, but versatility and quick-thinking can be valuable assets on occasion. Mike had a long association with Burghley Horse Trials: he rode there six times (finishing second on Skyborn in 1969) and commentated every year from 1990–2017, except for 2014 when he was engaged with the World Equestrian Games. However, he had not expected to be the course designer in 2001. **Elizabeth Inman**, who is director of Burghley, explained: '2001 was foot and mouth year. It was touch and go whether we were able to run as foot and mouth was confirmed the week we were due to place our abandonment insurance (I will never forget as I was negotiating the cover that very week and of course it became excluded from the cover). We were one of the very few outside "shows and events" that ran that season, with financial underpinning arranged by Bill Henson and British Eventing with the formation of "Friends of Burghley", Horse Trials Support Group and the trade stand exhibitors who, of course, were desperate for us to go ahead as their whole season on the show circuit was ruined.'

At *very* short notice, Mike was appointed as course designer. A quote from the time shows him saying:

'I could never have dreamt on the first of February this year that six months on I would be working with Philip Herbert to put the Burghley cross-country course together. Prior to this Wolfgang Feld had been appointed course designer, but the onset of foot and mouth disease and ensuing problems, together with closure of Burghley Park until July necessitated a re-think. Hence my last-minute appointment to design a course in a relatively short time, requiring the minimum amount of construction.

'If it had not been for the unusually wet winter, plans would have been far more advanced but it meant there were more fences left standing from last year than had been envisaged. With a good number of portable fences, we have been able to show a different course to last year but yet maintain Burghley as a four-star (Championship) test.'

Of the outcome, **Elizabeth** remarked: 'In the event we ran an amazingly successful competition as everyone flocked to Burghley, having been unable to attend other shows that year.' She also told the story of how a particular feature of course design originated from Mike.

'When Mike first designed the course at Burghley he particularly wanted to build a fence on an uphill slope. Eventing rules state that the height of a cross-country obstacle must be measured from a point where the average horse would normally be expected to take off, which can be between one and two metres away. This means that a fence on an uphill slope is measured from a point that is lower than the ground on which the fence itself is standing, thus the fence looks (and will be) considerably smaller than the jump required to clear it actually measures.'

The appearance of an obstacle is just about its most important aspect and the course builders at Burghley explained to Mike that, given the rules on size and location, a fence where he wanted one would not look acceptable for a four-star event. He insisted that his plan required an obstacle in this location, so the only way to overcome the problem was not to change the fence, but to change the ground. Therefore, a teardrop-shaped hump was built in front of the fence, using hardcore covered in turf to raise the approach, levelling out for the last couple of strides prior to take-off. This meant that the fence, approached uphill, could be made to look a properly imposing obstacle.

This design was repeated by Mike on more than one occasion, then taken up by other course designers, and became known as the "Tucker Take-off".'

Some of Mike's roles as an 'official' were rather more to do with bureaucratic matters than 'hands on' endeavours such as course building – and different roles may have provided different levels of personal satisfaction at the time. Mike was, for example, chairman of the Olympia

Horse Show Organising Committee and commentated there for thirty years. Of this role, **Simon Brooks-Ward** observed: 'When the position of committee chairman came up in 2016, there was only one person on the nomination list. Mike became vice chairman and then chairman in 2017. He was quite simply brilliant at the job. He took it seriously and, because he understood the complexity of running an international event, there was no education required. He supported where necessary and questioned where he thought it was right to do so. His judgment was impeccable, and he carried the team. He was the bridge between the executive management and the volunteers who needed a soft hand and a guiding father-like figure. He was exceptional and I predict, confidently, that he would have been the best chairman Olympia will ever have. We will miss the humour, the inspiring and engaging commentary and, most of all, Mike's character and charisma. Olympia's Grand Hall will be an emptier place without him, but Tuck's legacy is that he will be remembered and universally adored by all of us who were under his protective wing.'

While this important position would have involved Mike in a lot of 'admin', it also allowed him free rein to commentate on such events as the dog agility classes and to shout home his grandsons in the Shetland Grand National. However, he was not always engaged in such light-hearted projects.

Hugh Thomas made the observation that: 'There is nothing less glamorous than being a sporting bureaucrat. But Mike's contribution is often overlooked. For I do not know how many years in the 1970s/1980s he was involved with the then Horse Trials Committee, the governing body; he was chairman of its Fixtures Committee and, with his *alter ego* Major Michael Ayshford Sandford, he had to arrange the fixture list and placate the egos of the organisers. He managed the task while still remaining respected and a friend – no mean feat! For a short while he took on the role of chairman of British Eventing – not a happy time as he was in charge when a particular event owned by BE lost a lot of money. He was very unfairly pilloried for much about which he knew very little and for a while the sport lost his input.

'A few years earlier he had been part of a mini pressure group urging change on what was a very outdated governing body. The then chairman, Major Laurence Rook, with the cunning often displayed by war veterans, asked the members of the ginger group to form a working party – usually the best way to smother the initiative of younger people! The subsequent report has, in fact, proved to be the blueprint of most of the governance changes introduced subsequently – not surprisingly, Mike was a key part of that group.'

John Tulloch offered further recollections of the machiavellian nature of committee life. 'There was one little story of Mike and my early days on the Combined Training Committee under Guy Cubitt. (The name was changed after Mike, Hugh Thomas and I did a report in the 1970s entitled *Horse Trials in the 1980s*.) Babe Moseley decided he should introduce two younger members to his Junior Selection Committee and Mike and I were put on. All went well until the FEI decided to introduce the category known as "young riders" and, when discussing the cost of supporting them, and the juniors, at a main committee meeting Mike, with my support, said if we could only afford one such category the funding must go to the young riders. Babe did not agree! From then on he used to find out when Mike was away and call meetings at his house in Tetbury, at one, or two days' notice. After a summer of this, and our non-attendance at his meetings, he complained to Guy and had us replaced on his committee.

'Mike joined the Combined Training Committee of the British Horse Society (BHS) in the mid-1970s when he, Hugh Thomas and I were given the task of producing a paper on the way forward for the sport. In those days we just had a directorship of combined training (initially James Grose, later Peter Hodgson), which was originally a combined office with dressage). In the report we recommended, amongst other things, that the name be changed to "horse trials" and that a regional structure be established (which is the basis of the sport today). We managed to remove the name "eventing" from the British rule book for one year. Frank Weldon disapproved of the regional structure, and, as chairman of the Rules Sub-Committee (which Hugh sat on), immediately re-inserted "eventing" as he claimed that "horse trials" could not be translated into French. Mike and I used to pull Hugh's leg about it, saying he hadn't stood up to Frank – not an easy thing to do!

'Mike was appointed to the FEI Eventing Technical Committee during Pat Carew's [the Hon. Patrick Conolly-Carew] chairmanship. Mike, I seem to remember, served two full terms (eight years) when we were trying to get Hugh elected as chairman. There was strong pressure from the Germans and other federations that Mike should stand down, but Mike stood his ground, remained on the committee and Hugh was elected.

'Mike chaired the Events Sub-Committee for a number of years and put a huge amount of time into it, only reluctantly giving up because of the increased pressure of his media work. Throughout an incredibly complicated and drawn out "political process" from the late 1980s into 1990, which involved the reconstitution of the BEF (British Equestrian Federation) Mike was incredibly supportive and at the end of my term as chairman, was instrumental in organising a "thank you" dinner for me and presentation. He did point out that under the BHS banner horse trials had nominal reserves of over a million pounds while I was bequeathing them a new organisation with zero funds!

'Mike continued on the new horse trials board, serving as chairman for a two-year period. In his time, he served on various other sub-committees, including the Senior Selection Committee when Henrietta Knight was in the chair.'

If some of Mike's official activities were 'trying' at best, there were occasions when his contributions were highly praiseworthy and well received. **Giles Rowsell** underlined Mike's commitment to the sport in these terms: 'The best example of how he would put his hand up to help in difficult times was when, in the wake of a series of eventing tragedies, he took on the chair of the Hartington Committee for British Eventing in 2000. This committee included high-profile people from other sports where risk management was a vital component. It instigated fundamental research and produced guidelines that have shaped equestrian sports worldwide.'

Yogi Breisner, who was performance manager for the British eventing team from 2000–2016, commended Mike on his input to the Safety Committee. He said: 'In my view Mike really embraced the safety aspect and was the one person who instigated and made sure that the recommendations that came out of the Hartington Report were put into practice. Through British Eventing he got the funding together that was used for the research that led to the frangible pin. When he was chairman of BE's Safety Committee, Mike instigated the rule changes particularly for dangerous riding and the stewards' follow-up through the Incident List, and the system that is now used for remedial training of riders who have been pulled up for dangerous riding. Personally I think that Mike's enthusiasm and systematic working made the sport of eventing safer. I don't think that he has been given enough credit for what he did on the safety side of eventing. He always had a genuine concern for the best interests of the sport.'

Musing on changes to the sport since the turn of the century, **Mark Phillips** observed of Mike: 'One of his great passions in life was eventing. When the steeplechase phase went he was probably more upset than most because he knew that this was the beginning of the end of the sport as we all knew it prior to 2000. The intensity of the modern sport means that although horses are galloping for a shorter distance, it's now often eight hundred metres per minute on average footing, which puts extra wear and tear on tendons and ligaments (we seldom went out of a six hundred metres per minute "lick" except on the steeplechase course).

'Mike was also one of the moving lights on how and what could be done to make the sport safer and was instrumental in starting the Transport Research Laboratory development towards the frangible pin.'

Mike was given an award for the work he did on safety, which was presented by Peter O'Sullevan.

As ever with Mike, while there was a great deal of hard work involved in his official roles, it was by no means unusual for moments of humour to surface. **Elizabeth Inman** offered one example: 'On one of Mike's visits to Burghley the ground was quite wet. He had been driving round the course in his Subaru and slid into one of the course fencing posts, at a crossing, causing quite a bit of damage to his car. As he was always a good sport and happy to blame himself, he owned up to his mishap to the course building team. The thing he was most concerned about was that earlier that same morning, he had issued a severe telling-off to one of his farm staff for leaving a new farm Land Rover in a field where the bull had dented it!'

Hugh Thomas recalled that: 'It is well established that Mike was an Olympic animal – from his grooming in Mexico through to his commentary in London and Rio. For many years he was a very highly respected FEI official – course designer at Burghley (European Open Championships) and at Jerez (World Equestrian Games) for example. But there are several less glamorous aspects to his involvement. Prior to his elevation to senior BBC commentator, he was more than willing to play his part as a volunteer. He and I exchanged roles on many occasions but the most memorable for me were Seoul 1988 and Barcelona 1992. At the former he was the volunteer cross-country controller – a position of immense responsibility. We had a rather chaotic dress rehearsal during which, among other disasters, one of our sector stewards picked up a TV cable while driving on the course, cut off all transmissions and caused some twenty-five-thousand-dollars-worth of damage! Mike quite rightly took me (I was the cross-country course designer) to task.

'Four years later I, as controller, had the "pleasure" of reminding him of the past when his rehearsal at the Barcelona Olympics (at which he was FEI technical delegate overseeing cross-country control at the time) degenerated into farce when the motorbikes representing the riders ran out of fuel and none of the doctors turned up at all. He was generous in his admission that his disaster was worse than mine!'

Giles Rowsell recounted some more memorable moments during Olympic Games: 'At Barcelona in 1992 Mike was the cross-country course controller and achieved the distinction of initiating a musical ride crossover between a horse and an ambulance – how they missed each other was a miracle.

'At Atlanta 1996, where I was cross-country course controller, somebody out on the course stopped Marie-Christine Duroy and then, equally mysteriously, let her go again without taking any times. As you can imagine, she was not very happy about this so, finding the French team eating in the same restaurant as us that evening, Tucks presented her with a massive knife from the kitchen, brought her over to me and suggested that she got her own back on me. Later on, the bill for the French team's meal arrived at my table.'

Freelance journalist **Kate Green** was also party to some lighter moments: 'One of my funniest memories will always be when we were at some FEI safety conference in a dire hotel outside Copenhagen. There was a wedding going on with some tempting dance music so Mike and I just sauntered in, wove our way into a crowd of complete strangers, had a very jolly bop and left them all none the wiser! (Drink may have been taken!) There was also the time he was technical delegate and I was press officer at some hairy Europeans at Pratoni and I remember the pair of us shooing sheep off the dressage arena in the early hours.'

Kentucky was the scene of a couple of incidents that would perhaps not be addressed in guidebooks to officialdom. **Giles Rowsell** told this story of a wet day there: 'Another memorable incident occurred when Mike was technical delegate in Kentucky. It had been incredibly wet so he had asked course designer Mike Etherington-Smith to get him some better wet weather gear. All they could find was a bright yellow jacket and trousers, rather like an RNLI outfit. Next morning was wetter than ever and it was almost pitch dark just before the "test ride" that preceded the first competitor. The FEI steward, General Jack Burton, noticed that someone was still walking around in the arena and, on his radio, said "Would someone please get the canary out of the arena!" Mike wore the top and the bottom again separately but never together!'

Provider of canary gear **Mike Etherington-Smith** said: 'Over the years my wife Sue and I were lucky enough to have many great experiences with Mike in different parts of the world. If it was work it was always very professional; if it was play it was always great fun and full of mischief, whether it be dancing on tables (in Kentucky), singing and partying (in Sydney and many other places), or generally playing silly buggers.

'On one occasion when I was course designer in Kentucky we were having supper in Lexington with a group of about ten others, all well known in the eventing world. As always there was a lot of banter and nonsense being thrown around when Mike made some cheeky comment to Sue. Sue drew herself up to her full five feet four inches and said "Right, Tucker …". I then said "Watch out Tucker, now you're in trouble, it's tits on the table time." Mike responded "You call those tits, I've seen bigger tits on my dry old cows!" (You get the level of conversation that evening.) Much hilarity and several unprintable exchanges took place.

'So, the next evening, supper time again, same group of people. Sue, not having much by way of boobs, had put on a cardigan unbuttoned to a point of showing a bit of cleavage and had stuffed some socks in her bra for some pretty obvious enhancement. We made a plan whereby Mike would sit opposite Sue, moved the flowers from the middle of the table so there was a clear view, and waited. What was perfect was that Mike was last to arrive and everyone else was in on what was going on. Roger Haller arrived and gave Sue a hug and said "Gosh, I like that, I'll have another one please" and Sue replied "Roger, get over it, they are socks!" Mike then arrived, sat down, and the usual banter is going on. Mike did not notice a thing despite Sue's best efforts of showing off as best she could. So, comments such as "Things are looking up" and "Tucker, you really need to get abreast of things" started flying around and everyone was almost crying with laughter. Eventually Mike got there! From that moment on, "tits on the table" has been in the vocabulary of some twelve people who fully understand its meaning.'

CHAPTER TWELVE

Field Master
and Steward

Hunting and racing, both longstanding passions of Mike's, were other areas of interest in which he, for some years, took on official roles.

Mike followed the family tradition of embracing hunting and the local hunting community. He hunted with his local pack, the Duke of Beaufort's, all his life and also enjoyed visiting other packs, particularly the Wynnstay, when he would take up his horse and stay with his old friends Jonathan and Sue Clark.

He had many friends from the hunting field and enjoyed days out with the people he'd known from Pony Club days, including **Mark Phillips**, who recalled: 'In the 1960s and 70s, following Mike out hunting was an amazing experience. We used to get into terrible trouble. We went hunting, yes, to follow hounds, but really to educate the young event horses and to jump. If hounds went right, we went left, finding the biggest walls and hedges. One day we jumped a hedge that was so big you couldn't see what was on the other side. Unfortunately, we landed in a seed field and of course we were way beyond the headland and couldn't just turn quickly back. The first person to see us was "Master" – and did we get a telling off!

'We landed in ditches together; jumped into bomb craters – the stories are endless.

'It would be true to say that a lot of my cross-country skills developed from the many experiences following Mike out hunting. He was well-mounted – sometimes on one of my horses – was fearless, and always totally respected the countryside.'

Mike's daughter **Emma** mentioned a family involvement: 'Hunting was the activity that Dad and me did together. He was the one who took me out as a young girl on the lead rein – there is a black and white photo in the tack room of Dad and I jumping a rail alongside each other with the lead rein between us and me looking a little unsure! I soon progressed from the lead rein to following on behind him most Saturdays on an amazing 12.2hh chestnut pony called Monarch owned by the Tilly family. I went hunting with Dad right up until 2017 and in recent years he also enjoyed going out with his eldest grandsons, Josh and Harry, on their ponies. Dad nearly always managed to be in the right place to see what was going on and for some jumping.'

Many working pupils learned their trade in the Tuckers' yard, and some accompanied Mike in the hunting field. **Lorenzo Soprani Volpini** from Italy said of his days at Church Farm: 'Some of the best fun I had with Mike was when he took me out hunting in 1999/2000. Often I was riding a fairly green youngster who needed looking after. Mike was brilliant and always kind. He shared his flask with me: whisky mac was a favourite and I soon grew a bit too fond of it – sometimes when it was particularly cold and wet I got a bit greedy with it. I think he thought this was funny!

'One day we were hacking back through Tetbury. It was a Monday afternoon, and Mike was riding Smokey. We stopped in front of Lloyds Bank where Mike drew some cash from the cashpoint, then he got back in the saddle and fished a sausage out of his hunting coat pocket. He offered me half and off we rode home … I still remember all of it like it was yesterday.

'I was honoured to have known him: all the memories and precious time he spent with me will be treasured forever in my heart.'

Captain Ian Farquhar hunted the Duke of Beaufort's hounds from 1985 to 2011 and was highly respected for his knowledge of hunting and hounds as well as his riding skills across country. Of his long and close association with Mike, he said: 'Mike Tucker had always been a friend and a foxhunter. Though he was a hell of a horseman he didn't just hunt to ride, he took a huge interest in what the hounds were doing (and the huntsman I might add!) and was also fastidious in making sure his own farm was rideable.

'So in 2001, when the post of field master for half the Monday country became available, Mike was an obvious choice. He was a brilliant horseman, a proper hunter and a very capable farmer, the three prerequisites that go a long way to making a good field master. Before 2001 he had always intimated he was just too committed to take on a full-time role but when asked again I remember him saying in that pragmatic way of his "If I don't say yes now I will be too old, so yes I'm on for it."

'As well as his other abilities he was, of course, also great fun and a slightly devilish sense of humour was never far below the surface. I can still see the slight look of uncertainty on the faces of a number of important visitors who were not sure if they were being admonished or having their legs pulled – probably a bit of both!

'Mike was wonderfully supported by Angie, Andrew and Emma, and Church Farm was the venue of some memorable teas and parties. It was a sad day when, in 2009, Mike announced that again the pressure of work was building up and he thought it time to retire. I personally will always remember him on a grey horse quietly negotiating the country as though it just came naturally – which, of course, in his case it did. Thank you Mike, from all of us, for your fun and your friendship and for a job well done.'

However, as recalled by **Peter Sidebottom** (Beaufort field master on a Saturday for ten seasons) and his wife Debbie, a subscriber, Mike's role as field master had an inauspicious start! 'It was Mike's first Monday as a field master – so there was much banter at the meet. It was not very long before we had to pop a little wall and needless to say Mike's horse did a very strange jump and he fell off right in front of me!

'There was further banter and "Welcome to the pressure of field-mastering!". Going forward, not even an hour later, he sent my wife and me on point and we were sitting very quietly waiting for some action … when suddenly Mike's horse appeared without him – so we took great delight in handing back his horse to a very cross and red-faced Mike! We could not contain our laughter one bit. Going forward again about two hours or so after second horses, I was following him into a stone cattle barn yard – my horse exited to the right and Mike's to the left – but Mike went straight ahead, alone yet again! This time, when handed back the horse all I got for thanks was "You bloody Sidebottoms are jinxing me – bugger off and go home"! Well, we laughed all the way home!

'He was actually a fantastic field master, who gave us many a fun Monday following him – rarely falling off again! A legend of a man whom we shall miss very much.'

Jane Tuckwell – daughter of Major Gerald Gundry, legendary master of the Beaufort and assistant director at Badminton Horse Trials – also has fond memories of days out hunting with Mike: 'We all had a lot of fun hunting with Mike, especially when he was the Monday field master. There was a day when he was standing with the field at the end of a long valley. I was often lucky enough to be told to go ahead, which I was doing on one particular occasion. Having cantered on, I heard hounds behind me and looked back to see not only hounds but also the fox! All Mike said when he caught up with me was "Seen the fox Miss Gundry?" and this would always be his greeting when he first saw me on the days we hunted together in the future!

'Always, when Mike was involved, events ended with a jovial twist to them!'

Janie Dear, a Beaufort Hunt subscriber told me: 'I remember when my children were little and out hunting, Mike would be field-mastering on his grey TB, D'Argent, who kicked ferociously. A red ribbon was always *in situ* but quite often at the top of the tail, completely out of sight to a child on a 12.2hh. Even so, the children all knew. They all wanted to be upsides him and, as far as I know, contact was never made!

'When Mike was not acting as field master, he took his own line. On many occasions, hounds would be running and he would be out there two fields to the left, or right, frolicking over a line of hedges and up there in exactly the right place. I can picture him now – black coat, leggy grey horse, ears pricked, easy fluid jumping.'

Jane Sale, who acts as cross-country timekeeper at Burghley, was another rider who emphasised Mike's willingness to engage with young hunt followers and Pony Club members: 'When accompanying The Elms prep school on hunting trips as "hunting nanny" to follow the Duke of Beaufort's hounds, I was so impressed that Mike would always take considerable time to chat with and compliment the young pupils, despite having the responsibility of being field master for the day. The warm welcome and encouragement received by the young visitors, always accompanied by his friendly smile, meant that this outing became the highlight expedition of each season.

'Mike gave his time to commentate at plenty of Pony Club events. It was a joy to hear his well-informed and familiar voice at smaller local events – there seemed a genuine understanding that each performance, however junior, mattered hugely to each competitor, and when things went awry there was always a kind and encouraging comment.'

She also referred warmly to his influence as a commentator and his ability to combine a capacity for fun and mischief with a never-failing work ethic: 'Mike's voice and commentary were synonymous with every top equestrian occasion I had attended for as long as I can remember. I felt incredibly lucky to have enjoyed meeting him latterly whilst staying at Fishponds Farm for Burghley. Never short of an entertaining story, with a self-deprecating humour, he was excellent company, recounting many hilarious tales of high jinks from days long past late after supper, but never failing to prepare for the following day's work.'

Mike always loved the chance to get back on the stage and, when he had time, would enthusiastically join in fund-raising activities. **Fi Mitchell,** an old friend and neighbour, recalled a couple of those occasions. 'Mike was involved with a few Beaufort Hunt fundraising events. In 2012 *Beaufort's Got Talent* was staged at the theatre (now The Barn Theatre) at Ingleside House, Cirencester, by kind permission of Ian Carling. Mike had joined the Cirencester Operatic Society in this same theatre while he was at the Royal Agricultural College. He compèred this event with great panache and a large amount of humour and also gave a rousing rendition of "Ain't Nothing like a Dame". The lyrics may not have been recognised by Rodgers and Hammerstein! The presiding judges were Martin Scott and Nigel Peel, and the Beaufort showed a great deal of talent!

'In 2013 Tim Sage and I made *Gone in the Wind*, a film with seven sketches. Mike agreed to play the lead role in "The Dream", which was about a commentator who falls asleep and is commentating on a very unusual dressage competition. It turns out to be a nightmare! Angela too, played her part, dressed as Maria von Trapp on an Olympic dressage horse, no less!

'When Mike arrived for filming, he apologised for being a bit late. He sat down, read through the script, asked a couple of questions and then delivered the script without mistake whilst watching the already filmed section to link the two together. Not until he was leaving did he mention that the reason for his delay had been because his favourite hunter, D'Argent, had been injured in the field. Mike had played his part in the film as though it was his day job, quite brilliantly.'

D'Argent, the grey horse mentioned by Ian Farquhar, Janie Dear and Fi Mitchell, ranked as one of Mike's favourite hunters. A former racehorse, acquired from the Bunters who had him in training with Alan King, he was a wonderful jumper, allowing Mike to take his own line over the biggest country. Here is an extract from an article Mike wrote on retired racehorses from Alan King's yard:

> "D'Argent, by Roseliere (Fr) out of Money Galore (Ire) (Monksfield) has hunted with the Duke of Beaufort's for three seasons now and is being prepared for his fourth. Having jumped around most

of the Grand National (2008) there was never any doubt that he had the jump, but with quite a lot of our country being stone walls and post and rails the first two seasons were taken quite quietly to settle down his enthusiasm and get him to jump carefully enough, particularly over the stone walls.

Although quite spooky he was a super ride from day one, with a lovely mouth, which has always made him easy to hold even in company out hunting. When in off grass or when particularly fresh, he loves to throw a decent buck or two, so one can't relax too much. In his first season when out on exercise he was quite savagely attacked by two Staffordshire bull terriers which certainly left their mark with twenty stitches needed to repair the damage. Not surprisingly he is now pretty timid with dogs but is improving all the time. He was a very good patient and is also a lovely horse to do in the stables, making him the clear favourite in the yard.

Last season was the first that I took him up to the front of the field and on two occasions we cut loose and flew, once over most of the cream of the Beaufort Saturday country, with the second time being with the thrusters of the Wynnstay where he more than held his own over some very decent old-fashioned country. There really haven't been many better rides in my hunting experience and D'Argent was a superstar."

It was a sad day for all the family when, the week before Mike died, the necessary decision was taken to have the horse put down following a severe leg injury.

In the light of initial tributes to Mike that he had read, **James Crosbie Dawson**, a Beaufort regular, wrote this letter to *Horse & Hound*, which underlines how much Mike was valued in the hunting world as a true countryman, just like his grandfather before him.

Sir

> *One aspect of Mike Tucker's very busy life that has only been mentioned briefly in the various tributes to him, is his field-mastering in the Beaufort Monday country. During his eight or so seasons, he kept the area open, largely due to the fact that he knew all the people responsible well, and he farmed an important part of it himself. This was always well foxed and easy to cross. His sound farming knowledge was a big asset. Mike had a relaxed attitude to the job and made sure it was fun for everyone involved. Almost never a cross word or raised voice, he was particularly tolerant of genuine fox hunters. I only remember him getting wrong-footed once, just after he took over. The dog hounds slipped over the Cirencester Road from Georges' Gorse and took a bit of catching on the way to Newnton Gorse, his covert. He had a good eye, along with the advantage of being a brave and excellent horseman. I do not remember him frightening us, but he crossed the country with ease. In quiet moments he had a uncanny knack of following conversations, often coming up with a knowing remark and a smile several fields on! Inevitably hunting has changed, but those of us who followed him were lucky.*

> *James Crosbie Dawson*

Mike's involvement with hunting is perhaps best summarised by his long-time friend and colleague **Giles Rowsell**: 'He was first and foremost a farmer and countryman, with his roots firmly in the Beaufort Hunt country. His mother was born on the estate and hunting became central to his life. He became an outstanding field master with all the attributes to help people to enjoy themselves whilst maintaining proper standards in the field.

'Mike's hallmark was that any job should be done properly – high standards, honesty and integrity dominated every part of his life, plus enormous energy – but ensuring that whatever you did should be fun.'

In addition to his love of hunting, Mike always nurtured a passion for racing but his early enthusiasm as a point-to-point jockey was thwarted, as explained by his childhood friend, **William Alexander**: 'Mike toyed with point-to-point racing and rode in five races. This would have been fifty if he'd had his way but his mother's sheer terror completely banjaxed that idea. I think he would have been disinherited if he had continued!'

His dream of General Bugle being a successful racehorse failed to come to fruition but it did establish a long friendship with local trainer **Alan King**, who recalled: 'I first met Mike when I started with David Nicholson in 1985. He sent General Bugle to him to run over fences. (Ran rather slowly at Stratford in a three mile plus novice chase, I think.) We would meet fairly regularly in later years either racing or eventing and he would try to come to the gallops at Barbury once a year and it was always a pleasure to have him here. Rachel and I were having dinner with him a few years ago and I mentioned we were going to retire D'Argent. Mike knew the horse well, having followed his racing career. I put him in touch with Nigel and Penny Bunter. The rest is history and they enjoyed nine years of exciting hunting. Nigel and Penny also became great friends with Mike as they developed Barbury Horse Trials and Mike was heavily involved with the commentary over the years.'

It was my husband, Malcolm, who persuaded Mike that with his love and knowledge of the game he should apply to become a racecourse steward. **Malcolm** explained: 'Towards the end of my time with the Jockey Club as the executive director responsible for stewarding, I recommended to Mike one evening that he should give it a go, knowing how passionate he was about racing. Mike accepted the challenge with all his usual fervour, doing loads of research into the rules and regulations of racing and the way in which the Jockey Club (and, subsequently, the bodies that superseded it) wished them to be interpreted. Needless to say, Mike was a first-class steward, officiating on the Flat and under National Hunt rules. Regrettably, because he started late in life, he wasn't able to do it for very long, having to retire at seventy, but nevertheless, finished his stewarding stint as chairman of the Cheltenham panel for the National Hunt Festival. I received a call from him on his way back from his final day in the stewards' room. He was almost in tears, being the emotional man he was, always wearing his heart on his sleeve, and he thanked me profusely for suggesting he put himself forward as a steward. He told me it was one of the most fulfilling chapters of his life.'

Mike was held in high regard by all those who were fortunate to know him in the racing world; stewards, clerks of the course, trainers and jockeys all had great respect for him.

Trainer **Charlie Longsdon**, also a family friend, said: 'Apart from the fact that Mike was the father of one of my great old friends, Andrew, I also have my own memories of Mike, which revolve around his enthusiasm and interest in what we were doing with our lives as we grew up. We were never the best behaved while staying at Church Farm, but I think that reminded Mike of his youth! More recently, before Mike retired from stewarding, he always had time for a good catch-up on the racecourse and I am probably very lucky that I never got called in front of the stewards while he was in charge!'

Fellow steward **Cherry Jones** commented on Mike's willingness to (literally) 'go the extra mile': 'In 2009 the new racecourse at Ffos Las was opened and there were no "local" stewards. The BHA asked for volunteers to steward there – there were not many takers as it is a long way to travel and not a very fashionable place! Of course Mike volunteered – they always say you should ask a busy person to do something. Often, if I was rostered on the same day, I would leave my car at Church Farm and he would drive on. The long journey was never dull, with his phone ringing constantly and lots of chat. Mike was one of those rare people who was interested in others, enquiring about our little stud and grandchildren. He even invited two grandsons into the commentary box at Olympia. What a special man – I was so sad when he hit the age of seventy and had to retire from stewarding. I do miss him on my drive to Ffos Las.'

Bath racecourse was a little closer to Mike's home, and he was in situ there when **Katie Stephens** arrived: 'I came to Bath as clerk of the course in 2010 and Mike was an established member of the Bath stewarding panel. Obviously I was hugely familiar with "the voice of equestrianism" as I had spent my childhood growing up listening to his commentaries on so many equestrian disciplines. So when I came to work with him as a steward I sort of felt like I knew him already and this was how it was when I actually met him. Mike was always hugely supportive and seemed to have a good level of respect and appreciation of the plight of a clerk's role, and this was always reassuring as it gives you confidence if you believe your stewards demonstrate such understanding. In my experience of Mike, his vast knowledge of the horse and his horsemanship meant that he was so very balanced in his opinions and decisions, which made him a great steward. On a personal level, Mike was a very kind and warm individual and always took time out to ask about my family and how my children were getting on with their riding. I always felt that these were genuine enquiries too, not just conversation fillers, as he would recall with ease what we had chatted about previously. Mike had been retired from stewarding for a couple of years and I missed him from our panel, but was always pleased after his retirement that I still got to hear "the voice" commentating on the world of equestrianism.'

Keith Ottesen, clerk of the course at Chepstow, echoed the way in which Mike would put people at ease upon a first meeting: 'I had never met Mike Tucker and was in awe when I did first meet him but he could not have been a more friendly and helpful individual and above all he was a good and fair steward.'

Mention of Bath and Chepstow triggers a reconnection of an old friendship from Mike's childhood and teenage years. **Richard Smith** was National Hunt amateur champion jockey in 1974 and is a now a steward at both Bath and Chepstow. He farms on Badminton Estate at New House Farm, just six miles from Church Farm and explained that thus the 'Smith and Tucker families go back a long way as Mike's mother Betty was great friends with my uncle.'

Furthermore, he recounted of Mike, 'We were in the Beaufort Pony Club together, although Mike was a couple of years older and in another ride. We had great fun. Most of our activities centred around Highgrove. The Bullen family were with us, as was Andy Turnell (another National Hunt jockey, renowned for riding very short).

'I loved my racing and Mike went eventing but I was always impressed by his knowledge of and interest in racing, especially jump racing. It was great when he joined us as a steward, for which he had a natural flair. He was a good race-reader and, as ever, very fair. He was a delight to spend a race day with and to work alongside.

'What always impressed me about Mike was the number of people he knew, and the fact that he always found time to stop and exchange a few words.'

Simon Claisse, clerk of the course at Cheltenham, had common interests with Mike, and was another individual who benefited from his steadfast support in times of difficulty: 'A shared love of hunting and farming meant that our course walks round Cheltenham were rarely limited to discussions about racing but, when needed, Mike's knowledge and experience were invaluable to the racecourse when we faced challenging circumstances – and we had a few of those. The 2013 Festival springs to mind when, despite the covers being down over the course, the ground was frozen underneath after temperatures dropped to -12°C overnight. At ten-thirty, with Mike's support we gave the go-ahead for a delayed start at two o' clock, both of us putting our heads on the block as it was still below freezing, with the ground still frozen in places. The next couple of hours passed, oh so slowly, but come two we were just okay! Every year when pre-season the BHA put together the stewards' rosters, I always tried to make sure that Mike was in the chair on the days we knew we could expect challenges.'

(Later, in a tribute to Mike in the Cheltenham racecard for the eighteenth of April 2018, Simon added to these thoughts with the following words: 'Mike was a brilliant steward, the guy you wanted in the chair and by your side when things got tough; his knowledge and experience were invaluable to a clerk of the course, and within racing circles he was held in very high esteem. Thoroughly professional in his approach, impeccable in manner, he was someone whose judgement you could trust and, even when faced with serious challenges, he was always fun to be with. Our thoughts are with Angela and all his family.')

Lord Rathcreedan, a fellow steward of Mike's at Cheltenham, was also a fellow enthusiast for cattle and another person who appreciated having Mike at his side in tricky moments: 'I got to know Mike initially through his farming activities. He was a most enthusiastic and talented cattleman and I always enjoyed my conversations with him on the fascinating world of cattle breeding. He thought deeply about the subject and developed a fine herd of Holstein cows, which we eventually sold for him before he and Andrew turned their attention to breeding Wagyu cattle. He was also an excellent racecourse steward – one of the best I have officiated with in many years. Stewarding with Mike was always fun and his impish sense of humour was never far from the surface. However, I felt safe when Mike was alongside me, as he was always both sensible and decisive. The enquiry into the finish of the Cheltenham Gold Cup of 2014 was one of the most testing I have faced in many years of stewarding with the first two horses Lord Windermere and On His Own veering across the course on the run to the line before the former won by a short head. I couldn't have had anyone better than Mike next to me and after much deliberation we allowed the result to stand. I think most people believe we got it right!'

Simon Cowley, a stipendiary steward (a professional steward employed by the BHA), said 'Mike brought a wealth of expertise and experience to racecourse stewarding from his time in other equestrian disciplines and applied that wisdom with great tact and fairness. Above all it was a pleasure to work with him because of his great good humour and ready smile; if he was on duty you knew that whatever troubles the racing produced, you would enjoy the day because he was there. I hope that these poor words can give some idea of how much we all enjoyed working with him.'

Long-time friend **Giles Rowsell**, who worked extensively with Mike in official roles in eventing, was also an observer of his rapport with trainers and jockeys, that somehow managed to transcend his sartorial idiosyncrasies: 'I know how much the trainers (and jockeys) respected Mike for his sensible judgements and fairness and they even managed to keep a straight face when he wore his trademark leather sleeveless jacket.'

He also recalled that Mike's enthusiasm for racing continued beyond his official role: 'After his retirement on reaching seventy we had a wonderful day's racing with the whole family and the Killingbecks at Cheltenham in a private box – a day I shall always remember, not least as a very rare day when I made some money. Mike's grandsons thought I knew what I was doing, so before each race they asked: "What are we backing this time, Mr Rowsell?" They eventually found out that I did not have a clue.'

Another long-time friend of Mike's, with whom the racing connection transcended the mere Thoroughbred and entered the exalted realm of the Shetland (ask Mike's grandsons, if you're unsure on this point) was **Philip Mitchell**, a racehorse trainer, formerly based at Epsom and best known for his exploits with the multiple Group race winner, Running Stag. He is now based in Lambourn with his wife Trish, where they run a successful horse transport business. Philip recalls that: 'We first met Mike about thirty years ago at a dinner with "The Duke" (David Nicholson) and immediately a friendship blossomed as we were clearly on the same wavelength, with a similar mischievous sense of humour!

'We became more involved with him again when our sons, Jack and Freddie, were riding in the Shetland Grand Nationals at Olympia. This led to us retaining a strong involvement with these races and the series that leads up to Olympia. Mike played such a big part in making them so popular amongst those watching through his enthusiastic commentaries.

'In 2012 Mike approached me to see if Trish and I could help his young grandsons, who were then in Australia, get involved with the Shetland racing as he said he'd love to see them competing at Olympia. First we had Josh, who was successful on Snowman winning at Olympia in 2015 and then in 2017 it was Harry's turn winning on Lilly. In reality this was a great achievement that came to fruition as a result of Mike's forward thinking and planning but, more importantly, through his great enthusiasm. Trish and I have not only enjoyed all our involvement with the boys and the Shetlands but, more importantly, our friendship with Mike and Angela.'

To further emphasise the importance of Shetland racing, not only as a high point in Mike's commentary career, but in the great scheme of things overall, National Hunt jockey **Sam Twiston-Davies** recalled an anecdote from his days as a budding jockey in the Shetland Pony Grand National at Olympia. 'Mike was always incredibly good with all us young jockeys taking part in the Shetland Grand National and would take time to get to know us and offer a few kindly words of support and advice. I can remember one quite funny moment. It was at Olympia and the Shetland Pony race had taken place and we were doing our lap of honour when my pony bolted with me and hurled me, at some speed, into the side of the arena … not put off by the whole thing I leapt up, dusted myself down, whereupon the kind words of Mike rang out, "Never mind, Sam, it's not the worst thing that will happen to you in your future life as a jockey" – and rest assured he was absolutely right! We always galloped around to the tune Reach for the Stars, which is for me forever synonymous with the Shetland Grand National – that day I did not reach for the stars but found myself rolling around on the deck!'

CHAPTER THIRTEEN

Farming and Family Life

As explained in Chapter Eight, Mike and Angela were married at the very start of 1972, and their daughter Emma soon arrived. In this final chapter, I am going to focus on Mike and Angela's family life centred on Church Farm because, while he embraced a number of roles successfully, with grace, integrity and good humour, Mike was, at heart, a great farming and family man.

Angela, clearly, has been a major source of information about family matters. Having, herself, competed whilst unwittingly carrying Emma as a 'passenger', she remarked pragmatically that 'Mike was hunting the day Andrew was born in February 1976, but managed to get out of his dirty breeches and arrived with flowers just in time.'

She provided a succinct yet affectionate summary of how the workload was shared in the family home: 'Home life? Well, Mike never changed a nappy. Mind you, along with neither grooming nor plaiting his horse nor cleaning his tack, he wasn't much good at cooking either (but neither was I in fact to start with!). He could sort of muck out in "cattle fashion" … but then I never seriously drove a tractor! However, putting out the rubbish was a bit of a discussion point which is probably the same in every household!'

Commenting on the subsequent process of raising young children in a household dominated by equestrian and farming activity, she said: 'Our children were amazing at amusing themselves with a wonderful array of grooms who would double up as nannies. I was always busy with the horses and running the house and Mike was non-stop with the farm and riding when he could. It was difficult for the children when both parents were riding at events but they were brilliant and used to go off and find friends to play with and would return periodically to ask if Daddy had gone wrong in the dressage again or if Mummy had gone too slowly cross-country to win a rosette! Our grooms were fantastic in looking after them and we never seemed to have any dramas with them when we were at a competition, which is incredible.

'Looking back, it could be tricky when both Mike and I were competing because it was unlikely we would both go well on the same day. Driving back in the lorry was hard because one of us would be on a high whilst needing to commiserate with the other – never easy!'

Andrew explained that 'Emma and I always joke that it was our grandmother and the working pupils who brought us up because Mum and Dad were so busy with other things. Because Mum and Dad were still competing we were either dragged along to events or stayed with Granny Tucker, who lived at Slads Farm.'

Regarding the times when she and Andrew accompanied their parents to events, **Emma** recalled that 'Andrew and I spent a lot of time with Mum and Dad travelling to one-day events in a car or a horsebox. Dad enjoyed music and singing (although I don't believe he could play a musical instrument) and I have fond memories of singing along with him to songs by the Carpenters, Neil Diamond and Abba. [The same music that Mike used to help maintain his concentration on late-night drives home from commentary work.] A particular favourite of ours was the last song on one Abba album called, "Thank You for the Music".'

Returning to the topic of working pupils, **Andrew** explained: 'We grew up around a lot of the working pupils and had so much fun. I put a lot of Emma's and my social skills down to our upbringing. I was never interested in horses and was put off from a young age. I was much more interested in motorbikes, tractors, rugby and shooting. I had a mini motorbike when I was younger and I loved it. I would take it to the various events and do slip collecting, which was fun and yet served a purpose!'

Emma recalled that: 'Most of Andrew's and my days started with breakfast with Dad in the kitchen, which comprised Frosties and milk and a cooked breakfast from the Aga's bottom oven. Mum was already out doing the horses and/or tidying up the house at this time. Sometimes we would help Dad to make up the milk for the newly weaned calves before going to school. Dad milked dairy cows at Church Farm until 2008.

'Christmas was always at the farm as there were horses to look after and cows to milk. My Mum's sister, Felicity (Flick for short), my uncle Robert and my cousins, Charlotte and Beth, used to come most years to stay. There was always the big decision as to when to have the Christmas meal. We, the children, were always keen to have Christmas lunch so that we could open our presents as early as possible, but Dad understandably used to hate the thought of having a big Christmas turkey lunch and then having to go out and do the milking so, in later years, we had the Christmas meal in the early evening.'

Andrew's recollections of family meals embraced his father's insistence on good manners: 'I would say Dad was a lot stricter than Mum. Especially with manners, which he clearly got from his Mum, Granny Tucker, who was also very strict on table manners and often used the phrase, "One day you may have tea with the Queen!". We were told only to cut the butter from one end and to take your teaspoon out having stirred your tea and not put elbows on the table, etcetera. Dad also drilled into us about please and thank you – something that I do with the twins, Jack and Ned, now.'

With reference to the children's early schooling, **Angela** explained that 'Emma was a weekly boarder and I remember those awful Monday mornings of tears when I had to take her back to school. Andrew was at a local day school and then went off to Wycliffe where Mike had been.'

Andrew's proudest moment as a schoolboy was when he was playing rugby: 'Because Dad was so busy he was rarely able to come and watch me play sport at school so it was a real highlight when I knew he was coming. One of the most memorable occasions was when I was playing rugby for the second fifteen at Wycliffe against Bristol Grammar School (who we had never beaten) and he came to watch and I scored the winning try playing at scrum half. I think I was probably a bit like him when it came to sport, in that I wasn't naturally talented, but keen and passionate. I just loved playing team sports and going on tour and the team spirit which I know is what Dad enjoyed with the big events – it's being part of a team.'

This shared father-son interest in various sports continued far beyond Andrew's schooldays: 'Dad and I both loved our sport and followed it when we could. Whether it was athletics or Bath Rugby or the Six Nations we just loved watching it, either on the telly or even better, live. Dad and I made several trips to The Rec at Bath and to Twickenham to see England in the Six Nations and Autumn Internationals, especially when he was with the BBC and we could "blag" the odd ticket from Johnnie Watherston when the BBC was covering it! We were incredibly lucky to attend several very special sporting occasions. Emma went to the opening ceremony for the Barcelona Olympics (Emma and I had to toss a coin to see who went!) but Dad's work has enabled us to see some incredible sporting events, including the Olympics.'

On one occasion, getting into a major event provided a moment that Andrew never forgot. He explained: 'At Badminton one year, I clearly remember turning up at the gate and Dad didn't have the right passes. He stopped by the man at the gate and immediately greeted him warmly: "Good morning. How are you? I haven't seen you for ages …" They had a bit of a chat and then the man said, "You haven't got your passes have you?" and Dad said, "No, I've forgotten them, but I promise I've got them at home." And in we went. I remember asking Dad who the man was. He said he didn't know his name but explained he always stopped to have a chat with him on the way into Badminton every year. Dad always stressed to us that being polite and friendly and saying "please" and "thank you" gets you everywhere in life, and here was an occasion which really proved that.'

This story is a perfect example of the code of conduct that Mike followed throughout his life which, coupled with his zest for hard work, enabled him to achieve so much.

Although Emma had fewer sporting interests than her brother, she did, as mentioned in the previous chapter, ride and go hunting with her father – although riding was not always without incident, as **Angela** recalled: 'I remember one occasion when Emma would have been about eleven years old. We were cross-country schooling at home down by the pond. Emma was jumping her pony over a little drop fence and was jumped off. Having dusted her down, I encouraged her to get back on board and have another go. Anyway, she turned a bit green so was taken off to hospital where, after an X-ray, we discovered she had a greenstick fracture. The doctor told me that this was not to be taken lightly and was quite a serious break. I got a proper rap on the knuckles and I felt awfully guilty as you can imagine!'

Meanwhile, 'Andrew decided that three members of the family riding were enough, so he had dogs. Cracker, who arrived at Christmas one year when Andrew was quite small, probably about nine, was his terrier. She was wonderful, a really tough character who survived a number of mishaps. One time, she was enthusiastically joining in a cricket match at home when she managed to get knocked out by a cricket bat, another time she fell off the front of a quad bike and her third life-threatening experience was when she killed a rat in the cow sheds. The rat was by an open bag of hydrogen peroxide and she must have got some in her mouth which burnt her throat. She could never swallow properly after that and had to wear a muzzle to stop her eating things that would hurt her throat. She and Dikler (the Lurcher we were given as a wedding present by Robin Gundry) were great hunting companions and all the pupils and grooms were always worried in case they inadvertently let them out together and they slipped off hunting. Phillip Dutton was with us for a couple of years on and off and he recalls the mortification when he let them out by mistake on more than one occasion! Dogs were such a large part of our family life. I remember once leaving Dikler behind at Claughton Horse Trials. Imagine the horror when we realised we hadn't got him and there were no mobile phones in those days to let anyone know we'd forgotten him. Anyway, fortunately someone rescued him and Jonathan Turner returned him to us, unscathed!'

Of his association with dogs, **Andrew** added: 'Dogs have always been a big part of the Tucker family and in my younger days Dad and I would occasionally take them rabbiting on a Sunday morning. We had one Lurcher called Sky who was amazing.'

Of the family home, he said: 'Church Farm was (and still is) a very busy place. When I was around seventeen and eighteen we had several great summers as the students were all my age. We would all go down for tea at Granny's or go to the pub. Sometimes I would come back from school and go into the fridge and Mum would tell me not to touch the beers as they were for Toby (Toby Lee was a working pupil), which always made me laugh that the pupils got preferential treatment on the fridge!'

Referring to the students, **Angela** explained: 'We have had so many pupils over the years including the Subaru Scholars[1] Polly Gundry, Mark Rimell, Toby Lee, Polly Williamson (who, as Polly Lyon, won both Junior and European gold medals), Sophie Newman and Beanie Sturgis. Alice Lozeman and Dag Albert (who was brilliant at building and mending things – which was not Mike's forte!) were also with us for a while as well as many others who have remained lifelong friends. It was always such fun having them with us.'

Toby Lee, whose beer Andrew had coveted, was a recipient of the Subaru sponsorship in the late 1980s. He said: 'I think when I first met Mike he was dubious as to whether I was the right candidate to receive the prized Subaru Scholarship. The turning point, I believe, was on a fantastic day's hunting where I had to try to follow Mike over some of the biggest hedges which, still to this day, I believe I've ever jumped!'

---

1   Subaru provided funds for a pupil to spend some time training with the Tuckers.

Another working pupil, an Italian named **Lorenzo Soprani Volpini**, who arrived in later times, recalled: 'It was the summer of 1999 when I arrived at Church Farm. I did not speak English very well and it was a totally different experience that would change my life forever. Angela and Mike made me feel at home from the very first moment and I will treasure those memories for the rest of my life.

'That summer Mike taught me how to drive the tractor. In August we went to Larkhill to turn the hay, then he showed me all his Friesian cows. I was in charge of counting them all and adding some funny liquid [a copper supplement] in their water: it was something totally new for me and I loved it.'

One person who became involved with the Tuckers through a roundabout connection with the Subaru Scholarship was **Alice Plunkett**, who later married William Fox-Pitt. She reminisced: 'The Tuckers have been a huge family in my life. I first went to Church Farm when my dear friend Beanie Sturgis (then Hughes) won the Subaru Scholarship to train with the Tuckers when she was sixteen. She had left school but I stayed, and going to visit her there felt like the most exciting experience ever.

'Mike and Angela were heroes, the Japanese were training there, as were Swedish riders Dag Albert and Erik Duvander. It all felt so glamorous and successful.

'Through Beanie I got to know this wonderful family and when I got a place at Bristol University, Angela and Mike agreed that I could keep my Young Rider European team horse with them and train with them alongside studying. So began a very special time. I would travel up to ride in the evening, stay with the Tuckers and then work the horses in the morning before heading back to uni. They totally adopted me. I would have tea and a gossip with Granny down in Estcourt Park. She was wonderful and doted on her devoted son. She was like Mrs Tiggywinkle, tiny, twinkly, kind and fun – I loved her. Mike would be in and out to see her all the time he was home. Meanwhile Angela was caring for her mother just down the road.

'There was always a feeling at Church Farm that things were done properly, whether it was people or horses or cows. Everyone was busy but had time for everyone else.

'I graduated from Bristol and was supposed to move away but we suffered a terrible tragedy when my sister died very suddenly of cancer aged sixteen. So, having moved home, I returned to the bosom of Church Farm again to continue my eventing.

'Trying to juggle the beginning of a media career, racing and eventing was a bit tricky and led to the most memorable bollocking of my life! I ran into a logistical nightmare when I was asked at the last minute to work on the Racing Channel but didn't have the time to get back to do evening stables. I solved the problem by paying one of Angela's team to cover me. I didn't ask. The next morning Mike came to find me. Safe to say he was not jokey that day! Quite rightly he tore a strip off me. I was horrified and thought it would be the end of a great relationship but, by the afternoon, the cloud had shifted and normal service resumed. There are not enough people like Mike whom one holds in high enough esteem to listen to, who don't hold a grudge and who are clear about what is right and wrong and are not scared to tell you! I learned so much from that, about being honest and straight, but also looking back how lucky I was to have someone prepared to teach me rather than simply turf me out.

'When I told this story to William he laughed and said his most serious bollocking had also come from Mike! Whilst away at his first Senior European Championships in Aschelswang he was eliminated in the cross-country and, rather than stay and support his team on Sunday, he flew home. Mike found him the following week and gave him a few home truths about team etiquette and general behaviour! Like me, William looks back mortified but grateful at a lesson well learned – if a bit scary at the time! Mike may have been small – but my God he could get cross!'

Angela told me: 'Mike loved having young people around and although he did not get involved on the teaching front, he would often walk the course with them. I have subsequently received lots of letters from people saying what fun they had with Mike, jumping round the farm with him.'

In addition to students and working pupils, there were other visitors from the equestrian world. **Angela** explained that, while she and Mike were still competing, 'David Hunt was a regular visitor. He trained both of us in dressage and would always stay for Badminton when we were riding. Thanks to him, I led the dressage on two occasions but sadly didn't remain there!'

She went on to recall that, actually, Badminton week in those years could be pretty demanding: 'If I'm honest, trying to ride and have people to stay at the same time meant it could be a bit fraught! Additionally, we ran the Riders' Ball on the Saturday night, held at Westonbirt School, which was really well supported. After cross-country we were usually a bit weary and then had to go dancing (which Mike loved and always wanted to dance with everybody!). Any foreign riders used to be put up in the dormitories at the school and they were always on for a party on the Saturday night.' (The Saturday night parties were also part of **Mark Phillips's** memories from that time: 'In the 1970s, part of competing at Badminton was attending the Ball, which was held in Westonbirt School on the Saturday night and we would never get to bed before two or three in the morning and had to showjump that day! Nowadays, everyone has large horseboxes and so the parties take place in the horsebox park. We didn't have lorries with living or pop-outs, therefore we would stay in pubs or hotels, or with friends. I wouldn't necessarily say it was more fun, just different!')

Tetbury Horse Trials was a family run affair, as **Angela** explained: 'Mike, with his usual passion and enthusiasm, started Tetbury Horse Trials in 1977 and we ran it for fifteen years. I was in charge of the dressage and Mike's mum used to help in the secretary's "tent" (actually the back of our horsebox), handing out numbers. Mike's father carried on with the farming side of things while Mike was busy organising the event but would come and muck in with secretarial duties if required. It was a wonderful way of getting the hedges cut and the farm tidied up!' Daughter **Emma** added: 'Tetbury Horse Trials always came at the end of the summer holidays. Dad was always rushing around getting the farm tidy as well as designing a course and running the horse trials and the ride and drive challenge.'

Angela explained further: 'It started as a novice event, then ran a five- and six-year-old championship class. It was a really good novice track designed by Mike and built by the Willis brothers and, over the years, some very good horses won it. Then we progressed to an intermediate track and then ran all three levels. In those days, the cattle had to stay out until the last minute so the grassland could be a bit bare and if the ground was hard in those days we didn't have the equipment to improve the going sufficiently. Most big events nowadays are run over parkland with lovely old turf, but this was a working farm. The event used to provide a good run before Boekelo.'

Mike always had enterprising ways of getting in plenty of spectators, as recognised by **Mark Phillips**: 'Mike was an all-time great commentator and a great mover, shaker and protagonist. I used to call him Lord Tucker of the Golden Voice and he always called me The Captain! When he ran Tetbury Horse Trials, he wanted to put on an entertainment in the hope it would attract a bigger crowd, which it did. He would always go out of his way to do something special in every walk of life, but it was all for the good of the horse and the sport.'

One of Mike's innovations was the Subaru v Land Rover ride and drive challenge. As described by **Angela**: 'We invited celebrities to come and take part in the competition where they had to ride a horse round a few small fences then leap into a car and drive round another course. It was always great fun and certainly drew in the crowds, who thoroughly enjoyed what was often a hilarious spectacle. The celebrities included names such as Steve Cauthen, Richard Dunwoody, Tommy Steele, Mike Rutherford, Allan Lamb, Fraser Hines and Mark Phillips. They were all so competitive, and one year I recall one of them wiping out a brand new Land Rover round a gate post! I'm amazed we were provided with cars year after year!

'Lots of the competitors would stay with us and we would invariably play silly games in the evening, which were instigated, of course, by Mike! Games such as picking up a cereal box with your teeth (I seem to recall

Steve Cauthen was brilliant at it!) and other daft contests. One year a lot of foreign riders were in England at the time, including Bruce Davidson and Andrew Hoy. They all drew for horses then did a novice event which Andrew Hoy won on a lovely young horse. An amusing moment was when Bruce went to get on his horse, stuck his toe in its ribs by mistake causing the horse to almost lie down, and they parted company!

'We also ran a dog agility class, which was very popular. This prompts memories of another occasion when, after a certain amount of wine had been taken, quite a few of our guests decided it would be good fun to have a go in the dog agility – well, someone got stuck in the tunnel, which caused a certain amount of hilarity! Then I remember the time Mark took a brand new Land Rover through a pond to test it out. He drove it in, for some reason opened the door and the inside got absolutely soaked!

'In those days, things were a little more relaxed and one incident I remember is when Ginny Holgate, who was riding two horses, was running late, and when she arrived on her second horse at the showjumping, she discovered that the fences had all been dismantled. She was totally laid back about it and Charlie Cottenham, who was the horse trials steward, decided that she would have jumped her customary faultless round, so gave her a "clear" and off she went across country!'

Hugh Thomas recalled another amusing anecdote in which time was a factor: 'I commentated for many years at the event Mike and Angela ran on their farm near Tetbury – he was always innovative in the attractions he laid on and persuaded many jockeys and other celebrities to take part in a ride and drive or some other silly venture! One year he was so keen to start his celebrity event on time that we left one rider at the start, all ready to ride round Mike's advanced course, which he had just shut down to get ready for his "attraction"! Eventually she was postponed for three-quarters of an hour, then allowed to start – and judged by Mike and a couple of helpers pursuing her round the course in cars – the fence judges had long since left!'

Although there was all this equestrian activity going on around him, **Andrew** explained that 'I had no interest in the equestrian side of things.

So I remember Dad asking me, "Do you want to go farming?" And I said, "Yes I do." He told me the farm couldn't support two families, so encouraged me to go off and do something different, but the farm would always be there for me to return to. I had always wanted to do something in sports marketing and so took the decision to go to Newcastle and study food marketing which I hoped would cover both bases in terms of basic farming and also the principles of marketing. Dad had always been keen for me to go to the Royal Agricultural College at Cirencester but, having gone to school round here, and having already got a good friend base of farming mates, I wanted to explore further afield and not be on the doorstep where Dad would know exactly what I was up to! Whilst I think Dad was quite disappointed initially, after a year or so he saw where I was coming from and loved it when I brought mates down from Newcastle for weekends. Dad would ask me every few years whether I was still keen to go farming but never put any pressure on me and so, when having worked in London for four or so years, I set up an office for myself on the farm and started doing the sponsorship for Gatcombe Horse Trials and then Badminton, I think he was delighted.'

Over the years, as is often the case with farming, the enterprise at Church Farm underwent changes and challenges. As described in earlier chapters, Church Farm had been essentially a dairy farm and, as **Giles Rowsell** recalled, 'Mike's quest for breed improvement led him to commentating at breed society events and major agricultural shows. Here he was at his best when explaining to the general public the important facts about farming. He was at the forefront of embryo transplant technology and breeding of dairy cows to produce high Omega Three milk.'

Recollecting his involvement with the farm during that period, **Andrew** said: 'I wouldn't say Dad taught me about farming as such but I just used to work on the farm to earn money during school and university holidays. I vividly remember when we were having the new milking parlour being built having to milk in a temporary shed and it being a complete nightmare and so I went milking with Eric (still our herdsman) for every day of the holidays. I was shattered by the end of it but really enjoyed it and it was a really good bonding time with Eric who, I think, thought I was a lazy oik before! I also remember during foot and mouth Dad, Eric and I had to do the milking between us as we couldn't use our usual milkers because they had been working on a farm that went down with foot and mouth. We actually lost some young cattle to foot and mouth that were down at a rearing unit in the Severn Valley. It was a pretty stressful time and I remember watching the news every day as it got closer and closer to us. Luckily we got away with it.'

Despite all this hard work, the time came when a decision was made to sell the dairy herd. This, said **Andrew**, was not an easy decision: 'Selling the dairy herd was a massive thing for Dad. He had spent a large part of his life building up a pedigree dairy herd that was very respected but the sums just weren't adding up. We had explored every avenue but in the end he knew that we needed to finish with the dairy cattle and look to do something else. The sale at the farm was a sad day.'

What was *not* a sad day, was Andrew's decision to become permanently involved with the farm. Mike told me one day that, after a family discussion with Andrew, he had been surprised but delighted that Andrew wanted to take on the farm. Andrew's own business had prospered and I think Tucks had thought that was the way he was going. To know that a Tucker was going to continue at Church Farm gave him a real thrill.

Furthermore, it was not to be too long before a new bovine venture had its genesis many miles from Gloucestershire. As **Nick Brooks-Ward** explained: 'Many people wouldn't know how Mike became so enthused about breeding Wagyu cattle. He had sold his prize herd of dairy cattle in 2005 and really missed having cows about Church Farm.

'During the 2008 Olympics in Hong Kong there was a typhoon – the highest rating at number nine. Hong Kong is used to these and every shutter came down on the hotels and shops – but we weren't daunted. Off went the intrepid explorers – Mike and I to a shopping centre a mile away from the hotel – and everything was deserted apart from a single restaurant serving Wagyu beef. We had never tried it before and we both said that it was the most amazing beef that we had ever eaten – and that was the end of that – or so I thought. But inevitably, as always with Mike, an idea was brewing.

'Three days later, it was a rest day at the Olympics and Mike had arranged, via Peter Phillips, who was working out there at the time, that we should all go on a Chinese junk around the South Sea Islands. In typical Tucker style he had rounded up the great and good from all the FEI disciplines and off we went, realising that if the boat sunk the equestrian Olympics wouldn't have continued – everyone from the FEI directors, ground jury, course designers, commentators and Appeal Committee were on that boat and it was a thirsty and very jolly affair.

'Unbeknownst to any of us – apart from Mike – the owner of the boat was also the owner of the chain of restaurants where we had eaten three nights earlier. As Mike got chatting he discovered that they also bred the cattle in Australia – the plan and dream were born. Three months later these unruly cattle arrived at Church Farm – the rest, as they say, is history.'

Actually, there was somewhat more to the story than suggested by Nick. **Giles Rowsell** noted that, in typical Tucker fashion, he not only 'built up a sizeable Wagyu herd, but involved himself in trying to establish a reputable breed society for the breed and this became a real and time-consuming challenge. He was so committed to the quality of the beef that he often acted as the meat delivery man.' This was confirmed by hunting colleague and regular customer **Janie Dear**, 'a big supporter of his beef – totally delicious and yummy. He was always there, delivering a box of steaks or whatever. He was one of the busiest people imaginable, still taking the time to see a few customers.'

Andrew said of this new venture: 'When I became involved in the sales and marketing side of the Wagyu I think it was at this point Dad maybe realised that I had in fact learned something at university! We loved working on it together and there were times that we didn't necessarily agree but as far as I was concerned it was Dad's baby and he had the final say. Being a "foody", I get more and more excited about it and get real satisfaction when a really marbled beast comes to fruition.'

Although the farm and the many other demands on his time kept Mike and the family very busy, they would take holidays when circumstances allowed. **Emma** explained: 'As summer was not a good time for holidays in our family, with harvesting on the farm and the eventing season, Mum and Dad decided when I was about nine or ten to try a family skiing holiday. Our first trip was to Avoriaz in France with the Thomases and Lochores who had all skied before –apart possibly from Hamish Lochore. Anyway Hamish seemed to be as novice at skiing as us! This turned out to be an hilarious week, not without some drama, particularly as we all learned how to negotiate button lifts and chair lifts for the first time. Andrew managed to cut his chin on a camp bed and had to be taken to a French hospital for stitches. Dad, in particular, barely knew any French and just tended to speak louder in English, so we had to rely on the Lochores and the Thomases.

'As first timers on snow, none of us found skiing easy to begin with (apart from Andrew) but we all enjoyed the skiing and the *après ski* and went on quite a few more trips after that. I think it is fair to say that our cross-country characteristics came out on the mountain, with Dad and Andrew being fast but quite often out of control and Mum and me being more stylish (or so we claimed) but more cautious.'

Despite his unscheduled contretemps with the camp bed, **Andrew** clearly enjoyed the actual skiing, which he described as 'a lot of fun'.

Angela reiterated Emma's and Andrew's memories: 'Hamish and Polly Lochore introduced us to skiing when the children were quite small and we then went on to many happy and fun trips with Hugh and Mandy Thomas, Giles and Jill Rowsell and Charlie and Sarah Bullen in France, at the resorts of Courchevel, Avoriaz and Meribel, where Giles had access to a lovely chalet that was right on the side of the piste. The skiing holidays were always such fun – it was a bit like as we were cross-country on the piste – Mike would just set off, go flat out and probably fall over whereas I "accumulated a lot of time faults"!'

Not surprisingly, the Tuckers' friends had fond memories of skiing parties. **Hugh Thomas** said: 'We used to take the same chalet in Meribel for many years – originally found by Giles and Jill Rowsell. The party of eight each year was made up of close friends – not always the same, but drawn from Rowsells, Tuckers, Bullens (various), Claphams, a few non-horsey friends, and sundry "occasionals"! At Mike's Memorial Giles told the story of Tucker disappearing in the fog after lunch; we also had some major snowball fights on the way back from our evening out, e.g. at a local restaurant; there was the famous occasion of his split salopettes displaying very blue/red/cold thighs on the run into Courchevel when Mandy had to try to zip him up; the brass doorstop that he put in the freezer and then into our bed just before we retired for the night; and of course many memories of him wiping out into a snowdrift!'

In addition to his tale of Mike lost in the fog, **Giles Rowsell** recalled that: 'Some of our best moments came on regular skiing holidays in Meribel where the leg-pulling and party jokes were at their worst and woe-betide you if you were not "on the ball" from dawn to dusk. You never felt safe! But finding Tucker upside down under two feet of snow, unable to move, was too good an opportunity to miss! We laughed so much that there was no chance of rescuing him!

'Angela also reminded me of an occasion when we came out of a restaurant after lunch into a total whiteout where you couldn't see a foot in front of yourself. Tucks got his skis on, adjusted his goggles and bounced up and down, facing the opposite direction from the rest of us, keen to get going. And then disappeared backwards over a sheer drop! It took him ages to rejoin us because we could not see a thing. But a couple of days later, at the same restaurant in perfect light, it was plain to see that he had only been just a few yards from us all the time!

'The ready supply of snow was too much for Mike to resist – it came through windows, finished up in pyjamas, came off roofs just above where somebody happened to be standing. This ensured that a holiday was not somewhere to get rest, but a place where you were permanently on guard.

'One year, he had just become chairman of the BE board, so decided that he had to have a laptop. Where would be a good place to learn how to use it? Yes, on holiday – but the ribbing ensured that it never came out of its case even once!

'Party games after dinner were legendary, with the rules (if there were any at all) changing all the time and cheating being obligatory. Talk about horses was banned until after eleven, the theory being that, by that time and after a few drinks, nobody had any idea what we were talking about, people had fallen asleep and certainly no one could remember anything about it the next morning!'

Although both Emma and Andrew emphasised that family holidays were usually planned around other commitments, **Angela** mentioned that: 'We did once try to combine holiday with work when we drove to Barcelona when Mike was technical director for all three events and had to go out early. I then drove out with Emma and Andrew. It was there, during a practice run, with the jump judges in place, that the motorbikes, which were being used to collect the slips, ran out of petrol! The next day, Patrick Conolly-Carew was one of the members of the ground jury and it was at the start of the dressage phase, when the guinea pig rider was doing his test, that they all discovered that the writers' command of English was more or less non-existent! After the test all three judges stormed out of their boxes at the same time, saying they couldn't cope with their writers. So, an announcement came over the tannoy and Judy Bradwell and I were called for to step in.' This may have been a case of a 'busman's holiday' too far!

Time has a habit of passing, and **Angela** explained that 'As we got older and Mike was having trouble with his knee while skiing,[2] we started going to Cornwall instead for our winter break. Holidays were often spent with friends such as the Rowsells, who had a lovely cottage down there. We always went in the winter when it was empty. Mike and Sue Etherington-Smith came too and Jennifer and Bruce Millar and lots of family. We loved Cornwall because we could take the dogs for long walks on the beach, and it would be our only chance to write Christmas cards (always a point of discussion as to who should write them!) and our "round robin letter" that we used to include.'

---

2   Mike eventually had his knee replaced in 2015 and, the following year, had a replacement hip. He chose to have both operations done in January so he could hunt until Christmas and to avoid interfering with his commentary commitments.

Giles Rowsell confirmed that: 'The Tuckers had our house near Padstow in Cornwall on several occasions and loved seeing their dogs charging around on the beach. They went point-to-pointing at Wadebridge and hunting on foot with the Four Burrow so, while it was a break, horses and hounds were never far away and people down there knew who Mike was, partly from his commentating at the Royal Cornwall Show.'

Holiday time was by no means rest time for Mike's sense of humour. It seems that parties involving the Tuckers and Rowsells sometimes stayed at a hotel in Cornwall. Joining them on one occasion, **Nick Brooks-Ward** remembered: 'The six of us had a splendid lunch and walked the dogs on the beach at low tide and then I stupidly said we should take a look at our room, which had wonderful sea views. Whilst I went and sorted out afternoon tea, yet again the curse of Tucks struck — we got back upstairs to find clothes in different wardrobes and no pyjamas — never to be seen again — and we had looked everywhere.'

Andrew confirmed that 'Cornwall was a big part of holidays in the last few years. It was always difficult to get us all together so quite often we would be down for a few days and then the Barkers would follow. Dad loved their early morning walks on the beach and visiting the many great restaurants and he even found time to go and visit a local farm where we had sent cattle to check up on them.'

Mike and Angela had what was to prove their final time away together in November 2017. **Angela** recalled 'A really lovely little break Mike and I had was for his birthday, when we went to stay with Ian and Jenny Stark. On the way we visited Cotton Hall at Holmes Chapel where I did my initial "finishing school" training with Eddy Goldman. I spent hours in the indoor school without stirrups learning to ride a corner, along with many names from the past such as Sheila Wilcox, Lorna Clarke, Judy Bradwell and others. Stephen Clarke has been there for a long time now and the field is full of houses, but it brought back many memories. Driving in the car is always catch-up time — "You never told me about …!" — and we meandered through the Yorkshire Dales and the Lake District looking to see if there were any Patterdale terriers as pretty as mine!

'On arrival at the Starks the warm welcome far outweighed the cold weather, and long walks, good food and plenty of banter ensured we felt refreshed when we returned home to get the horses back into work again. (The Japanese riders return to Japan for the winter).'

This last comment refers to the fact that, while Mike was busy with his mixed career of commentating, course design and various official roles in the equestrian world, **Angela** has, over many years, built up a long association with the Japanese eventing team and has been hugely successful in their training. She explained, 'Through our Australian friend, Peter Winton, we were approached to help the Japanese riders in their quest to field a team for the Seoul Olympics in 1988. This was too much to take on by ourselves as we were still competing, so Tomi Gretener had them based with him and we shared the management. He helped find the horses and I did some schooling and dressage training. The riders came from the Japan Racing Association and Riding Club Crane and had more of a showjumping background, so educating them in the art of cross-country riding was some challenge!

'After Seoul and Barcelona, they returned to Japan but one of the riders, Kazu Iwatani (now in a very senior managerial position in Riding Club Crane, a company that has over forty riding schools in Japan) approached us again to have some riders to try to qualify for London. Kazu competed at Seoul, Barcelona and Atlanta during the time he was based with us for training and I went as groom!

'Blenheim put on an Asian Pacific qualifying competition for three nations and, by an amazing stroke of luck, the Japanese team beat the Australians and in so doing, qualified for London.

'Kazu has been such a loyal friend and Crane sent another rider who qualified for Rio as an individual and now we have two riders and ten horses based here preparing for the Asian Games. Of course, this is a big undertaking and I could never have managed without the help of Matt Glentworth, who has been an invaluable member of our team for years.'

As will be evident, Church Farm has always been a hive of activity, with a constant flow of people coming and going with their horses, and visitors were welcomed when they dropped in, as explained by retired veterinary surgeon **Ray Williams**: 'The kitchen at Church Farm always has a warm, calm, welcoming feel, plus of course a warm, milky coffee with the addition of a little dram! Mike was an expert at catching that boiling milk as it promised to boil over. Whenever we met over work or socially, there was always a bit of banter! I'd try to keep up, but the barrage kept coming and I'd have to concede (mostly).

'Who will I get to bet with now? Our rugby bets on the "big game" or the Six Nations were memorable and nowhere more than IOU evenings at the Cat and Custard Pot at Shipton Moyne, when the loser paid. And guess who that was …?

'In fact, one such session was followed by an early farm visit and I think I retired, with the inevitable effects, only to find that milky coffee on offer! Mike was bouncing around, chuckling with Eric (Mike's herdsman of nearly forty years) at my obvious discomfort.'

In addition to welcoming those who simply visited in passing, Church Farm has played host to numerous supper parties over the years as **Hugh Thomas** recalled: 'Mike and Angela came to supper with us (and we with them) on innumerable occasions over the years. We always put the world, especially the world of eventing and horses generally, completely to rights. I will never know if there was more good sense or more rubbish talked on those evenings. Mark Phillips was usually the other participant – we were in one or other of our kitchens – but the problem was always driving home. Mike was lucky – Angela had usually very sensibly slept through our ludicrous discussions, but was absolutely fit to drive; Mark was never fit to drive –though sometimes he knew the way home via the off road options.'

Hugh's foggy recollections of these suppers are pretty much supported by **Mark's** version of events: 'Tucker's kitchen table suppers were legendary and you would never get to bed before midnight. After a few glasses of wine and a couple of whiskies we would put the sport to rights, celebrating or lamenting changes, discussing what was needed to try to maintain standards of old.'

Mike Etherington-Smith was also a guest at some of these suppers, although his memories of them seem a little more sober than those of Hugh and Mark: 'We also spent a lot of time over the years discussing safety in the sport, another passion of both of ours, and would regularly meet up for supper to chew the fat.'

In addition to his attendance at the 'legendary' suppers, **Hugh Thomas** was, latterly, invited to some shooting days at Church Farm: 'In recent years I had the huge pleasure of a day's shooting at Church Farm, invited either by Mike or Andrew. Mike was not brought up to shoot and I first remember him at a day, courtesy of Mark, at Gatcombe. He did not shoot very well – nor did the rest of us, but he was in a class of his own. We stopped for elevenses. Someone said "I bet you couldn't hit your own hat" – and threw it in the air. He missed. He tried three more times – and missed every time. I don't know if that was the day he gave up shooting – but it could have been. He was a wonderful host but sensibly never picked up his gun when we went to shoot with him.'

While he greatly valued his many friends, Mike's greatest love was, quite rightly, that of his family. On the first of November 1997, Emma had married Paul Barker, whom she had met at a dance at the Royal Agricultural Society. The wedding, like that of her parents, took place at four o' clock in the local church at Long Newnton. The reception, dinner and dancing took place in a marquee, and Angela recalled a moment of panic about the heating, because it was rather windy. Paul, who had been in the army, was not horsey (although he was to become a 'good Pony Club Dad') – his main sporting interest was shooting, and now runs the family shoot with Andrew. The couple's first child, Josh, was born in 2004 during the Athens Olympics – at which moment Mike announced his birth on BBC television – and Harry followed three years later.

The shoot aside, Paul's involvement with the farm had moments of mixed fortunes. **Emma** recalled: 'Dad was very proud of the farm and did like to keep it tidy. In more recent years, when he was at home a little more, he spent a lot of time on the sit-on mower. Not many people were allowed to do mowing for him. Paul, however, was allowed on a few times until he sheared off the steering wheel going under an apple tree. Despite that, Dad was very fond of Paul (he was a proud man at our wedding) – and he appreciated Paul's assistance with technology!'

It is possible that Mike was relieved that, for once, someone other than himself had damaged a machine – and he was not, himself, a dab hand with computers! Mike's mower was not, however, always the victim. Mike and Fiona Mitchell were long-time neighbours, friends and hunting companions of Mike's, and **Fiona** recalled the occasion when 'Hubby and I were driving past Church Farm on a summer's evening, and stopped to hurl some friendly abuse at Mike, who was on his ride-on mower coming out of his gateway. We had a good chat and were about to drive off when suddenly the mower jumped forward and slammed into the passenger door of our car. We got complete hysterics, while Mr T just reversed away as though nothing had happened!'

In 2016, there was a family visit to the South of France. As **Andrew** explained, 'This was for my wedding to Georgie in Provence, which was a very special day for us and I think for Mum and Dad. It was just so good to be surrounded by family and friends. I actually met Georgie on Tinder, which is a dating app! I'm not sure Mum or Dad knew what that was, given their technophobe nature! I think Dad was very relieved I met Georgie, who has very strong family principles and is always willing to muck in and get her hands dirty on the farm.'

Mike's close friend **Giles Rowsell** observed that 'Tucks was very proud of his family and, despite being so busy, he gave them a great deal of his spare time – his grandsons worshipped him, but they all knew that high standards were expected at all times, something I know was instilled in him by his mother Betty.

'When Emma, Paul and the boys went to Australia for two years Mike's biggest regret was not seeing the boys grow up. However, his computer skills had improved by then and regular Skype sessions proved invaluable. He was thrilled when they came back to the UK and he could cheer them on in the Shetland Pony Grand National and on the rugby field.'

Angela confirmed that 'Mike loved having the grandchildren around and we are so lucky as a family to live close to each other with Paul and Emma one field away with Josh and Harry, and Andrew and Georgie and the twins Jack and Ned three fields away in the other direction.' However, she added: ' He did have a bit of a habit of winding them up before bedtime just like he did with our children!'

Andrew's comments reinforced those of his mother: 'Dad often dropped in for a catch-up, more so in the last few years when I had become more involved in the Wagyu and the farm as a whole. He had a knack of always arriving just as we were trying to quieten the boys down before bedtime and winding them up into a fever of excitement, which was never ideal and it would take Georgie and me about two hours to calm them down again!'

Both sets of grandchildren soon became involved in typical Tucker family pursuits. **Angela** reported that: 'Andrew's twins love helping on the farm feeding the cows and going beating on the little shoot that Andrew and Paul run on the farm during the winter. Josh and Harry's ponies live up at the farm most of the time and the boys really enjoy being part of the Beaufort Pony Club tetrathlon team. One of Mike's triumphs was warming them up for the show jumping phase – they loved it that he kept it simple: "One pull here, two kicks there, get straight, learn the course and wait for the bell." Two clear rounds was the result!'

Emma stressed Mike's support for her two sons: 'Dad hunted with both Josh and Harry and supported them in their Shetland Grand National racing careers. He had the pleasure of calling them both home in this event at Olympia. Dad also came to watch the boys ride at Pony Club events whenever he could' and, she adds, 'He was in charge of warming up Josh for the tetrathlon riding phase at Summerhouse only a month before he died.'

Mike's work ethic and willingness to 'get involved' included many activities that are not widely known about, but nevertheless significant. In his eulogy, **Nick Brooks-Ward** recorded that 'One of his proudest moments was when he was installed as an Honorary Fellow of his *alma* *mater*, the Royal Agricultural University, from which he graduated in 1964. The Fellowship is the highest honour the University can confer and is reserved for those who have made the most distinguished contributions to the land-based sector and industries.

'In the early years of equine education at RAU Mike was a passionate promoter of equine activities on the College/University Council and also on the School of Agriculture Advisory Board. He was never afraid of being the "lone voice" for equine education in RAU and his belief and drive in this for twenty-plus years, culminated in the setting up of the School of Equine Management and Science in 2014.

'Mike was incredibly supportive of the students. He gave numerous guest lectures, helped organise work placements, and promoted the graduates across the globe and, as chairman of the Advisory Council helped the university develop an identity and strong reputation for educating the future "movers and shakers" in the equine industry.'

Not content with all his other commitments, Mike also took on the role of trustee of the Retraining of Racehorses, and was hugely influential in the promotion of the hunting and eventing series.

Such commendable work notwithstanding, it is very telling that, in crystallising their thoughts of Mike, close friends emphasised his absolute commitment to friends and family.

Jim Wofford, fellow competitor and friend, wrote the following:

Tuesday, April 17

Dear Angela,

Given the small number of actual participants, I suppose it was inevitable that in the spring of 1968, those two young oafs, Mike Tucker and Jim Wofford, would wind up leaning on the competitors' bar at Tweseldown's event. And it was inevitable they would immediately fall into an amiable disagreement regarding the relative qualities of UK and US beer.

Tucker: 'US beer is far too cold.'

Woff: 'UK beer is like making love in a canoe, hot and effing close to water.'

By the summer of 1968, given the secluded nature of the Olympic eventing training facilities at the Valle de Bravos and the lack of any form of entertainment other than whisky and conversation, it was again inevitable those amiable disagreements would continue and expand. And, perhaps, their experiences at the debacle of the 1968 Eventing Olympics convinced them that, like war, eventing was too important to be left to the generals.

However, one should notice that as their friendship grew, their areas of disagreement grew, even after they left the Mexico Olympics behind. And as they grew in experience, and stature in the horse world, and as the scope and nature of the issues they were caused to grapple with grew, and then as their girth grew while their shadows shrank, and as they became more and more follically challenged, yet through all of this, one should not miss that by this time in their now firm, life-long friendship, their agreements by far outweighed their disagreements. Indeed, to a listener, a discussion between them would be similar to discussions of Talmudic scholars, true believers disputing the smallest of points regarding unknowable mysteries.

Those many agreements are the clearest manifestations of their similar beliefs, and form the bedrock of their friendship.

~ Both agreed they had demonstrably over-married.

~ Both agreed that family came first.

~ Both agreed that a few moments on the back of a horse were far better than any day in an office.

~ Both agreed they felt an inescapable obligation towards the betterment of horses, the environment wherein horses thrive, and indeed of all God's creatures.

~ Both agreed that it is not given to mankind, to know the number of his days. Given a choice, they would go a few days early, quickly, without fanfare or warning, still active to the last moment, still caring for

*their creatures, and satisfied to know their families were safe insofar as the
human condition will allow.*

*When we are at a loss for words, we must turn to others, the better to
express ourselves, as here by Father Joseph Roux: 'We call that person who
has lost his father, an orphan; and a widower that man who has lost his
wife. But that man who has known the immense unhappiness of losing a
friend, by what name do we call him? Here every language is silent and
holds its peace in impotence.'*

*We know that in losing Michael Tucker, the horse world has lost a
guiding light, yet we should not fear we might lose our way. As Sir Harry
Lauder said, 'I could tell where the lamplighter was by the trail he left
behind him.'*

All my love,

Woff

Giles Rowsell said: 'Mike's amazingly varied life was dominated by
the importance of his family life – Angela who was such a support and
foil to his antics, Emma with Paul and their boys Harry and Josh living
just across the field from Church Farm and Andrew and Georgie with
the twins Ned and Jack only a stone's throw away. Their presence in Long
Newnton will be Mike's proudest legacy, along with Andrew being so
involved in the future of Church Farm.'

Very similar thoughts were uttered by **William Alexander** in his
eulogy at the family funeral: 'I now come to the two most important things
in Mike's life – his family and his farm. He was so very proud of Emma
and Andrew and, in recent years, of his grandchildren, Josh and Harry and
Jack and Ned. But throughout it has been that tower of strength, Angela,
whom he married on the first of January 1972, who has seen him through
the highs and the lows.'

While **Hugh Thomas** said: 'What else can I say? Mike was the truest
of friends – if ever I was in trouble, I could completely rely on Mike. He
was a wonderful supporter of everything I did at Badminton – while also
a private and honest critic. He was such fun to be with – yet also serious

when needed. I and many others miss him so much.'

A regular church-goer when circumstances allowed, Mike was the third generation of Tuckers to serve as churchwarden at Long Newnton Church, a duty he carried out for twenty-five years, stepping down in 2015. It is wholly fitting that Mike is now buried in its peaceful churchyard.

Overleaf is a poem that was written and read out by Georgie Tucker at Mike's memorial service.

An Ode to Mike

Mr T, Tucks, Dad, Grampie or Mike
The equestrian voice 'The man with the mic'
We can't quite believe, you're not here any more
Still expecting in vain you'll walk back through our door.

We've come here today each to pay our respect
And your family just want this last chance to reflect
On some of the *personal* memories you shared
Don't worry, I'll make sure some details are spared!

You've stood here before giving noble advice
Like *'Just give it a go'; 'Say thank you'; 'Be nice'*
And if ever in doubt *'Kick on and hold tight!'*
You'd call to the grand-kids, as the Beaufort took flight.

A late-comer to riding, at eight years of age!
Found the Pony Club such a great way to engage
With the girls, with whom you refined a great knack
Of favours returned, for them cleaning your tack!

You grew up and built your young life around horses
Either jumping or racing, or building their courses
In the tack room at Burghley, you first met your wife
In *Angela* whom you would be with, for life.

So elegant and beautiful, so talented and tall
You still caught her eye despite being quite small!
And moved to Church Farm, with a slight disregard
For her father who'd just built her new stable yard.

We've seen what a legendary pair you both made
And we're sure that whenever in doubt, you 'obeyed'
But perhaps it was wise you did never agree
To a lesson, in dressage, from your Mrs T!

'It's all circles and bumps' it's been known that you said
But despite this, on Bugle (dear horse that you bred)
You were second at Badminton, to Lucinda Green
And honoured, accepting your prize from The Queen.

Cooking was *not* your great strength, it transpired
Though your signature breakfast was always admired,
Yet Angela's cooking (a sensation itself)
Meant you never were left just to fend for yourself.

The skin of the custard - your joint guilty pleasure
Not shared by your children, in Andrew and Emma
Growing up with the dairy which meant that the norm
Was their Frosties, with milk, so fresh it was warm.

Your love of *all* sport was impressive, inspiring
With no sign of slowing, despite your retiring
Yet heaps more to give, so much wisdom to share
You have touched many lives, in the world, everywhere.

You're the voice of Olympia, so your last curtain call
Means Christmas will never be the same for us all
The Shetland Grand National, 'Tucks' on the PA!
Cheering Harry & Josh; great memories will stay.

Your dogs were like children, but more spoilt of course
(Though perhaps not as much as your favourite horse)

There's been Dikler, and Holly, Sky, Kite and now Mo
Who've *all* slept in your bed - we pretend not to know!

You were blessed with your Ems and your shared love of riding
You would take her out hunting – no time for deciding
If that hedge was too big for her teeny 12.2 –
Young Ems, riding Monarch, kicked on behind you.

Your reputation for manners will go on forever
No exceptions for adults or kids what-so-ever!
God forbid should you rest, elbows out on the table
Or drive on his verges or mess up the stable.

We'll keep up these standards, Paul won't let them go
Any signs of a lapse, he will soon let us know!
But we'll try, as you'd wish, to recall the good fun
That you shared in your life, now it's all said and done.

Your record of crashing each machine that you bought
Was extensive (expensive) and by your wife caught!
But prompt with excuses and admissions of guilt
You ensured that each gatepost was quickly rebuilt!

Your successes were vast and impressive, it's true
But by *far* the most celebrated one that *we* knew
Was your gin rummy 'legend' – it was never defeated
(Except that one time, when your grandson had cheated!)

The cows were your love – though they tended to injure
But quickly forgiven after whisky and ginger
And with Andrew enjoyed this shared passion and vision
He'll now take the reins, without *your* supervision.

Your shadow in Eric will be by our side
'A champion cow-man', and willing to guide
Your dear Wagyu along to the next generation
Ensuring we build on your solid foundation.

We'll miss bedtime visits, to young Jack and Ned
When you'd lift them both up, by their feet, on their head
To the laughter and shrieks in response to your tickles
Making bedtime a challenge, as they wound up in giggles.

It was only last month that you bid your goodbye
To D'Argent, your horse, who left life on a high
Just like you Mr T – although much less well trained
Catching him in the field kept poor Matt entertained!

But today, as you're laid down, for your final rest
We're here for each other – we'll all do our best
To make you feel proud and continue your dream
As this last week has proved we're a bloody good team.

We trust where you are, you're surrounded by mates
A new dawn in Heaven, inside Pearly Gates
Horse & Hound at the ready, *Racing Post* by your side
Milky coffee with breakfast before taking a ride.

Georgie Tucker
10 April 2018

The Wallace Family's Recollections of Mike

Mike and Angela have been friends of Malcolm and mine for many years, and Mike (and Angela, when not otherwise engaged) had stayed with us at Fishponds Farm for some twenty years during Burghley Horse Trials week. Since the idea for this book had its origins on the last of many occasions when Mike stayed for Burghley, it seems appropriate that it should conclude with some of our family reminiscences from those times.

Charlie, our younger son, said 'As a young man growing up in a horse-mad family, one of the great highlights of my calendar was the annual reappearance of Burghley Horse Trials at the end of my summer holidays. Our home is only half an hour from Burghley, and thus for a few days each summer, Fishponds Farm is transformed into a "Fawlty Towersesque" hotel for some of Mum and Dad's closest friends. With a guest list over the years boasting names such as Hugh and Mandy Thomas, Chris and Jackie Tar, the late Mrs Rook and of course Mike Tucker (Angela was usually officiating, I seem to remember) it was inevitably a raucous affair, characterised by bad jokes, stories of old, and of course, a significant depletion of Dad's alcohol supply.

'At the age of seven, however, I was far too young for all that nonsense and had other intentions. Instead, Tom, my year-older brother, and I had bought a worryingly realistic "fake dog poo" from the joke store at Burghley and made it our aim to sneak it onto the floor of Mike's bedroom, before finding a suitably unsubtle hiding place in order to view his reaction.

'Despite the fact that this hilarious little joke may have started to lose its edge by the fourth day, Mike's characteristic chuckle every time he spotted the immaculately placed defecation on his carpet was something that was absolute gold dust to my seven-year-old self and to eight-year-old Tom. With the poo stashed safely away for another year, this joke continued for many years to come and never failed to disappoint!

'With our homes at opposite ends of the country, my encounters with Mike were few and far between. However, Burghley week was always one of great anticipation and, despite only seeing Mike for four days a year, he made an impression that will last a lifetime. He always took such a genuine interest in all aspects of my life whilst being quietly humble about his own. Indeed, I will never forget his ability to make me feel so comfortable in his company, despite a fifty-year age gap.

'To me, it is this that made Mike such an inspirational person and whether it be "dog poos" or world-class commentary, my Burghley week will never quite be the same again.'

Our elder son **Tom** relished his farming chats with Mike: 'Burghley Horse Trials was always a particularly hectic time at Fishponds Farm. With Dad acting as chairman for nine years and Mum on the committee, the event was highly anticipated. This excitement was added to by the large array of guests who came to stay for the Burghley weekend. This had accumulated to quite a number over the years and Mike and Angela were early additions, who stayed at Fishponds for Burghley for over twenty years. Mike was an integral part of the Fishponds team and, with the likes of Major Chris Tar (main ring steward), Jane Rook (widow of Major Laurence, a former chairman of Horse Trials), Hugh Thomas (director of Badminton) and my father, there were some cracking dinner parties.

'Despite being the first to leave the house in the morning and last to return after what was probably a particularly eventful day of commentary, Mike was always interested to hear how I was and what I had been up to.

As well as hunting and riding, which we discussed at length, one of our greatest passions was cattle and beef farming. I had worked on cattle farms both in England and across Australia and New Zealand as well as studying agricultural business management at the University of Reading, which Mike enjoyed hearing about.

'I remember one such time whilst enjoying a couple of glasses of red wine in front of the log burner, Mike and I embarked on a full-scale overview of the beef industry. It started with the science of marbling in cattle breeds, backed up by Mike's expert knowledge of Wagyu cattle. The conversation then drifted towards the effects of supermarkets on the beef industry. Since I had just started work for a company whose main customers consisted of the likes of M&S and Aldi, we had two sides of the argument to fight! I tried my best to justify some of the reasoning behind it but Mike's passion and enthusiasm for the beef industry was incredible. We debated this for almost an hour and, despite various members of the party trying to enquire about the day's eventing, Mike was determined to continue our conversation!

'Mike would always make the utmost effort to come and have a conversation regardless of the company. His ability to be so accommodating and show such an interest in my life and what I had to say is what made Mike such a fantastic person. Burghley will not be the same without him.'

Burghley holds many, many special memories for me from my time there as a rider and official and for Malcolm as chairman. The most fun, however, was having such special people to stay and the company, stories and laughter will be treasured forever. There is one story that is retold time and again …

As Tom has mentioned, Mike stayed with us for Burghley Horse Trials for some twenty years. Angela sometimes came too, but all too often she was holding the fort at Church Farm in the years when she wasn't on the ground jury. One year (2011) we were all sitting having a drink before dinner, waiting for Mike's arrival. The phone rang: "Hallo, I'm afraid I'm going to be a bit late. You see, I've had a bit of a mishap. I've just put petrol in my new car. The problem is, it's diesel." Well, you can imagine the varying reactions from the assembled crew of Malcolm, Jane Rook, Chris and Jackie Tar and our sons, Tom and Charlie. So we all sat and waited, relishing the leg-pulling opportunities to be had from this latest escapade. Finally, when the low-loader, complete with flashing yellow lights, arrived down our little lane with Tucks perched high up on the passenger seat and his smart new Audi tethered on the trailer behind, we were all lined up as a reception committee. Flustered, sheepish and dishevelled, he was given a large drink and took all the ribbings with his usual good humour. We then all settled down to the usual fun evening enjoyed at Fishponds Farm during Burghley week. However, that was one story he was never allowed to forget – recorded for posterity, by him, in our visitors' book!

In years to come, our house will be so much the poorer without him.

Epilogue

Writing this book has proved to be an emotional roller-coaster. It took a while for Mike to get into the swing of using voice recognition, but once he'd mastered it, he was off!

I so looked forward to receiving his latest episode, which I would thoroughly enjoy sorting out and 'tweaking' here and there. Everything was going swimmingly well. Mike had selected all the photographs, the captions had been written and he was delighted with the design of the front cover. It then all came to a sudden, shattering halt after about 50,000 words.

However, with the support of Mike's family, and in the knowledge that Mike himself would have wished it, I persevered in meeting the deadline to get his book finished. Had it not been for the help of all those who willingly and readily supplied such wonderful stories, I would not have succeeded. Many of those contributors expressed their appreciation in having the opportunity to share their own recollections of Mike.

I would like to thank Andrew and Gilly Johnston of Quiller Publishing for being very sympathetic in the aftermath of Mike's death, for supporting the completion of the book and extending the deadline. Gratitude is also due to designer Becky Bowyer who has juggled the photographs and captions and general lay-out to great effect. Also, thanks to Martin Diggle, the editor, who has shown forbearance beyond all expectation and has expertly guided me as I grappled with each chapter. Despite the huge sadness at Mike's sudden and untimely passing, we managed to retain a sense of humour whilst finishing the book, which I know Mike would have expected.

I must also thank husband Malcolm and sons Tom and Charlie for their patience, as I ignored them for long periods whilst immersed in concentration at my computer!

I would like to finish by quoting the final two paragraphs of Malcolm's and my eulogy, which we gave at Mike's family funeral in Long Newnton Church.

'In the time allotted to us, we have only managed to touch the surface of Mike's life in which he achieved so much and was admired and loved by so many.

'Last autumn he decided that he would like to record his memoirs in a book. When he asked if I would help, he explained he hadn't a clue where to begin. So I asked him what he wanted to say – was it to be a straight biography? And he replied "No, I would like to convey the message that if you really work hard and are pleasant to everyone, you can achieve in life whatever you set out to do."'

I fervently hope that the stories told in this book will be able to portray this, as it now becomes a tribute to Mike for all the family.

Index